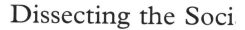

Dissecting the Soci

On the Principles of Analytica

Peter Hedström
University of Oxford

CAMBRIDGE
UNIVERSITY PRESS

CAMBRIDGE UNIVERSITY PRESS

Cambridge, New York, Melbourne, Madrid, Cape Town, Singapore,
São Paulo, Delhi, Dubai, Tokyo, Mexico City

Cambridge University Press
The Edinburgh Building, Cambridge CB2 8RU, UK

Published in the United States of America by Cambridge University Press, New York

www.cambridge.org
Information on this title: www.cambridge.org/9780521796675

First published 2005

A catalogue record for this publication is available from the British Library

ISBN 978-0-521-79229-5 Hardback
ISBN 978-0-521-79667-5 Paperback

Contents

List of figures	*page*	vi
List of tables		viii
Preface		ix
1	The analytical tradition in sociology	1
2	Social mechanisms and explanatory theory	11
3	Action and interaction	34
4	Social interaction and social change	67
5	On causal modelling	101
6	Quantitative research, agent-based modelling and theories of the social (with Yvonne Åberg)	114
7	Coda	145
References		156
Index		170

Figures

2.1 Hypothetical decomposition used to answer the question
'Why do we observe a gender gap in earnings?'   *page* 22
2.2 Alternative mechanism definitions   25
2.3 Components of a programme explanation   30
3.1 Core components of the DBO theory   39
3.2 Dyadic interaction between actor *i* and actor *j* according
to the DBO theory   44
3.3 Sources of uniformity within groups of individuals   47
3.4 Belief-mediated interactions in coordination problems
(adopted from Lewis1969)   50
3.5 Decision tree illustrating a hypothetical choice situation
consisting of two possible courses of action, **A1** and **A2**   57
4.1 Initial patterns of beliefs, desires and actions in a
population of 2,500 actors   79
4.2 The structure of social interaction between Ego and
Alters   80
4.3 Typical patterns of beliefs, desires and actions in a
population of 2,500 actors who socially interact with
four neighbours   81
4.4 Typical patterns of beliefs, desires and actions in a
population of 2,500 actors who interact socially with
three neighbours and one randomly selected actor   85
4.5 Effects on typical actions of two different structures of
social interaction   86
4.6 Macro-level patterns to be expected under atomistic
and non-atomistic decision-making, according to
Coleman, Katz and Menzel (1957)   89
4.7 Decision situation in collective action problem,
according to Åberg (2000)   90
4.8 Social outcomes expected in a structurally
undifferentiated setting   92
4.9 Graph of a hypothetical four-category catnet   94

4.10 Social outcomes in a structurally differentiated setting   96
5.1   Blau and Duncan's (1967) path model of the process of
      stratification   103
6.1   Coleman's micro–macro graph   115
6.2   Unemployment as an endogenous process   122
6.3   Variation in unemployment levels among
      neighbourhoods that are similar to one another in terms
      of their unemployment-relevant characteristics   125
6.4   Social and individual components of the outflow from
      unemployment   127
6.5   Estimated strength of social interaction effects for an
      average person   130
6.6   Typical action patterns in a population of 2,500 actors
      who socially interact with four neighbours on the basis
      of an empirically calibrated action rule   133
6.7   Summary of the results of 5,200 agent-based analyses in
      which 2,500 agents interact on a lattice (torus) with 50
      rows and 50 columns on the basis of an empirically
      calibrated action rule   134
6.8   Actual and simulated unemployment levels in the
      Stockholm metropolitan area   139
6.9   Unemployment levels and social interactions in low and
      high unemployment neighbourhoods in the Stockholm
      metropolitan area   140
6.10 Effects of social interactions and education on the
      unemployment level in the Stockholm metropolitan
      area   141

Tables

2.1	Main types of explanations	*page* 14
3.1	Summary of some of the action-related mechanisms discussed in chapter 3	59
4.1	DBO patterns and associated courses of action	77
4.2	Summary of simulation results	82
4.3	Probabilities ($\times 100$) of different social outcomes with randomly assigned catnet parameters and varying number of actors acting at the onset	98
5.1	Main traditions of causal modelling	102
5.2	Logistic regression model of the BDA data of figure 4.3	110
6.1	Logistic regression model of the probability of leaving unemployment: regression coefficients, with z statistics in parentheses	128

Preface

In this book I seek to clarify what a mechanism-based explanatory strategy looks like. At the core of the approach is a set of mechanisms that specifies how individuals are influenced by those with whom they interact. Such mechanisms are not only the object of this book, they also explain why the book looks the way it does.

I have benefited greatly from interactions with numerous colleagues in Europe as well as in the United States. First of all I would like to thank Yvonne Åberg. Not only is she the co-author of one of the chapters, she has also served as a constructive discussion partner throughout this book project. Others who have made time to read and comment on the book include Peter Abell, Patrik Aspers, Filippo Barbera, Peter Bearman, Markus Berger, Michael Biggs, Raymond Boudon, Richard Breen, Magnus Bygren, Mohamed Cherkaoui, Christofer Edling, David Freedman, John Goldthorpe, Carl le Grand, Ann-Sofie Kolm, Fredrik Liljeros, Lars Lindahl, Renate Meyntz, Carina Mood-Roman, Krister Segerberg, Mattias Smångs, Ryszard Szulkin, Lars Udehn and Björn Wittrock. I am extremely grateful to you all.

I also have had the great fortune to be affiliated to several excellent academic institutions; the Department of Sociology at Stockholm University, the Swedish Collegium for Advanced Studies in the Social Sciences (SCASSS) and Nuffield College, Oxford. These institutions have allowed me to concentrate on my research for extended periods of time and have provided most stimulating intellectual environments. I am particularly indebted to SCASSS. Without its generous support at the outset of this project, this book would never have been written.

The research reported in the book also has been supported by generous grants from the following research councils: the Swedish Research Council, the Swedish Council for Working Life and Social Research, the Bank of Sweden Tercentenary Foundation and the NEST/Path Finder initiative of the European Community (MMCOMNET).

Last but not least I would like to express my gratitude to Sarah Caro, my editor at Cambridge University Press, for her patience and support.

Oxford
August 2005

1 The analytical tradition in sociology

Over the past several decades leading sociologists in Europe and in the United States have expressed strong reservations about the explanatory power of sociological theory and research (e.g. Abbott 1998; Boudon 2002; Coleman 1986b; Sørensen 1998). They are concerned that much sociological theory has evolved into a form of metatheorizing without any specific empirical referents, and that much empirical sociological research has developed into a rather shallow form of variable analysis with only limited explanatory power.[1] The main message of this book is that a path must be hewn between the eclectic empiricism of variable-based sociology and the often vacuous writings of the 'grand' social theorists.[2]

This approach to sociological theorizing and research, which I refer to as 'analytical sociology', seeks to explain complex social processes by carefully dissecting them and then bringing into focus their most important constituent components. The approach focuses on traditional sociological concerns but uses explanatory strategies more often found in analytical philosophy and behavioural economics. It is an approach that seeks precise, abstract, realistic and action-based explanations for various social phenomena.

As a general road map to this book, in this introductory chapter I give a brief overview of the approach adopted. The overview is organized under the following four headings:

- Explanation
- Dissection and abstraction
- Precision and clarity
- Action

---

[1] See also the various contributions in Hedström and Swedberg (1998a).
[2] I do not pay much attention to the 'grand' social theorists in this book. The secondary literature on these scholars is, in my view, already far too voluminous, and they do not have much to contribute to the agenda of analytical sociology. I return to the problems posed by variable-based sociology in chapters 2 and 5, however.

I will define the distinctive features of the approach in these terms. In addition, at the end of this chapter I situate it intellectually by briefly discussing the works of some of the most important contemporary contributors to the tradition.

Explanation

Analytical sociology focuses on explanation. Unlike descriptions, which typically seek answers to 'what' questions, explanations provide answers to 'why' questions. Explanations account for why events happen, why something changes over time or why states or events co-vary in time or space. As will be noted in chapter 2, there is no general agreement on what an acceptable explanation should look like. Many sociologists set an equals sign between explanations and predictive accuracy, for example, while many philosophers take the position that an acceptable explanation consists in subsuming the event to be explained under a general causal law.

The purpose of this book is to describe and discuss the logic of an explanatory strategy. Consequently, the notion of what an appropriate explanation should look like is at the very core of the enterprise. Once we have decided what we should aim for, much of the rest will follow. Had I, for instance, subscribed to the notion that appropriate explanations specify factors that seem to make a difference to the probability of observing the events to be explained, as Salmon (1971) and many statistically oriented sociologists do, this book would have looked very different. The position taken here, rather, is that mechanism-based explanations are the most appropriate type of explanation for the social sciences. The core idea behind the mechanism approach is that we explain a social phenomenon by referring to a constellation of entities and activities, typically actors and their actions, that are linked to one another in such a way that they regularly bring about the type of phenomenon we seek to explain.

Dissection and abstraction

As the title of this book indicates, one important characteristic of the analytical approach is that it aims to gain understanding by dissecting the social phenomena to be explained. To dissect, as the term is used here, is to decompose a complex totality into its constituent entities and activities and then to bring into focus what is believed to be its most essential elements. When focusing on what is believed to be particularly important for the problem at hand, we abstract from, or move out of focus, those elements believed to be of lesser importance. In this sense, dissection and abstraction are two aspects of the same activity, and they are core components of the analytical approach. It is through dissection and abstraction that the important cogs and wheels of social processes are made visible and intelligible.

In certain areas of the social sciences, most notably in economics, there is general agreement on the importance of abstract theories. But in these areas one also often finds rather instrumental attitudes towards theories: theoretical assumptions are often seen as mere instruments that can be freely tinkered with until one arrives at simple and elegant models. An important theme of this book is that one should resist such fictionalist temptations. An explanatory theory must refer to the actual mechanisms at work, not to those that could have been at work in a fictional world invented by the theorist.

In *The Structure of Social Action* (1937), Talcott Parsons likewise stressed the importance of making a clear distinction between abstractions and fictions. The methodological position he arrived at after analyzing the writings of Marshall, Pareto, Durkheim and Weber he termed 'analytical realism':

the general concepts of science are not fictional but adequately 'grasp' aspects of the objective external world . . . Hence, the position here taken is, in an epistemological sense, realistic. At the same time it avoids the objectionable implications of an empiricist realism. The concepts correspond, not to concrete phenomena, but to elements in them which are analytically separable from other elements . . . Hence it is necessary to qualify the term realism with 'analytical'. (Parsons 1937: 730)

Developing explanatory theory involves a delicate balance between realism and abstraction. Although it is difficult to specify a priori what should be considered a sufficiently faithful representation of a social process, the question is of fundamental importance. Explanatory theories can never be based on fictitious accounts, because such accounts cannot provide convincing answers to the question of why we observe what we observe. What must be aimed for is 'analytical realism' in Parsons' sense of the term.[3]

Precision and clarity

The quest for precision and clarity also characterizes the analytical approach. If it is not perfectly clear what a given theory or theorist is

---

[3] I return to the relationship between abstraction, realism and explanation in chapter 2, when discussing theories of explanations, and in chapter 3, when discussing instrumentalist tendencies within rational-choice theory.

trying to say, how can we then possibly understand and assess the potential merits of the theory being proposed? On an even more fundamental level, the purpose of theorizing, it seems to me, should always be to clarify matters, to make the complex and seemingly obscure clear and understandable. But if the theory itself lacks clarity, this goal cannot be attained.

My favourite example of a mystifying statement is the following, in which Pierre Bourdieu tries explicitly to define his master concept of *habitus*. According to Bourdieu (1990: 53), habitus should be understood as

systems of durable, transposable dispositions, structured structures predisposed to function as structuring structures, that is, as principles which generate and organize practices and representations that can be objectively adapted to their outcomes without presupposing a conscious aiming at ends or an express mastery of the operations necessary in order to attain them. Objectively 'regulated' and 'regular' without being in any way the product of obedience to rules, they can be collectively orchestrated without being the product of the organizing action of a conductor.

Ambiguous definitions like this are like mental clouds that mystify rather than clarify. From an explanatory point of view, they are clearly unsatisfactory. It seems as if Bourdieu is trying to say that individuals often behave in habitual ways without consciously reflecting upon what they are doing, and that individuals who occupy similar positions in some abstractly defined social space tend to behave in similar ways; but I must admit that I am not entirely sure whether this interpretation is correct. Nevertheless, the main point I wish to make is that his statement lacks clarity and precision. Not only is it unclear what *habitus* actually refers to, it is also unclear why he believes that *habitus*, whatever it is, operates the way it does. If we want to propose that one phenomenon partly or fully explains another, ambiguous statements like these are unacceptable. At least, it must be clear what phenomena we are referring to and how we believe they are interrelated.

Clarity, in the sense of precision, is important for a slightly different reason as well. As is discussed in later chapters, small and seemingly insignificant differences or events can sometimes make a huge difference to the processes we are trying to explain. If our concepts and theories are not sufficiently precise to pick up on such differences, they are not capable of explaining why we observe what we observe. For these various reasons clarity, precision and fine-grained distinctions are of crucial importance for the development of explanatory theory.

Action

When a complex totality is decomposed into its constituent components, the type of problem being analyzed will obviously dictate which entities and activities are considered important. In sociological inquiries, however, the core entity always tends to be the actors in the social system being analyzed, and the core activity tends to be the actions of these actors. Through their actions actors make society 'tick', and without their actions social processes would come to a halt. Theories of action are therefore of fundamental importance for explanatory sociological theories and, as is discussed at great length in later chapters, we can understand why actors do what they do if we assume that their behaviour is endowed with meaning, that is, that there is an intention explaining why they do what they do.[4]

To understand why actors do what they do is not sufficient, however; we must also seek to explain why, acting as they do, they bring about the social outcomes they do. Sociology as a discipline is not concerned with explaining the actions of single individuals. The focus on actions is merely an intermediate step in an explanatory strategy that seeks to understand change at a social level. As the term is used here, the *social* refers to collective properties that are not definable by reference to any single member of the collectivity. Important examples of such properties include:[5]

- typical actions, beliefs or desires among the members of the collectivity
- distributions and aggregate patterns such as spatial distributions and inequalities
- topologies of networks that describe relationships between the members of the collectivity
- informal rules or social norms that constrain the actions of the members of the collectivity

Since changes in such social properties must be either intended or unintended outcomes of individuals' actions – how else could they possibly be brought about? – they should be analyzed as such. But the structure of social interaction, that is, who interacts with whom, is of

[4] To avoid possible misunderstandings, it should be pointed out at the outset that this emphasis on action-based explanations does not imply a commitment to any extreme form of methodological individualism that denies the explanatory importance of pre-existing social structures. The position taken here is what Udehn (2001) refers to as 'structural individualism'. This is discussed further in chapters 3 and 4.

[5] For a similar definition of the 'social,' see Carlsson (1968).

explanatory significance in its own right. Therefore, social interactions and structures of interaction networks are recurrent themes throughout this book.

The analytical tradition in sociology

Although the term *analytical sociology* is not commonly used,[6] the type of sociology designated by the term has an important history that can be traced back to the works of late nineteenth- and early twentieth-century sociologists such as Max Weber and Alexis de Tocqueville, and to prominent mid-twentieth-century sociologists such as the early Talcott Parsons and Robert K. Merton.[7] Among contemporary social scientists, four in particular have profoundly influenced the analytical approach. They are Jon Elster, Raymond Boudon, Thomas Schelling and James Coleman. In order to place the analytical approach on the contemporary sociology map, I will briefly describe their respective contributions to the analytical agenda.

Jon Elster has had considerable influence on the philosophical foundations of the analytical approach. Starting with his early work, in which he used modal logic to analyze social phenomena (Elster 1978), and continuing with his critique of the logic of functionalist explanations in the social sciences (Elster 1983a; 1985), he demonstrated the relevance of the analytical-philosophy tradition for the social sciences. Much of his work during the last twenty-five years has been concerned with the logic of action-based explanations and the relationship between rationality, social norms and emotions (Elster 1979; 1983b; 1989a; 1989c; 1991; 1994; 1996; 1998a; 1999). His writings in these areas have established important links between sociological theory, the philosophy of action and behavioural economics.

As noted above, many scholars in the rational-choice tradition, not least the economists, tend to adopt rather instrumentalist attitudes towards theories. In contrast, Elster's position has always been that of an analytical realist. While arguing for the necessity of abstractions, he has

---

[6] Exceptions include Burger (1977), J. H. Turner (1987a) and Pearce (1994). Turner's and Pearce's uses of the concept are rather different from the one adopted here, however, and Burger's discussion of Parsonian analytical sociology concerns only the methodological and epistemological aspects of the approach. See also Barbera (2004).

[7] Swedberg (1998) discusses some of Weber's most relevant work, and Elster (1993) some of Tocqueville's most relevant work. Interesting discussions of Parsons' analytical approach can be found in Bershady (1974), Burger (1977) and Camic (1987), and insightful discussions of Merton's middle-range approach are found in Boudon (1991) and Pawson (2000).

always insisted that genuine explanations must account for what happens, as it happens (e.g., Elster 1989b), and he has expressed deep dissatisfaction with the instrumentalism and fictionalism that characterize some rational-choice analyses (e.g., Elster 2000).

In certain respects Boudon's role in the development of analytical sociology has been similar to Elster's. In numerous publications he has insisted on the importance of action-based explanations and the dangers of instrumentalism. In particular, he has emphasized the importance of basing explanations on realistic theories of action that recognize the cognitive limitations of real individuals (e.g., Boudon 1981; 1982; 1994; 1998b; 2003). But while Elster's point of reference has mainly been analytical philosophy and behavioural economics, Boudon has been primarily engaged in a dialogue with the classics of sociology, most notably with Durkheim, Tocqueville, Simmel and Weber (e.g., Boudon 1981; 1986; 1994).

Boudon's deeper grounding in the sociological tradition can also be seen in the close attention he has given to the micro–macro link, that is, to the social outcomes of individual action. Early on he used simulation models to analyze the link between the educational decisions of individuals and the social properties of the educational system at large (Boudon 1974), and he argued for the general importance of 'generative models' for explaining the social outcomes of action (Boudon 1979). He succinctly summarized his Weberian-inspired explanatory strategy with the following equation: $M = M\{m[S(M')]\}$. What he meant is that a social phenomenon, M, should be explained as a function, M, of actions, m. These actions should be seen as being dependent on the social situation, S, in which they take place, and these social situations, in turn, should be seen as being dependent on other social phenomena, M' (see Boudon 1986). The explanatory strategies advocated in this book follow similar principles.

Some of Thomas Schelling's work has also been concerned with the logic of action (Schelling 1984b), and he has made important theoretical contributions to the analysis of conflict (Schelling 1960). From the vantage point of analytical sociology, however, his most important contributions are those dealing with the micro–macro link. Although he is not a sociologist by training but, in his own words, an 'errant economist' (Schelling 1984a), his *Micromotives and Macrobehavior* (1978) is one the most important sociology books published in recent decades. In it he develops useful analytical tools and analyzes the social outcomes that groups of interacting individuals are likely to bring about.

Schelling's best-known study of the link between micro motives and macro-level outcomes focuses on patterns of racial segregation

(Schelling 1971). In it he shows that even open-minded and unprejudiced individuals can bring about highly segregated neighbourhoods. When individuals' actions depend on what others have done in the past, even highly integrated neighbourhoods can unravel because if one individual leaves the neighbourhood a chain reaction can be set in motion, leading many others to do the same. The general lesson to be learned from this and related analyses by Schelling concerns the apparent disjunction between the macro and the micro levels. Aggregate or macro-level patterns usually say surprisingly little about why we observe particular aggregate patterns, and our explanations must therefore focus on the micro-level processes that brought them about.

The micro–macro link was a major focus of James Coleman's writings as well. From his early research on diffusion processes to his rational-choice-based analyses in the 1980s and 1990s, the links between these two levels of analysis were a core concern (Coleman 1973; 1986b; 1990; Coleman, Katz and Menzel 1957; 1966). Like most sociologists, Coleman was primarily interested in social or macro-level phenomena, but unlike many sociologists he always emphasized that changes in them must be explained by reference to the actions that brought them about. In order to explain social or macro-level change it is not sufficient to simply relate macro-level phenomena to one another. To be explanatory a theory must specify the set of causal mechanisms that are likely to have brought about the change, and this requires one to demonstrate how macro states at one point in time influence individuals' actions, and how these actions bring about new macro states at a later point in time.

Another aspect of Coleman's work that is of considerable importance for analytical sociology is his view on how to link theory and quantitative research. Unlike Elster, Boudon and Schelling, who are predominantly theorists, Coleman was also an empirical researcher and as such interested in bridging the gap between quantitative research and sociological theory. While most quantitative sociologists use rather ad hoc statistical models in their research, Coleman insisted that statistical analyses are meaningful only insofar as they are based on plausible models of the processes through which the phenomena to be explained were brought about (Coleman 1964; 1981; 1986b). If this is not the case, the statistical estimates will have little bearing on the proposed sociological explanation.

Although Elster, Boudon, Schelling and Coleman are rather different types of scholars, they complement each other in important ways, and they all share a commitment to precise, abstract, realistic and action-based explanations. Building upon the foundations laid by them, an analytical middle-range approach to sociological theory can be developed that avoids the somewhat empiricist and eclectic tendencies of Merton's original middle-range approach (Merton 1967). This type of analytical theory is abstract, realistic and precise, and it seeks to explain specific social phenomena on the basis of explicitly formulated theories of action and interaction. This book is a modest contribution to that agenda.

Outline of the book

Chapter 2, 'Social mechanisms and explanatory theory', is a core chapter of the book. In it I discuss different types of explanations and present the arguments in favour of mechanism-based explanations. Adopting this notion means that an appropriate explanation consists in detailing the constellation of entities and activities that regularly bring about the type of outcome to be explained. The chapter is a core chapter in the sense that the other chapters are to a large extent concerned with working out what logically seems to follow from the positions taken in this chapter, that is, what consequences a mechanism-based approach has for an explanatory sociological theory.

The social-mechanism approach assigns a unique explanatory role to action. In chapter 3, 'Action and interaction', I take as my point of departure an action theory that explains action in terms of actors' desires, beliefs and opportunities, the so-called DBO theory. I then consider social interaction from the perspective of this action theory and identify various mechanisms through which the actions or behaviours of some actors can come to influence the actions of others. Social interactions are at the core of most sociological theories for the simple reason that actions often cannot be explained unless they are related to the actions of others. I conclude the chapter by briefly discussing rational-choice theory and what I consider to be an unfortunate instrumentalist tendency among many of its proponents. Knowingly accepting false assumptions because they lead to better predictions or to more elegant models threatens the explanatory value and the long-term viability of the rational-choice approach.

Theories of action are thus of fundamental importance for explanatory sociological theories. But to understand why actors act as they do is not sufficient; we must also seek to explain why, acting as they do, they bring about the social outcomes they do. Chapter 4, 'Social interaction and social change', therefore focuses on the link between individual actions and social change. First I critically discuss some positions that treat social reality as if it were stratified into different ontological levels that can be causally analyzed independently of each other. This sort of reification obscures rather than clarifies, and typically leads to rather superficial causal accounts and explanations. I then illustrate how one must proceed if one is to develop theories that explicitly consider the dynamic interplay between the individual and the social by using DBO theory as the foundation of a so-called agent-based simulation analysis. The analyses presented in the chapter underscore how important the structure of social interaction is in its own right for the social outcomes observed. Furthermore, they show that there is no necessary proportionality between the size or uniqueness of a social phenomenon and the size or uniqueness of its causes. Large-scale social phenomena may simply be the result of uncommon combinations of common events and circumstances.

Chapter 5, 'On causal modelling', discusses different traditions of empirical sociological research. The main message of the chapter is that, in order to have a direct bearing on sociological theory, sociological research must take theory much more seriously than is typically done today. Quantitative empirical research should be based on substantively meaningful models of the social mechanisms believed to be at work and not, as is common today, on generic statistical models that simply summarize the statistical relations found in a specific set of data.

Chapter 6, 'Quantitative research, agent-based modelling, and theories of the social', is co-authored with Yvonne Åberg and illustrates how one can go about testing and empirically calibrating the type of mechanism-based explanations advocated in previous chapters. The essence of the approach is to use statistical analyses to examine various bits and pieces of the mechanistic machinery, and then to specify an agent-based model on the basis of the results. The approach provides a micro-to-macro link that makes it possible to derive the social-level implications of a set of quantitative research results. We use unemployment in Stockholm during the 1990s as a case study to illustrate concretely how these ideas can be put into practice.

Chapter 7 concludes this book by briefly summarizing some of its most important themes and discussing some items high on the future agenda of analytical sociology.

2 Social mechanisms and explanatory theory

In this chapter I argue for the importance of a specific kind of abstract analytical theorizing that differs from many other types of sociological theorizing in its focus on social mechanisms. A social mechanism, as defined here, is a constellation of entities and activities that are linked to one another in such a way that they regularly bring about a particular type of outcome. We explain an observed phenomenon by referring to the social mechanism by which such a phenomenon is regularly brought about.

The purpose of the chapter is threefold. First, I very briefly discuss different notions of theorizing within contemporary sociology. Sociology is a fragmented discipline and theorizing means different things to different sociologists. Second, I consider at some length what 'explanation' entails. Sociologists differ not only on what they consider to be the objective of theorizing, but also on the meanings they attach to the concept of 'explanation.' Third, I discuss in some detail the main thrust of the mechanism-based approach developed here.

As this brief synopsis indicates, in this chapter I touch upon a range of difficult problems related to causation and explanation. It goes without saying that a discussion of such vast and difficult problems runs the risk of being perceived as shallow. But the purpose of the chapter must be kept in mind. My intention is not to contribute to the theory of explanations or to the philosophy of the social sciences. The purpose is to outline an explanatory framework that I believe to be of crucial importance for sociology, and in doing this I draw upon some of the relevant philosophical literature. This literature is of considerable importance for sociology because it identifies general criteria that can assist us in distinguishing between adequate and inadequate explanations. By being rigorous about what an adequate explanation should look like, we are likely to arrive at better theories and research than otherwise. Sociology is likely to benefit from a strict 'Ulyssean' strategy of precommitting itself to certain explanatory standards, or so I suggest here.

Varieties of sociological theorizing

In most scientific fields and in much of the philosophy of science literature, 'theories' are seen as abstract codifications of knowledge that allow us to explain and predict events and processes, and a 'theorist' is a person who contributes to the development of such theories. But this is not always the case in sociology. Some sociological theorists see it as their main mission to voice and give expression to deeply felt sentiments and concerns in society (e.g., Beck and Ritter 1992). Others see their role as interpreters of societal trends and conditions (e.g., Bauman 2001; Castells 2000), and yet others view social theory as a predominantly normative endeavour, the main purpose of which is to criticize and/or suggest alternatives to existing social, cultural and economic orders (e.g., Habermas 1987).

The fragmentation of the discipline is readily seen in recent 'hand-books' of sociological and social theory, such as those by B. S. Turner (1996), Sica (1998) and Ritzer and Smart (2001). The editors of these volumes seem to equate theory with everything from general reflections on modernity to exegetic digressions on the founding fathers of the discipline.[1] Whatever value these various non-explanatory traditions in social theory may have, they are not the concern of this book. In my view, too much social theory currently falls within these non-explanatory traditions, and it therefore appears more essential to try to develop and strengthen the traditional canon of explanatory theorizing.[2]

What, then, does it mean to 'explain' something? In answering this question, let me start with stating what an explanation is not. First of all, explanations are not *descriptions*. As emphasized by Sen (1980), the choices and judgements involved in producing good descriptions

---

[1] The former editor of *Sociological Theory*, Craig Calhoun, made a similar observation when trying to characterize the submissions he received to the journal. He noted that the submissions all too often were 'summaries of what dead people said (with no indication of why living ones should care or how the revered ancestor's work would advance contemporary analytic projects)' and 'criticisms of what other people have said that dead people said (with no more indication of why we should care than that those criticized are famous)' (Calhoun 1996: 1).

[2] A telling sign of the current state of the discipline, at least in Britain, is the official website of the British Sociological Association (http://www.britsoc.co.uk). The history of the discipline there is approvingly described as a movement from explanations to reflections. According to the BSA, in the nineteenth century there was a view of the discipline as offering 'explanations of the collective entities and relationships of human beings'. This by now outmoded view has been replaced by a 'modern' reflexive view: 'From this original purpose . . . sociology has moved on to more reflexive attempts to understand how society works.'

resemble those faced when one makes predictions or proposes explanations, but descriptions differ in important respects from explanations. A description of something tells us how it is constituted, or how it varies over time or between different groups or social settings, but it does not say *why* it looks, changes or varies as it does.[3] This also holds true for a common form of 'thick' descriptive work, where one 'interprets' a phenomenon by describing it with a vocabulary borrowed from some specific sociological tradition such as symbolic interactionism (see Charon 2001 for various examples). The exact boundaries between descriptions and explanations are not always clear-cut, but it should be noted that 'to explain' and 'to describe', although interrelated, provide answers to different types of questions.[4]

Second, explanations differ from *typologies* and *taxonomies*. Much sociological theory consists of typologies. We have class typologies (e.g., Wright 1997), welfare-state typologies (e.g., Esping-Andersen 1990), and typologies of historical trajectories (e.g., Therborn 1995), to mention a few. Such typologies can be extremely useful in that they can create order out of otherwise perplexing chaos. But typologies are not explanations. They are classificatory devices that allow us to attach labels to different phenomena in an orderly fashion, but they do not tell us why we observe the phenomena we observe. Thus, as the terms are used here, we can have a typology of explanations and we can have a typology based on explanations, but we cannot have an explanatory typology.

A basic characteristic of all explanations is that they provide plausible causal accounts for why events happen, why something changes over time, or why states or events co-vary in time or space. At least three types of explanations can be identified in the literature that differ in terms of the types of answers they consider appropriate to such why-questions.[5] These three types of explanations are (1) covering-law explanations,

---

[3] To avoid any misunderstandings, answers to explanatory *why* questions often consist in detailing *how* the phenomena to be explained were brought about.

[4] Descriptions and explanations are always interrelated in the sense that what social reality is held to be also is that which we seek to explain. See Archer (1995).

[5] A fourth view of what causality is and what an explanation entails is found in the counterfactual approach most closely associated with the writings of David Lewis (e.g. 1973). The basic idea here is that an event, C, can be said to be a cause of an event, E, if and only if it is the case that if C had not occurred E would not have occurred. This approach has not had much influence on sociological theory, however, and therefore it is not discussed here. It has had some influence on the statistical methods used by sociologists to test hypotheses about causal effects, and I will therefore have occasion to return to the counterfactual approach in chapter 5.

Table 2.1. *Main types of explanations*

	Covering law explanations	Statistical explanations	Mechanism explanations
Explanatory principle	To subsume under a causal law	To identify a statistical relationship	To specify a social mechanism
Key explanatory factors	No restrictions, except that the factor must exhibit a law-like relation to the event to be explained	No restrictions, except that the factor must be statistically relevant to the event to be explained	Action-relevant entities and activities and the way in which they are linked to one another

(2) statistical explanations, and (3) mechanism explanations. The main differences between them are set out in table 2.1.[6]

Before discussing these different types of explanations, we must deal with one terminological issue. Most philosophers of science insist that causes and effects must be *events*, while sociologists and other social scientists also refer to social states and various individual attributes as potential causes and effects. In many respects the former terminology appears more precise and appropriate for the simple reason that causes bring things about, and what is brought about (that is, the effect) cannot have been there before, and therefore what is brought about must be a change or an event. Similarly, it is difficult to see how change can be brought about except by another change, which suggests that causes are events too. Nevertheless, I use standard sociological terminology and refer to states and other non-events as potential causes and effects as well. Substantively this does not seem to be of much import. From an event-causation perspective, one would not view such entities as proper causes, but one could see them as conditions that make it possible for one event to cause another (Lombard 1990). Similarly, non-events could, as effects, be viewed as the aggregate (or otherwise combined) outcome of a series of events.

---

[6] Unless otherwise noted, I will use 'mechanisms', 'causal mechanisms' and 'social mechanisms' as synonymous terms. Also, although my choice of wording may be a bit ambiguous here and there, a 'mechanism' refers to the real empirical entities and activities that bring about phenomena. These should be distinguished from theories or models of mechanisms, since we otherwise are likely to commit what Whitehead (1930: 52) called 'the fallacy of misplaced concreteness'. Most of the discussions in this book are concerned with the models of or theories about real mechanisms.

Covering-law explanations

One of the most influential notions of what an appropriate explanation should look like is the 'covering-law model' most closely associated with the work of Carl Hempel (e.g., Hempel 1965). Assume that we have an event, e, that we seek to explain. In order to provide an appropriate answer to the question 'Why did e happen?' we subsume the event under a general law. That is, we explain e by pointing to one or several general laws and the conditions that make these laws applicable to the specific case.[7]

To illustrate the logic of his proposal Hempel often used the example of an automobile radiator cracking during a freezing-cold night. The general laws cited in the explanation would need to refer to how the pressure exerted by water varies with changes in temperature and volume, and the initial conditions referred to would be conditions such as the temperature during the night and the bursting pressure of the radiator. A proper explanation has been proposed if, and only if, the sentence describing the cracking of the radiator can be logically deduced from the sentences stating the laws and the initial conditions. From a covering-law perspective, the appropriate answer to the question 'Why do we observe phenomenon X?' is that X was *expected* given the existence of certain causal laws.

To the extent that general laws of the kind 'All A are B' exist, Hempel's proposal seems highly attractive. If B is a property describing society x, a perfectly reasonable answer to the question 'Why is x a B?' would be that society x is an 'A' and 'All A are B'. But although they are attractive in principle, such explanations are of limited relevance to the social sciences because we do not yet know of any general laws of the 'All A are B' kind, and human agency seems to render such laws highly implausible in the social and the cultural sciences.

The 'law-like' relationships that it might be possible to establish in the social sciences are instead of a probabilistic nature, and Hempel proposed a different explanatory model in such situations. The differences in the explanatory logic between these two models can be described in the following way:

---

[7] Although Hempel specified in detail the logic of this type of explanation, the basic idea behind the covering-law model has been around for a long time and was formulated in the following way by John Stuart Mill: 'An individual fact is said to be explained, by pointing to its cause, that is, by stating the law or laws of causation, of which its production is an instance' (1874: 332). See also Braithwaite (1953) for another influential work with a view similar to that of Hempel.

1. All A are B.
   $\underline{x\ is\ A.}$
   x is B.

2. Most A are B.
   $\underline{\underline{x\ is\ A.\ [p]}}$
   x is likely to be B.

The single line in (1) represents a deductive relation between the premises and the conclusion. The double line in (2) represents an inductive relation, and p states the conditional probability of the conclusion given the premises. Hempel referred to (1) as the 'deductive-nomological' model, and to (2) as the 'inductive-probabilistic' model.

Once again, Hempel's proposal seems reasonable as far as it goes. The problem is that it does not seem to go very far. First of all, as pointed out by Nagel (1961), Salmon (1971) and others, the covering-law model does not seem to describe adequately the defining characteristics of what are generally considered to be acceptable scientific explanations. First, there exist generally accepted scientific explanations – not the least in the social sciences – that would not be considered acceptable if we were to follow Hempel's model because of the difficulty of specifying any relevant laws. Second, there exist statements that fulfil all of Hempel's logical requirements but which nevertheless are not explanatory. The following 'explanation' is a case in point. If we wanted to explain the fact that Peter did not become pregnant, the following line of reasoning would appear to be acceptable from Hempel's perspective (adopted from Salmon 1971):

> No one who regularly takes birth-control pills becomes pregnant.
> Peter regularly takes birth-control pills.
> (Therefore) Peter did not become pregnant.

The fact to be explained can be logically deduced from the premises – both of which can be assumed to be true – but the explanation is nevertheless incorrect because it refers to the wrong causal mechanism.

Furthermore, and related to the latter type of objection, Hempel's model is not sufficiently restrictive in the sense that it does not rule out obviously superficial explanations. Hempel's form of explanation entails applying a law to a specific situation. The insights offered by this exercise depend on the depth and robustness of the 'law'. If this 'law' is only a statistical association, which is the norm in the social and cultural sciences (according to Hempel as well), the specific explanation will offer no more insight than the statistical association itself and will usually only suggest that an event is likely to happen but give no clue as to why this is likely to be the case.

Consider the following example. It would be possible to statistically estimate the parameters of an equation describing the relationship between the intake of, say, strychnine and the risk of dying. If the statistical model had the correct functional form and took into account relevant factors such as body weight, we could describe the result as a 'probabilistic law' of the dose – response relationship, and we could use this 'law' as one of the premises when explaining why individual x died after ingesting a specific dose of strychnine: given individual x's intake of strychnine and our 'probabilistic law', we could have predicted what would happen. In this sense we would also have explained the death of x because this outcome was expected given the initial conditions and the 'probabilistic law'.

Such an explanation seems wanting, however. When posing such questions in a scientific context we normally expect answers that not only state *that* the event was likely because this is what has happened in the past, we also want to know *why* this is so. Below I discuss in some detail the important role played by causal mechanisms in providing such answers, but it already seems clear that what is required is some form of mechanism that provides an intelligible link between the causal factor and the event to be explained. By pointing to how strychnine typically inhibits the respiratory centre of the brain and to the biochemical processes typically responsible for such paralysis, we provide a mechanism that allows us not only to predict *what* is likely to happen but also to explain *why* (Bunge 1967). For these reasons, I am inclined to agree with von Wright that it is better 'not to say that the inductive-probabilistic model [of Hempel] explains what happens, but to say only that it justifies certain expectations and predictions' (von Wright 1971: 14).

The covering-law model has encouraged and legitimized a type of theorizing that I do not think has been entirely conducive to the development of a rigorous body of explanatory theory. The problem is not with the mode of theorizing as such. In fact, the precision and clarity of those endorsing this mode of theorizing often greatly surpass those of other theorists. The problem is rather the aforementioned lack of restrictions on the content of the propositions. Let me examine one semi-classic example, Peter Blau's theory of organizational differentiation (Blau 1970).

Blau's theory of organizational differentiation, as noted by Calhoun, Meyer and Scott (1990), was in many respects a direct precursor of his later so-called macro-sociological theory of social structure (e.g., Blau

1977), and it exemplifies his approach to theorizing even more clearly than the latter theory. With reference to the work of Hempel and Braithwaite, Blau argued that general propositions of the aforementioned kind are at the heart of all explanations: 'Inasmuch as the generalizations [that is, the general propositions] subsume many empirically demonstrated propositions, that is, logically imply them, they explain these regularities' (Blau 1970: 202).

Blau's general 'law-like' propositions were the following:

1. Increasing size generates structural differentiation in organizations along various dimensions at decelerating rates.
2. Structural differentiation in organizations enlarges the administrative component.

Expressed more plainly, these propositions say that when organizations grow in size the elements of their internal composition – for example, the number of different job tasks and the number of departments – also tend to increase, but the increase will gradually level off the larger the organization gets. This 'structural differentiation', in turn, tends to increase the proportion of administrative personnel in the organization.

On the basis of these general propositions Blau then deduced a set of 'lower-level' propositions that follow from the simultaneous operation of these two law-like propositions. The details need not concern us here, however, since we are exclusively interested in Blau's theory as an example of a type of sociological theorizing that has been much influenced by the writings of Hempel and other logical positivists. According to Blau, theories are systems of general propositions, and explanations are arrived at by subsuming the events to be explained under the law-like regularities expressed in these propositions.

It is also of interest to note that theorists in this tradition often seem to consider it a strength if their explanations make no reference to actions or to 'psychological' phenomena such as beliefs and desires. In the words of Blau (1970: 203): 'The theory centers attention on the social forces that govern the interrelations among differentiated elements in a formal structure and ignores the psychological forces that govern individual behavior. Formal structures exhibit regularities that can be studied in their own right without investigating the motives of the individuals in organizations.' In similar vein, Donald Black (1979: 149–50) summarized his approach to 'pure sociology' in the following way: '[Pure sociology] has nothing to say about how people experience themselves, their freedom of choice, or the causes of their actions . . . It is a way to predict and explain the behavior of social life, and that is all' (see also Black 1976; Black 2000; Mayhew 1980; Mayhew 1981).

The type of approach advocated by Blau and Black follows rather naturally if one adopts the covering-law model. However, a basic flaw with this mode of theorizing, as I see it, is that it excludes from the explanation exactly those processes that would have allowed us to understand why social entities exhibit the regularities they do. In this respect, theories like these are wanting for the same reason that the correlation-based explanation of the relationship between the intake of strychnine and the risk of dying is wanting: they are both black-box explanations that exclude from focus those processes that would allow us to understand why a specific causal factor is likely to be of explanatory relevance.[8] What are lacking in the approach of Blau, Black and other methodological 'holists' are the basic entities and activities that generate these correlations. The most reasonable ontological hypothesis we can formulate in order to make sense of the social world as we know it is that it is individuals in interaction with others that generate the social regularities we observe. Hence, social interaction processes are the parallels to the biochemical processes in the strychnine example. Both constitute the intelligible links between the explanatory factors and the events to be explained that are required to answer the type of why-questions normally posed by explanatory sciences, and it is these types of processes that are missing in Blau's type of theory.[9] Even if one suspects that there are 'nomic' law-like social regularities, it seems more reasonable, as von Wright (1989: 838) once pointed out, to try to understand first *why* this is so before we accord explanatory force to the 'law' *that* it is so. For these reasons, and as is discussed in more detail below, we are likely to arrive at better and more precise sociological theories if they are based upon explicit theories of action.

Blau defended his methodological position with a line of argumentation common to many of those advocating similar holistic or pseudo holistic approaches: 'Social structures (and indeed all structures composed of subunits) have emergent properties that cannot be understood on the basis of the properties of the subunits' (Blau 1986: ix). Blau never explained why he believed this to be the case, that is, whether his belief was based on ontological or methodological considerations. Therefore

---

[8] As noted by Goldstone (1998), an explanatory logic similar to the one criticized here is also at the heart of much of contemporary comparative-historical work.

[9] See Harré (1985) for a similar view of the parallels between causal mechanisms in the natural sciences and reason-based explanations in the social sciences. See also Abell (2004).

his statement remained rather vacuous. Although it may be difficult to explain why we observe the social phenomena we observe, I fail to see why, *in principle*, it would be impossible to explain social phenomena on the basis of the properties and activities of subunits and the way in which they are linked to one another. I return the question about emergence in chapter 4.

Where, then, does this leave us? Although the covering-law model has many attractive features, I do not think that the model as such is particularly useful for sociology. The main reasons are the following:

1. The deductive-nomological model is not applicable because the deterministic social laws that it presupposes do not exist.
2. The inductive-probabilistic model is not useful as an explanatory model because (a) it allows for and thereby legitimizes superficial theories and explanations, and (b) it does not give action and intentional explanations the privileged role they should have.

Statistical explanations

While the covering-law model is often referred to in discussions of explanatory strategies in sociology, it is rarely relied on in practice. The type of explanation to be discussed next, statistical explanation, is its opposite in this respect: it is at the heart of most empirical research in sociology but it is rarely discussed in contexts such as this.

The statistical type of explanation differs in important respects from a covering-law explanation. Most importantly, while covering-law explanations are theory-based in the sense that they use existing theories or laws to explain specific events through a deductive argument, statistical explanations are much more inductively oriented and typically do not presuppose any well-specified theories.

The defining characteristic of what here is referred to as a statistical explanation is that an appropriate explanation is at hand when we have identified factors that seem to make a difference to the probability of the event one seeks to explain. The identification of such factors is typically accomplished by decomposing the relevant population into different categories. The logic is best described with a hypothetical example. Much sociological research seeks to answer questions such as: 'Why do we observe a gender gap in earnings?'; 'Why has the support for political party X eroded over time?'; or 'Why are revolutions more likely to occur in certain nations than in others?' The questions refer to a difference between different entities – in these examples between men and women, different time periods, and different nations, respectively – and the answers given are typically based on breaking down the relevant population into different subpopulations. In order to answer the question about the gender gap in earnings, for example, a decomposition as in figure 2.1 may be required.

In order to explain the observed difference in the average earnings between men and women, the population is decomposed. First we decompose it into four different groups based on gender and education, and we examine the average earnings within each of these groups. If at this point the gender differences disappear, that is, if men and women with the same educational levels are paid approximately the same, we may conclude that the explanation for the earnings gap might be that there are relatively more women than men with a low level of education (on the assumption that the highly educated earn more than the poorly educated). If the earnings gap does not disappear, we would further decompose the population. In this example, the next level of decomposition is in terms of work experience. If the gender differences disappear at this stage, we may conclude that the earnings gap is explained by gender differences in education and work experience. If not, we would continue the decomposition and introduce additional factors that could possibly explain the observed earnings differential.

This example is stylized. In reality, more fine-grained decompositions are used and partial accounts of observed differences are all that can be hoped for. In addition, such explicit decompositions are rarely seen in leading journals today; instead, some form of regression model is typically used to perform the same task. Nevertheless, the *logic* behind the analysis can best be understood in these terms: differences in some social states or events are considered to be explained if the decomposition eliminates them, and they are considered to be partially explained if it partially eliminates them.[10]

Unlike the search for 'social laws' discussed in the previous section, statistical analysis is a useful, and in many applied situations the most useful, strategy to pursue. In addition, when the objective is to develop explanatory sociological *theory*, such analyses may be important for 'establishing the facts' that need to be explained, as suggested by Goldthorpe (2000) and others. With reference to the previous example, for instance, rather different theories would seem to be needed if the

---

[10] In the context of regression analysis, the extent to which observed differences are eliminated is typically measured as the proportion of the variance in the outcome variable being 'removed' when the explanatory factors are introduced.

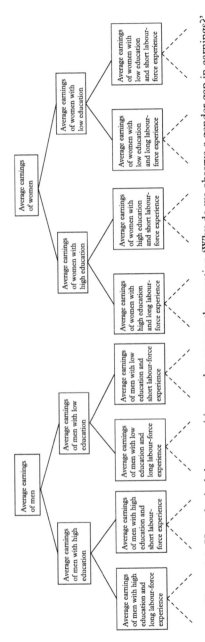

Figure 2.1. Hypothetical decomposition used to answer the question 'Why do we observe a gender gap in earnings?'

gender gap in earnings were due to educational differences between men and women rather than discriminatory practices at the workplace. Without a proper initial decomposition, we may end up focusing our attention on pseudoproblems or on problems that have little or no bearing on the empirical phenomenon that we seek to explain.[11]

Such statistical analysis is often described as a form of 'causal analysis'. If a factor appears to be systematically related to the expected value or the conditional probability of the outcome, then the factor is often referred to as a (probabilistic) 'cause' of the outcome. Although it makes little sense to quibble over words, I would like to reserve the word *cause* for a less casual notion of causality.

Richard Swedberg and I have discussed the limitations of this 'variable approach' in more detail elsewhere (see Hedström and Swedberg 1998b), and I will not repeat that discussion here (but I return to the variable approach and its limitations in chapter 5). In brief, however, I do not believe that a view of theories and explanations as lists of statistically relevant factors is conducive to the development of a rigorous body of sociological theory. Statistical regularities are rarely (if ever) as unequivocal and easily interpretable in causal terms as this view would seem to suggest. As Stinchcombe (1968: 13) once expressed it, 'A student who has difficulty thinking of at least three sensible explanations for any correlation that he is really interested in should probably choose another profession.' Phenomena such as gender differences in earnings, voting trends, political upheavals and most other concerns of sociologists are clearly the result of highly complex social processes. The belief that one should be able to 'read off' their causes by observing relationships between variables such as those discussed above has always seemed a bit naïve to me. Rather than trying to establish 'phenomenological laws' on the basis of statistical analyses, Boudon's suggestion (1976: 117) that we should 'go beyond the statistical relationships to explore the generative mechanism responsible for them' seems to be a more promising path forward, and it is the one pursued in chapter 6. Statistical analyses are important for testing proposed explanations, but it must be remembered that a statistical analysis is a *test* of an explanation, not the explanation itself. This distinction is often obliterated in the statistically oriented tradition.

---

[11] As is discussed in chapter 5, however, one should always be aware that statistical analysis, particularly when it is based on implausible assumptions or on ad hoc statistical models with numerous independent variables, can establish 'artifacts' rather than 'facts', thus hindering us rather than helping us to arrive at appropriate answers (see e.g., Freedman 1991).

Mechanism-based explanations

Although the search for law-like relationships between different social entities – in both their covering-law and causal-modelling guises – seems to be part of sociology's past rather than its future, this does not preclude the possibility of developing rigorous explanatory theories. By focusing on the mechanisms that generate change in social entities, rather than on statistical regularities between variables, a foundation for powerful explanations can be established. Such mechanism-based explanations are at the core of the analytical approach, and the rest of this book is, in one way or another, concerned with explicating and refining this type of explanatory approach. In the remainder of this chapter I focus on the abstract logic of mechanism-based explanations and show how such explanations differ from covering-law and statistical explanations, and in later chapters I give the idea concrete expression in empirical examples.[12]

The core idea behind the mechanism approach is that we explain not by evoking universal laws, or by identifying statistically relevant factors, but by specifying mechanisms that show how phenomena are brought about. Philosophers and social scientists have defined the mechanism concept in numerous ways (e.g. Bhaskar 1978; Bunge 1996; Elster 1999; Gambetta 1998; Glennan 1996; Hedström and Swedberg 1998b; Karlsson 1958; Little 1991; Mahoney 2001; Mayntz 2004; Mcadam, Tarrow and Tilly 2001; Pawson 2000; Salmon 1984; Schelling 1998). Figure 2.2 describes some of the currently most cited definitions of what characterizes a mechanism.

These definitions differ a great deal from one another. Some definitions refer to causal mechanisms in general, while others refer exclusively to social mechanisms; some definitions refer to concretely existing entities, while others refer to models or reasoning about such entities. Underlying them all, however, is an emphasis on making intelligible the regularities being observed – a mechanism explicates the details of how the regularities were brought about.

---

[12] A focus on mechanisms similar to the one advocated here can be found in the work of Bhaskar and other 'critical realists' (see Archer et al. 1998 for an overview). Much of what the critical realists have to say about explanatory strategies in the social sciences I find useful and interesting, but others have said most of this with greater precision. The set of ideas that can be said to be unique to the critical realists tends to be too vague and too normatively oriented to be of much scientific use. Hence, despite somewhat overlapping concerns, there are not many references to the work of the critical realists in the following pages, except in chapter 4 where I critically discuss their notion of a stratified reality.

Author	Definition	References
Bunge	A mechanism is a process in a concrete system which is capable of bringing about or preventing some change in the system.	Bunge (1997; 2004)
Craver	Mechanisms are entities and activities organized such that they are productive of regular changes from start to finish.	Craver (2001), Machamer, Darden and Craver (2000)
Elster (I)	A mechanism explains by opening up the black box and showing the cogs and wheels of the internal machinery. A mechanism provides a continuous and contiguous chain of causal or intentional links between the explanans and the explanandum.	Elster (Elster 1983a; Elster 1989b)
Elster (II)	Mechanisms are frequently occurring and easily recognizable causal patterns that are triggered under generally unknown conditions.	Elster (1998b; 1999)
Hedström and Swedberg	A social mechanism is a precise, abstract, and action-based explanation which shows how the occurrence of a triggering event regularly generates the type of outcome to be explained.	Hedström and Swedberg (1996; 1998b)
Little	A causal mechanism is a series of events governed by law-like regularities that lead from the explanans to the explanandum.	Little (1991)
Stinchcombe	A mechanism is a piece of scientific reasoning which gives knowledge about a component of another, ordinarily higher-level theory.	Stinchcombe (1991)

Figure 2.2. Alternative mechanism definitions.

The most satisfactory conceptual analysis of the mechanism concept is found in Machamer, Darden and Craver (2000). The spirit of their approach is very similar to the Elster I and Hedström–Swedberg approaches. If one builds upon these ideas, mechanisms can be said to consist of *entities* (with their properties) and the *activities* that these entities engage in, either by themselves or in concert with other entities. These activities bring about change, and the type of change brought about depends upon the properties of the entities and the way in which they are linked to one another. A social mechanism, as here defined, describes a constellation of entities and activities that are organized such that they regularly bring about a particular type of outcome. We explain an observed phenomenon by referring to the social mechanism by which such phenomena are regularly brought about.

From the mechanism perspective, correlations and constant conjunctions do not explain but require explanation by reference to the entities and activities that brought them into existence. The explanatory mechanisms that we seek to develop should be 'final' in Boudon's (1998a) sense of the term. That is to say, the mechanism should not include any glaring black boxes which simply give rise to additional why-questions. As discussed in chapter 3, this means that action-based explanations are at the core of all social mechanisms.[13]

According to Craver (2001), theories in the biological sciences typically refer to mechanisms that are hierarchically nested: that is, they refer to mechanisms nested within other mechanisms. This is also the case in the social sciences, and this is why Stinchcombe (1991) once defined mechanisms as theories-within-theories or as pieces of theory that give knowledge about components of another theory. As emphasized above, sociological theories typically seek to explain social outcomes such as inequalities, typical behaviours of individuals in different social settings, and social norms. In such theories individuals are the core entities and their actions are the core activities that bring about the social-level phenomena that one seeks to explain. The way in which these actors are linked one to another defines the structure of interaction, and this is likely to influence in its own right the social outcomes brought about. That is to say, the same entities (individual actors) strung together in different ways can be expected to regularly bring about different types of outcome.[14] In this sense, different types of structural configurations of actors can be said to constitute different social mechanisms.

Nested within these 'molecular' mechanisms are more elementary mechanisms that explain the actions of individual actors. Also in this case the mechanisms can be described in terms of their entities (and their properties) and the way in which the entities are linked to one another. The core entities are different, however, and now include the beliefs, desires and opportunities of the actors, but the explanatory logic is the same: we explain an observed phenomenon, in this case an individual action, by referring to the mechanism (that is, the constellation of

---

[13] It should be noted that the criterion of what constitutes a 'final' explanation varies from discipline to discipline. For example, while in sociology an intentional explanation can be considered final because it allows us to understand why actors do what they do, a neuroscientist would consider it to be a black-box explanation. I return to the issue of discipline-specific stopping rules later in this chapter.

[14] The ways in which social networks or relational structures influence the social outcomes actors are likely to bring about are examined in some detail in chapter 4.

beliefs, desires and opportunities) by which such phenomena are regularly brought about.[15]

One possible objection to explanations that seek to explicate generative mechanisms 'beneath' the surface of observed regularities is that they may lead to an infinite regress (e.g., Kincaid 1996; King, Keohane and Verba 1994). For example, is not the insistence on mechanisms as theories-within-theories simply a way of moving the 'black box' down a level – from that of the theory to that of the theory-within-the-theory? To be consistent, should not the mechanisms of the theory-within-the-theory also be specified in terms of yet deeper mechanisms (that is, with a theory-within-the-theory-within-the-theory), and these, in turn, in terms of even deeper mechanisms? This regress could *in principle* continue for ever, or at least until we have reached the level of inexplicable laws of nature. In the end, then, we may be forced to accept a traditional regularity view of causation, and the critical reader may wonder if it is not better, or at least more consistent, to adopt a traditional Humean approach from the very start.

What is perceived to be a 'black box' and a 'mechanism' certainly depends upon the resolution of the theoretical lens through which we view a problem. It also has an important historical dimension.[16] But from these observations it does not follow that the insistence on mechanism-based explanations is unfounded or that a traditional regularity view of causation and explanation would be preferable. Even if it were possible to carry out a reduction in the manner described in the previous paragraph – impossible in practice – the resulting explanation is not likely to be of much sociological relevance. There exist discipline-specific relevance criteria and 'stopping rules' (Miller 1987) that at least roughly stipulate what types of explanatory factors are considered relevant within different academic disciplines. Although, as noted above, sociologists differ in what they consider to be the most appropriate stopping rules – Blau and Black, for instance, advocate different stopping rules from those that I do – non-explainable laws of nature are far outside the domain of sociological relevance. For this reason I would

---

[15] The way in which different constellations of beliefs, desires and opportunities are likely to influence individuals' actions is examined in chapter 3.

[16] As noted by Patrick Suppes (1970: 91), 'From the standpoint of either scientific investigation or philosophical analysis it can fairly be said that one man's mechanism is another man's black box. I mean by this that the mechanisms postulated and used by one generation are mechanisms that are to be explained and understood themselves in terms of more primitive mechanisms by the next generation.'

not consider the infinite-regress objection to be of much importance, and I would therefore maintain that mechanism-based explanations are what sociological theory should be all about.

Why, then, is it so important to specify the mechanisms that are supposed to have generated observed outcomes? From the perspective of sociological theory, one important reason for insisting on a detailed specification of mechanisms is that it tends to produce more precise and intelligible explanations. Another important reason is that a focus on mechanisms tends to reduce theoretical fragmentation. For example, we may have numerous different theories (of crime, organizations, social movements or whatnot) that are all based on the same theory-within-the-theory, that is, they all refer to the same set of mechanisms of action and interaction. Focusing on the mechanisms as such avoids unnecessary proliferation of theoretical concepts and may help to bring out structural similarities between seemingly disparate processes. Finally, it is the knowledge about the mechanism as such, that is, knowledge about why the constellation of entities and activities referred to in the explanation can be expected to regularly bring about the type of outcome we seek to explain, that gives us reason to believe that there indeed is a genuine causal relationship between a proposed cause and its effect, and not simply a correlation.

Although the explanatory focus of sociological theory is on social entities, an important thrust of the analytical approach is that actors and actions are the core entities and activities of the mechanisms explaining such phenomena. There are at least three important reasons why this is the case. First, it is a well-established scientific practice that theories should be formulated in terms of the processes that are believed to have generated the phenomena being studied. In sociology, this realist principle assigns a unique role to actions because actions are the activities that bring about social change. The causal efficacy of actions would be readily seen if we were able to press a pause button that suddenly froze all individuals and prevented them from performing any further actions. All social processes would then come to an immediate halt.[17] Second, action-based explanations are, in one particular respect, more intellectually satisfactory than the available alternatives. Focusing on actions and explaining actions in intentional terms provides a deeper and more emphatic *understanding* of the causal process than do other

---

[17] As is discussed in more detail in chapter 4, this does not mean that 'social structure' is unimportant, only that 'structural' effects need actors in order to be instantiated.

non-action-based explanations.[18] Third, action-based explanations tend to reduce the risk of erroneous causal inferences. As noted by Skog (1988) and others, there is considerable risk of mistaking spurious correlations for genuine causal relationships when one focuses on macro-level trends and correlations. One telling example used by Skog is the high correlation often found between sunspot activity and various social phenomena. The correlation between sunspot activity and the prevalence of intravenous drug use in Stockholm during the period 1965–70, for example, was as high as 0.91. Action-based explanations can help to eliminate such spurious causal accounts in the following way: if it proves impossible to specify how the phenomenon to be explained could have been generated by the actions of individuals, or if the account must be based on highly implausible assumptions, one's faith in the proposed causal account is sharply reduced.

A concern often raised is that a focus on actions and micro-level mechanisms may lead to a loss of valuable information and therefore to a biased understanding of the phenomena being studied. Sometimes it is even suggested that macro-levels and micro-levels are partly independent of each other, or that it is at least useful to assume this to be the case (e.g., Brante 2001). A similar view seems to have motivated Jackson and Pettit (1992b) to advocate a particular type of explanation called a 'programme' explanation. They describe their core idea in the following way:

The idea is that a structural factor may explain a given social fact, not through producing it in the same basic way as individual factors, but through more or less ensuring that there will be some individual-level confluence of factors – perhaps this, perhaps that – sufficient to produce it. (Jackson and Pettit 1992b: 120)[19]

The situation Jackson and Pettit describe is illustrated in figure 2.3. The solid lines represent causal processes through which C_1 and C_2 can bring about E, and the dotted line represents the 'ensuring condition', which states that in situation S, should C_1 fail to occur, C_2 would occur, and C_2 would bring about E (and vice versa should C_2 fail to occur).

While I find the argument that social entities sometimes have these 'effects' to be persuasive, I do not find the arguments for 'programme' explanations equally so. The reason for this can be stated as follows:

---

[18] The notion of 'intentional explanations' is discussed in chapter 3.

[19] See also Jackson and Pettit (1992a). A well-known sociological work that rests on this type of argument is Skocpol's (1979) so-called structural theory of revolutions.

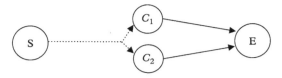

Figure 2.3. Components of a programme explanation.

1. Most of us would agree that the empirical observation that E is more likely to be brought about in situation S than in *not–S* provides important and useful information (although many of us would not think of it as explanatory).

2. Most of us would agree that detailing the mechanisms through which various Cs can bring about E is of obvious explanatory importance. This is also true in situations of causal overdetermination (like the one described above) because we thereby reduce the causal possibility space.

3. Given the empirical information in (1) and the information about the causal processes in (2), the introduction of the programme explanation does not seem to add any new information unless the causal processes linking S and the Cs are explicated, but then we are not talking about a programme explanation any more.

Thus, it seems that reasonable programme explanations can be expressed as mechanism-based explanations, albeit of a more complex nature. If this is not possible, the programme explanation does not provide any information not already available from (1). This conclusion can, I believe, be generalized to any problem describable in these terms.

Differences and similarities

Let me highlight some of the most important differences and similarities between the three explanatory traditions discussed. With their focus on theory and systematic deductive arguments, mechanism-based explanations are in many ways closer to covering-law explanations than to statistical explanations. While a statistical explanation consists of an assembly of factors that appear to make a difference to the probability of the event being studied, a mechanism-based explanation, like a covering-law explanation, can be characterized as a theoretical deductive argument. The theoretical arguments differ in numerous ways, however. For instance, covering-law explanations typically refer to causal factors and not to causal processes (Mayntz 2004). Furthermore, the laws of covering-law explanations are typically seen as perfectly general and without exceptions while the mechanisms of mechanism-based explanations are not (Elster 1989b), and mechanism-based explanations are action-based while covering-law explanations typically are not.

An obvious difference between statistical explanations and mechanism-based explanations is that randomness and the stochastic nature of social processes are more central concerns of the statistical tradition. Although I certainly do not wish to deny the importance of randomness, I believe it is useful to formulate theories and explanations as if the world were deterministic. One important reason for this is that only as a last resort should one attribute the unexplained to the unexplainable. As we all know, all cats look grey at night, and we should therefore evoke randomness as an explanation only when all plausible alternatives have been proven unsatisfactory. Second, a deterministic language is preferable because of its economy of expression. As long as we are aware that theoretical statements refer to tendencies and not to actual processes, a deterministic language seems better suited to communicate the core ideas about the mechanisms assumed to govern the processes.[20]

A mechanism should thus be seen as an empirical commitment on the part of the theorist as to how a process would unfold if the assumptions upon which it rests were well founded. Even if the mechanism were well founded, however, we may not observe the outcome suggested by the mechanism. One important reason for this is that social phenomena are generally the result of several different causal processes operating simultaneously, and these processes can influence and even counteract one another. For this very reason, John Stuart Mill emphasized the importance of treating all theoretical statements as statements about empirical tendencies and not about actualities:

Doubtless, a man often asserts of an entire class what is only true of a part of it; but his error generally consists not in making too wide an assertion, but in making the wrong *kind* of assertion: he predicated an actual result, when he should only have predicated a *tendency* to that result – a power acting with a certain intensity in that direction. With regard to *exceptions*; in any tolerably advanced science there is properly no such thing as an exception. What is thought to be an exception to a principle is always some other

---

[20] It could be argued that using a deterministic language to describe a stochastic world represents a form of fictionalism. As is discussed on page 62, one should make a distinction between descriptively false and descriptively incomplete sentences, and I would consider the use of a deterministic language to be an example of the latter.

and distinct principle cutting into the former: some other force which impinges against the first force, and deflects it from its direction. There are not a *law* and an *exception* to that law — the law acting in ninety-nine cases, and the exception in one. There are two laws, each possibly acting in the whole hundred cases, and bringing about a common effect by their conjunct operation. (Mill 1844: 161–2)

Following Mill, mechanism-based explanations should be viewed as propositions about particular aspects of a causal 'totality', with no claim that the tendency in question is the dominant one.[21] For this reason, to quote Mill once again, all mechanisms 'in consequence of the liability to be counteracted, require to be stated in words affirmative of tendencies only, and not of actual results' (1874: 319). In more modern language, mechanism-based explanations can be described as propositions about probabilities of different outcomes conditional upon general *ceteris paribus* clauses (see Gibson 1983).

A concrete example may help to identify the distinguishing features of the three types of explanations. As mentioned above, one of Peter Blau's concerns was to explain why the formal organizational structures of different organizations vary as they do (see Blau 1970). His strategy was to specify general covering laws that could subsume, and in this respect explain, his concrete observations. From the point of view of the statistical approach, one would not seek to specify general laws, but instead use data about a large number of organizations to find statistically relevant factors that appear to make a difference to the probability of the organizations having a specific formal structure. The mechanism perspective, finally, would explain the change in organizational structures by referring to a constellation of actors and their actions that typically bring about such changes in organizational structures, and would then use statistical and other types of empirical analyses to test the assumptions and predictions of the theory. The details of how such mechanism-based explanations and empirical tests are carried through is the main focus of the rest of this book.

Summary

Let me close this chapter by briefly recapitulating the main thread of the argument. I started by noting that theories, in order to be explanatory, must provide at least partial accounts of why events happen, why

---

[21] In practice, of course, the reason that we focus on one tendency and not on another is likely to be based on a belief that the tendency in question is more important than the other. But 'important' is not always the same as 'dominant'.

something changes over time, or why states or events co-vary in time or space.

I then distinguished between three types of explanations that differ in terms of what are considered to be appropriate answers to such why-questions: (1) covering-law explanations, (2) statistical explanations, and (3) mechanism-based explanations. The discussion led to the conclusion that mechanism-based explanations are the most appropriate ones for sociological theory. Statistically oriented variable approaches once were a progressive force that moved sociology forward. But, as Abbott (1999: 216) has noted, this approach now 'is old and tired'. To move out of the current impasse it seems essential to bring mechanism-based explanations to the fore. A social mechanism is a constellation of entities and activities that are organized in such a way that they regularly bring about a particular type of outcome. We explain an observed social phenomenon by referring to the social mechanism by which such phenomena are regularly brought about, and this entails a focus on the social outcomes that interacting actors are likely to bring about. In developing such theories we must not forsake the high standards set by the statistical tradition. We need to use the most appropriate statistical techniques when testing our theories, and we need to be as precise in formulating our theories as are the best sociologists in the statistical tradition when they specify and diagnose their statistical models.

3 Action and interaction

In the previous chapter I focused on the characteristics of explanatory theories. I made a distinction between covering-law explanations, statistical explanations and mechanism-based explanations, and I suggested that the advancement of sociological theory largely hinges on our ability to develop precise mechanism-based theories. The main reason for this is that we arrive at more intellectually satisfying answers to the question of why we observe the social phenomena we observe if we specify the individual-level mechanisms likely to have brought them about. Furthermore, and as a side effect, this is likely to lead to more useful theories in that detailed knowledge of how things are brought about is useful if one wants to alter a process in a more desirable direction.

The most viable alternative to the mechanism-based approach is a statistical approach that directly examines the relationship between variables describing different entities. As the discussion in the previous chapter suggests, such an approach to *theory building* is prone to difficulties, and a 'deeper' causal account can be obtained by explicating mechanisms through which social patterns are likely to have been brought about. The types of mechanisms we are looking for are those concerned with the causes and consequences of individual actions, because, as Popper (1994) expressed it, actions are the 'animating principles' of the social.

Jerry Fodor (1994: 294) once noted that the theoretical strategy adopted here is useful for explaining many different types of phenomena:

If you are specifically interested in the peculiarities of aggregates of matter at the Lth level (in plants, or minds, or mountains, as it might be) then you are likely to be specifically interested in implementing mechanisms at the L-1th level; . . . this is because the characteristics of L-level laws can often be explained by the characteristics of their L-1th level implementations.

Although, as discussed at some length in the previous chapter, I do not think it is appropriate to talk about causal laws in the social sciences, the logic of Fodor's approach is basically the same as that of the mechanism approach. Such a 'multi-level' approach is also a core characteristic of the Weberian tradition in sociology. In my view, the most valuable aspect of Weber's methodological writings is his insistence that one should never accept aggregate correlations as explanatory until they have been broken down into intelligible patterns of individual action (see S. Turner 1983; Weber 1949). In this respect there is a close affinity between the Weberian approach and the mechanism approach.

Theories of action and interaction thus provide the foundation for explanatory sociological theories, and the type of action theory that we are looking for should at least satisfy the following three basic desiderata: (1) it should be psychologically and sociologically plausible; (2) it should be as simple as possible; and (3) it should explain action in meaningful intentional terms.

The theory should be psychologically plausible, because otherwise we would simply be telling an as-if story, not detailing the actual mechanisms at work. For example, billiard players may act as if they based their shots on highly complex mathematical calculations, although they obviously do not. Using a theory that assumes that billiard players make such calculations may allow us to predict what they will do, but it will not provide a correct explanation of why or how they do it. In the terminology of the preceding chapter, in order to explain the actions of a billiard player we need an abstract and realistic theory of action. I return to this issue of instrumentalism versus analytical realism in the penultimate section when discussing instrumentalist tendencies within rational-choice theorizing.

The theory also should be sociologically plausible, by which I mean that it should take into account the structure of social interaction. The reason for this, to be discussed in more detail below, is that the actions of any given individual often cannot be understood and explained unless they are related to the actions of others. Ignoring the structure of interaction would render the theory lacking for the very same reasons as those discussed in the previous paragraph, namely, that we would then be giving an incorrect account of the mechanisms at work. As discussed in great detail in chapter 4, ignoring or misrepresenting the structure of social interaction also makes it difficult to properly explain the social or macro-level outcomes that individuals bring about through their actions.

Within the restrictions imposed by psychological and sociological plausibility, we should seek a theory that is as simple as possible. This is partly because we prefer clear and transparent theories that abstract away from all that are inessential to the problem at hand. But in addition, as emphasized by Coleman (1990), we often face complexity trade-offs between different components of a theory. Sociological theories of the kind focused on here can be said to contain three types of components: (1) an individual-action component; (2) a component describing the structure of interaction; and (3) a component linking micro-actions to macro-outcomes. To allow greater complexity in the latter two components, which are typically of greater sociological interest, one must keep the action component as simple as possible by abstracting away all elements not considered crucial.

The theory should also explain action in intentional terms. This means that we should explain an action by reference to the future state it was intended to bring about. Intentional explanations are important for sociological theory because, unlike causalist explanations of the behaviourist or statistical kind, they make the act 'understandable' in the Weberian sense of the term.[1] In addition to providing deeper and intellectually more satisfying explanations, intentional explanations are likely to reduce the risk of erroneous explanations because they force the theorist to clearly specify a set of plausible mechanisms that tightly link the proposed cause to its effect (see the discussion in chapter 2).[2]

One important implication of this brief discussion is that for a theory of action to be appropriate for our purposes it must avoid the one-sidedness found in many sociological and economic action theories. For example, Dahrendorf (1968: 30) once argued that an action theory suitable for sociology should view the individual 'as a bearer of socially predetermined attributes and modes of behavior'. In such a theory actors are assumed to be passive subjects whose behaviour is explained by causal factors (psychological or social) of which the individuals themselves are usually unaware. As Wrong (1961) rightly suggested, this is an 'oversocialized' view of the actor. Individuals act; they are not merely pushed around by anonymous social forces; and in order for a theory to be explanatory it must consider the reasons why individuals act as they do.

Homo economicus, as traditionally conceived, is an atomized actor equipped with unlimited cognitive abilities that allow 'him' to consistently choose the optimal course of action. While such theories are clear and simple and explain action in intentional terms, they lack

---

[1] See von Wright (1971) and Elster (1983a) for excellent discussions of the role of intentional explanations in the social sciences.

[2] To avoid any misunderstanding it should be emphasized that a focus on intentional action does not imply that the unintentional is seen as unimportant. As we all know, the road to hell is paved with good intentions, and therefore unintended consequences of intentional actions are crucial for understanding how social processes unfold. See Merton (1936) and Popper (1961) for two classic statements about the importance of unintended effects in social-science explanations.

psychological as well as sociological realism. The type of theory that we are looking for should avoid the 'atomized' and 'heroic' assumptions of traditional economics as well as the 'causalism' of traditional sociology, because, as Mark Granovetter (1985: 487) has expressed it,

> Actors do not behave or decide as atoms outside a social context, nor do they adhere slavishly to a script written for them by the particular intersection of social categories that they happen to occupy. Their attempts at purposive action are instead embedded in concrete, ongoing systems of social relations.

This statement should *not* be understood as an endorsement of some form of eclecticism or theoretical pluralism. Many contemporary theorists base their work on the assumption that a pluralist approach that incorporates elements from a range of different theoretical traditions is in itself something desirable (see, for example, Alexander 1982; Ritzer 1991). As far as I can see, this assumption is entirely groundless. Theoretical pluralism may be a valuable property of a discipline since it is likely to entail competition between different approaches, and this competition may stimulate further theoretical development. But pluralism within a particular theory or theorist usually produces anything but desirable results. Typically, it leads to long lists of potentially important factors and to no clearly specified mechanisms at all.

The rest of this chapter is organized as follows. First, I describe a well-established and venerable theory of action, here referred to as the 'DBO theory', which offers an appropriate micro-foundation for the type of sociological theory of concern here. Then I discuss social interaction from the perspective of the DBO theory and identify various mechanisms through which the action of one actor can come to influence the actions of others. Finally, I discuss explanations based on rational-choice assumptions. These explanations are abstract, precise and action-based. Yet their explanatory status can be called into question because of an overly instrumentalist attitude towards theorizing.

Before describing the DBO theory, I want to say a few words about the ontological status of the 'actors' focused on here. There exist at least three types of action theories, and it is essential to clearly distinguish between them:

1 Action theory as an *interpretive tool* for understanding the behaviour of a concretely existing actor (e.g., von Wright 1971).

2 Action theory as a *predictive tool* to anticipate the behaviour of a concretely existing actor (e.g., Dennett 1981).

3 Action theory as a *theoretical mechanism* of a sociological theory (e.g., Hernes 1998).

In the first two types of action theories, the objects whose behaviour the theory refers to are real, concretely existing actors. It is the third type of action theory that we are primarily concerned with here, however, and this type of theory does not refer to concretely existing actors but to abstract *ideal-typical actors*. The intentions ascribed to these ideal-typical actors are not (necessarily) identical to the intentions of any concretely existing actor, but rather should be seen as typical intentions that could motivate typical actors to behave in specific ways. Believing that theories can accurately represent reality in all its complexity is an empiricist illusion. Action theories should be seen not as abstract replicas of concretely existing actors but as analytical-realist models of the type of actors involved in the action. These models are analytical because they intentionally move out of focus all elements that are deemed inessential to the problem at hand. They are realist because the elements that are retained are believed to reflect the real processes at work (this is discussed further in the penultimate section).[3]

The DBO theory

Desires (D), beliefs (B) and opportunities (O) are the primary theoretical terms upon which the analysis of action and interaction will be based. As figure 3.1 illustrates, the desires, beliefs and opportunities of an actor are here seen as the proximate causes of the actor's action.[4]

The concept of *action* refers to what individuals do intentionally, as distinct from mere 'behaviours' such as snoring during the night or accidentally tripping over a stone, which are not actions. As the term is used here, I act if and only if what I do is explainable (in an appropriate way) by my desires, beliefs and opportunities (see Davidson 1980).

A *belief* can be defined as a proposition about the world held to be true (Hahn 1973),[5] and a *desire* as a wish or want.[6] *Opportunities*, as the term is used here, describes the 'menu' of action alternatives available to the

---

[3] Although the distinction between the three types of action theories is important, it should be recognized that the third type of action theory must be reasonably close to the first type if it is to explain anything in the real world.

[4] Unless otherwise indicated in the text, arrows in figures such as these should be interpreted as 'and' and not as 'or'. That is to say, desires, beliefs *and* opportunities are the proximate causes of actions.

[5] Two important classes of beliefs are (1) beliefs about existing action alternatives, and (2) beliefs about the likely consequences of performing different actions. An important subclass of type (1) beliefs that currently receives a great deal of attention in the psychological literature is the so-called self-efficacy beliefs of Bandura (e.g., 2001).

[6] Sometimes I also distinguish between different desires and beliefs in terms of how strongly they are felt or entertained by an actor.

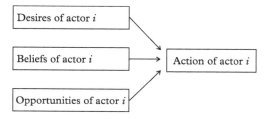

Figure 3.1. Core components of the DBO theory.

actor, that is, the actual set of action alternatives that exists independently of the actor's beliefs about them.[7]

Beliefs and desires are mental events that can be said to cause an action in the sense of providing reasons for the action. As suggested by von Wright (1989), a particular combination of desires and beliefs constitutes a 'compelling reason' for performing an action. Desires and beliefs have a motivational force that allows us to understand and, in this respect, explain the actions. The cause of an action is a constellation of desires, beliefs and opportunities in the light of which the action appears reasonable.[8] Action mechanisms differ from one another in terms of how these entities are linked to one another.

The following everyday example illustrates the logic of a DBO explanation. If we want to explain why Mr Smith brought an umbrella today, we can point to a specific set of desires, beliefs and opportunities, such as (1) he believed that it would rain today, (2) he desired not to get wet, and (3) there was an umbrella for him to bring. Given this set of desires, beliefs and opportunities, we have made the action intelligible and thereby explained it.[9]

---

[7] Although opportunities exist independently of an actor's beliefs, they must be known to the actor and hence they can be said to influence actions via the beliefs of the actor.

[8] In the philosophy of mind literature, much of the discussion has centred on whether mental states indeed can be said to cause one another, or whether it is rather the physical properties on which the mental states supervene that cause one another. These discussions are interesting, but I do not believe that anything of sociological importance hinges on which of these positions one adopts.

[9] The fact that beliefs and desires, as well as other mental states and events, are unobservable makes it difficult for us to verify their existence and to analyze their effects. Although they cannot be observed, even casual introspection suggests that they are real and that they causally influence our actions. The position adopted here is the traditional Davidsonian position that beliefs and desires indeed cause our actions (Davidson 1980). That is to say, beliefs and desires are not merely concepts or theoretical instruments that we use in as-if stories to interpret already performed actions or to predict future actions, as Dennett (1981) and many economists (e.g., Friedman 1953) argue; desires and beliefs are (believed to be) real and to be causally efficacious.

The causal efficacy of beliefs, desires and opportunities can be illustrated by the following set of examples focusing on the action complementary to the one just described, namely, on the reasons why Mr Smith did not bring an umbrella today. There are three ideal-typical explanations:

- *Belief-based explanation*   Mr Smith desires not to get wet and he had an umbrella that he could have brought, but by mistake he read yesterday's weather column in the newspaper which made him believe that it would not rain today. Therefore he did not bring an umbrella today.
- *Desire-based explanation*   Mr Smith believed that it would rain today and he had an umbrella that he could have brought, but he has somewhat unusual desires: walking in heavy rain always makes him feel like Gene Kelly in *Singin' in the Rain*, and feeling like Gene Kelly is something he really desires. Therefore he did not bring an umbrella today.
- *Opportunity-based explanation*   Mr Smith believed that it would rain today and he had a strong desire not to get wet, but when he was leaving for work in the morning he found that his son had, once again, taken his umbrella and there were no other umbrellas in the house. Therefore he did not bring an umbrella today.

Not only can desires, beliefs and opportunities be said to cause actions as described in these examples; there are also important causal interconnections between them. As discussed in detail by Elster (1979; 1983b), the mind plays many tricks on us, and some of these tricks are the result of causal interconnections between desires, beliefs and opportunities. Three patterns appear particularly important: (1) *adaptive preferences*, causal connections from beliefs to desires that lead actors to desire only what they believe they can get ('sour grapes'); (2) *counteradaptive preferences*, causal connections from beliefs to desires that lead actors to desire only what they believe they cannot get ('the grass is always greener on the other side of the fence'); and (3) *wishful thinking*, causal connections from desires to beliefs that lead actors to believe only what they desire to be the case.[10]

One of the most important reasons for using the DBO theory as a micro-foundation for sociological theory is that it has a great deal of phenomenological truth to it. Individuals around us behave and move in quite mysterious ways. Nevertheless, we are often able to predict what

---

[10] As discussed below, cognitive-dissonance theory also suggests important links between an actor's past actions and his/her current beliefs and/or desires. To reduce cognitive dissonance, 'is' can become 'ought' by beliefs and desires adjusting to the actions.

they will do, and we manage to do this by treating them as subjects with mental states that cause them to behave as they do (Braddon-Mitchell and Jackson 1996). As Fodor (1988: 4) expressed it when discussing the success of belief–desire psychology: 'If we could do that well with predicting the weather, no one would ever get their feet wet; and yet the etiology of the weather must surely be child's play compared with the causes of behavior.'

In my view, the most viable alternatives to the DBO theory are rational-choice theories and various forms of learning theories.[11] As discussed below, rational-choice theory can in certain respects be seen as a specific type of DBO theory. When this theory is applicable it is highly useful, but there are numerous situations in which it is not applicable (unless we make it tautologically true by definition). Were we to use the theory in such a situation, we would be telling a non-explanatory as-if story. Because of this I do not think that rational-choice theory is useful as a general point of departure for sociological theory (for more on this, see the penultimate section). Learning theories in which actors are seen as deciding future courses of action based on their own past actions or those of others (Bandura 1977) may initially appear rather different from the DBO theory. While the DBO theory assumes that actors are forward-looking, learning theories assume them to be backward-looking. Learning theories should not necessarily be seen as an alternative to the DBO theory, however. In my view they should be seen as a specific type of DBO theory that is applicable when actors use information about the past to decide what to do in the future (see Hedström 1998 for a more detailed discussion).

Churchland (1981), Stich and Ravenscroft (1994), and other cognitively oriented philosophers have noted that the DBO theory, or the 'folk psychology' model as they call it, is likely to be replaced by better and more 'scientific' theories in the future. This may well occur. However, it does not follow, as these authors argue, that the DBO theory should therefore be abandoned. Theories should be replaced only when better ones appear, not when expectations about better theories exist. At least for the purposes discussed here, I cannot see any alternative theory that is clearly preferable to the DBO theory. As David Lewis (1994: 416) once remarked, 'It is not the last word in psychology, but we should be confident that as far as it goes – and it does go far – it is largely right.'

---

[11] Multifactorial motivation theories such as that of J. Turner (1987b) may be psychologically and sociologically realistic, but they lack the compelling simplicity and clarity one seeks in an action theory which is to provide an explanation that is adequate at the level of meaning.

This does not mean that the use of the DBO theory will always allow us to predict correctly how individuals will act. Often we do not know which set of desires, beliefs and so forth are in operation at a particular moment.[12] Similarly, if an actor has a specific set of desires, beliefs and opportunities that provide a strong reason for him to do X, he may have even stronger reasons for doing Y. Furthermore, even if we knew an individual's 'dominant' desires, beliefs and opportunities, the DBO theory is not infallible, as demonstrated most vividly by the phenomenon of akrasia, or weakness of the will, that makes individuals unable to resist the temptation of small immediate rewards even at the cost of larger delayed rewards (Davidson 1980).[13] But infallibility is not something we should require of a theory of action. What seems reasonable to aspire to is not 'token' faithfulness but 'type' faithfulness, that is, abstract but realistic ideal-types of the logic of action.

The DBO theory may be psychologically plausible and it may provide a useful micro-foundation for sociological theory, but in and of itself it may not appear particularly exciting. Compared with theories evoking such colourful terms as 'fluid identities', 'demonic societies' and the 'age of reprimitivization', to cite a recent reader in social theory (Ritzer and Smart 2001), it certainly sounds rather dry and sterile. Theories should not be judged on the basis of their colourfulness or smartness, however, and the value of the DBO theory will, one hopes, become apparent once it is used to analyze how the social situations in which actors are embedded are likely to influence their beliefs, desires and opportunities, and how groups of actors, acting on the basis of these beliefs, desires and opportunities, bring about various intended and unintended outcomes.

Social interaction

Up to this point I have not said much about the causes of the causes of actions, but getting a handle on how beliefs, desires and opportunities are formed in interactions with others is an essential part of any explanatory

---

[12] But if we knew which beliefs and desires were operative, and if we knew what the structure of interaction looked like, we should be able to predict fairly well how individuals are likely to act. This is the main reason why it is meaningful to engage in the type of theoretical agent-based simulations discussed in chapter 4, which try to assess what would happen if individuals had certain beliefs, desires and opportunities and they were influenced in certain ways by the actions of others.

[13] As suggested by Ainslie and others, we need to consider in detail the temporal dimension of desires if we are to understand weakness of the will. In this book I do not have much to say about how individuals discount future events. See instead Ainslie (2001) and Loewenstein and Elster (1992).

theory. Simply assuming that beliefs and desires are fixed and unaffected by the actions of others may be plausible in some very specific situations. However, since social action, in the Weberian sense of the term, is at the very core of the sociological enterprise, and since it is well-established empirically that individuals' attitudes and beliefs are moulded in inter-actions with others (for overviews see Fiske and Taylor 1991; Ross and Nisbett 1991), this would be an untenable assumption in the general case. Therefore, we must problematize and try to specify the mechan-isms through which the actions of some actors may come to influence the beliefs, desires, opportunities and actions of others. I have little to say about the specifics of these beliefs and desires – whether, for example, one individual desires or believes p rather than q. The type of interaction mechanisms that I focus on are of a more general kind and deal with the centripetal forces that tend to make interacting individuals coalesce around a certain p or a certain q, whatever that p or q may be.

At first glance, the explanatory framework described in the previous section, with its focus on intentional action, may not seem to take us very far since we usually do not decide what to believe or to desire. Beliefs and desires are usually the result of causal processes not directly under our intentional control. However, since these causal processes are, in turn, often set in motion by the actions of others, the DBO theory, applied to their actions, is also central to explaining states and events that from a focal actor's point of view may appear as 'social facts' in the Durkheimian sense of the term. Take beliefs as an example. As empha-sized by Williams (1973), deciding to believe something because we want it to be true is an incoherent project. The mechanisms through which beliefs are formed tend to be 'causal' (as distinct from inten-tional) from the focal individual's point of view, and typically operate 'behind the back' of the individual.[14] Dissonance reduction, to be dis-cussed later in this chapter, is an important example of a process in which the actions of some bring about dissonance and subsequent changes in the beliefs of others. Although the process is an unintended outcome of other individuals' actions, actions nevertheless are what make them tick, and therefore analyses of social interactions between intentional actors are the core concern. This was certainly an important reason why Weber explicitly defined sociology as a science that concerns itself with understanding and explaining the causes and consequences of social action (Weber 1978).

---

[14] Deciding to desire something is not incoherent, but it usually operates via some inter-mediary steps. Typically one decides to set in motion a process that one hopes will eventually alter one's desires (for example, character planning).

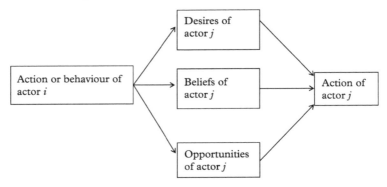

Figure 3.2. Dyadic interaction between actor *i* and actor *j* according to the DBO theory.

There are numerous ways to conceptualize social-interaction processes, but from the perspective of the DBO theory it appears essential to distinguish between three broad types of social interactions: (1) desire-mediated, (2) belief-mediated, and (3) opportunity-mediated interactions. In the dyadic case we can describe the interaction between two actors as in figure 3.2.

To the extent that the action of one actor, actor *i*, influences the action of another, actor *j*, this influence must be mediated via the action opportunities or mental states of actor *j*. In terms of the DBO theory, the action (or behaviour) of actor *i* can influence the desires of actor *j* and thereby the actions of *j*, it can influence the beliefs of *j* and thereby the actions of *j*, and/or it can influence the opportunities of *j* and thereby the actions of *j*.[15] And the properties of *i*, such as what status he or she has or born trustworthy he or she looks, often influence the extent to which the actions of *j* influence the actions of *i*.

As far as the unidirectional form of influence depicted in figure 3.2 is concerned, the actor labelled *i* could also be some form of 'generalized other' who represents typical standpoints or actions of groups of individuals. If that is the case, then we do not have interaction between two individuals but between one individual and a social aggregate.

---

[15] In most of the cases discussed here, actor *i* is assumed not to be aware of or not to care about the influence (s)he has on actor *j*. In other words, most of the processes discussed here do not assume strategic behaviour on the part of the actors. The reason for this is partly that I believe that non-strategic processes are more important in everyday life, and partly that strategic processes already are so well covered in the game theoretical literature.

The difference is well described in the following everyday example of Schelling (1998: 33): 'I interact with an individual if I change lanes when his front bumper approaches within five feet of my rear bumper; I interact with a social aggregate when I adjust my speed to the average speed on the highway.' It also is important to note that actors may know what other actors do without necessarily knowing them. This knowledge of or belief about the actions of others may influence their actions even if they do not directly interact with any of them.[16] In this chapter I mainly discuss dyadic interactions between individuals, but in chapter 4 I consider in some detail how interactions between individuals and social aggregates evolve over time.[17]

Dyadic interactions between individuals are complex, and large literatures in social psychology, micro-sociology and decision theory deal with various mechanisms likely to be at work. Therefore I confine myself to discussing a few mechanisms that I believe are particularly important because they illustrate different types of mechanisms. I organize the discussion in the following way. First, I introduce some distinctions that will allow me to more clearly differentiate social interactions from other behavioural patterns that they otherwise could easily be confused with. Second, I describe some belief-based, desire-based and opportunity-based mechanisms that appear particularly central to sociological theory. Finally, as mentioned above, I conclude the chapter by discussing what I consider to be an unfortunate instrumentalist tendency within contemporary rational-choice theory.

Social interactions and related behavioural patterns

When we observe a group of individuals who appear to act or think in a similar manner, one possible explanation for this is that they do so because they have interacted and influenced one another's beliefs and desires (e.g., Latane 1981). However, it is important to recognize that individuals often act in a similar manner without this having anything to do with social interaction. With respect to a specific group of individuals at a specific point in time, one can distinguish between at least three types of processes that may result in the individuals' acting in a similar manner, and only one of these has anything to do with social interaction. We can use another umbrella example, this time

---

[16] As suggested by Rydgren (2004), mechanisms like these also are important for explaining xenophobia.
[17] See also Abell (2003) for a somewhat related discussion.

an example of Weber's, to clarify the differences between these types of processes:

Social action is not identical with the similar actions of many persons . . . Thus, if at the beginning of a shower a number of people on the street put up their umbrellas at the same time, this would not ordinarily be a case of action mutually oriented to that of each other, but rather of all reacting in the same way to the like need of protection from the rain. (Weber 1978: 23)

This piece of everyday behaviour is not 'social action' explained by some form of social interaction between the people on the street, but is due to an *environmental effect*, in this case rainfall that makes all actors adjust their actions in a similar manner. Outcomes of such environmental processes can easily be mistaken for the outcome of social interactions. Assume that Weber's rainfall started at one end of the street and gradually spread along it. The pattern of umbrella use would then 'diffuse' in a way that could easily be seen as the result of a genuine interaction process, where one individual's umbrella use increased the likelihood that neighbouring individuals would use umbrellas as well.

Even if during said rainfall we observed that the frequency of umbrella use was higher among those walking on one street than on another, this would not necessarily mean that we were observing the outcome of some sort of interaction process. It could simply be due to a *selection effect*: in this case, individuals without umbrellas for some reason ended up walking on one street rather than on the other.[18]

A *social interaction* effect exists if, and only if, the actions or behaviours of others influenced a focal individual's action. A little introspection suggests that I sometimes hesitate to use my umbrella because of vanity; being the only person using an umbrella could indicate to others that I am excessively concerned with my appearance, and this is something I do not want. Although I would like to use my umbrella, I decide against it in order not to send such signals. But once others start to use their umbrellas, I quickly follow suit. This would then be an example of a social interaction effect, because it was the actions of others that influenced my choice of action.

Social interactions do not always reinforce behaviour as in this umbrella example; they may have the opposite effect as well. So-called 'snob effects' in consumption are obvious examples of this (see Leibenstein 1950), but it can also operate in indirect and non-status-related ways.

---

[18] Such a pattern could, for example, be observed if the stores on one of the streets catered exclusively to young people and young people were less likely to use umbrellas.

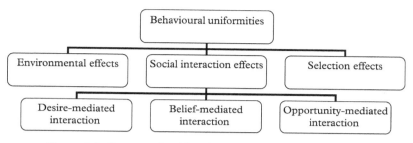

Figure 3.3. Sources of uniformity within groups of individuals.

For example, in her analysis of the role of social interactions in the spread of sexually transmittable diseases, Åberg (2000) argues that condom use is likely to follow such a pattern. If most people use condoms, the risk of acquiring a sexually transmittable disease in a casual sexual encounter is low, and the focal individuals may therefore decide not to use condoms. But if condom use in the relevant population decreases, the likelihood that they will use condoms increases.

The distinctions introduced so far are summarized in the upper part of figure 3.3, and, as mentioned above, different types of social interaction effects can, in turn, be analytically distinguished from one another on the basis of how the interaction effect is mediated. We have a desire-mediated effect if the action (or behaviour) of actor i influences the action of actor j via the desires of j. We have a belief-mediated effect if the action of i influences the action of j via the beliefs of j. And, we have an opportunity-mediated effect if the action of i influences the action of j via the opportunities of j.[19]

Belief-mediated social interactions

My favourite everyday example of a belief-mediated social interaction is the 'wolf-pack' behaviour often observed on highways.[20] Although the road and weather conditions remain the same, it can often be observed that cars within eyesight of each other suddenly reduce speed as if instructed to do so by an invisible authority, and then return to normal speed a few moments later as if on command. This pattern is repeated

---

[19] See Manski (2000) for a similar analytical distinction.
[20] Since it is my favourite example, I have used it in previous publications. See Hedström (1998).

numerous times: the cars suddenly slow down only to resume their
original speed a short while later.

The reason for this coordinated behaviour is obviously not that the
drivers have access to radio devices that allow them to communicate.
The mechanism that generates this sort of interdependent behaviour is
of a non-verbal kind; through his actions one driver gives off signals to
the others, and their interpretation of these signals generates the social
behaviour observed. When one driver reduces his speed, this may be
interpreted by others as indicating that he has observed something that
gave him reason to slow down, although the real reason may simply have
been a sudden itch on his right foot that forced him to slow down while
he scratched. But given the possibility that the reason might concern
them as well, the other drivers decide to 'imitate' the first driver, only to
find out a moment later that they could just as well have continued at
their original speed.

This wolf-pack behaviour is an example of a belief-mediated social
interaction; through their behaviours or actions, some individuals influence the beliefs and subsequent actions of others. Although the belief may
be factually incorrect, actors have good reasons for subscribing to it, and it
therefore brings about the same action as it would have had it been
correct. It is a form of rational imitation that illustrates the wisdom of
the so-called Thomas Theorem, which states that 'if men define situations as real, they are real in their consequences' (Thomas and Thomas
1928: 572).

The same basic idea is also at the heart of Merton's notion of the self-
fulfilling prophecy (Merton 1968b). Merton focuses on the case in
which an initially false belief evokes behaviour that eventually makes
the false belief come true. The example he uses is a run on a bank. Once
a rumour of insolvency gets started, some depositors are likely to withdraw their savings, acting on the principle that it is better to be safe than
sorry. Their withdrawals strengthen the beliefs of others that the bank is
in financial difficulties, partly because the withdrawals may actually hurt
the financial standing of the bank, but more importantly because the act
of withdrawal in itself signals to others that something might be wrong
with the bank and the actors act on the principle that there is no smoke
without fire. This produces even more withdrawals, which further
strengthens the belief, and so on. By this mechanism, even an initially
sound bank may go bankrupt if enough depositors withdraw their money
in the (initially) false belief that the bank is insolvent.

These cases are examples of a belief-mediated interaction mechanism
where one individual's belief in the value or necessity of performing a
certain act is influenced by the number of other individuals who have

already done so.[21] The general logic of rational imitation is the following:

1 Others do **A**.
2 If I believe that they have good reasons for doing what they do, their actions will influence my beliefs about their beliefs in the value of doing **A**.
3 In an uncertain decision context, my beliefs about their beliefs are likely to influence my beliefs about the value of doing **A**, particularly if I believe that they may have access to relevant information that I do not have.
4 Therefore, the likelihood that I will do **A** increases with the number of others doing **A**.[22]

As far as this type of interaction is concerned, it is the behaviour of others that enables us to be influenced by them, but it is not the behaviour as such that constitutes the reason that we are influenced. Our beliefs about the beliefs of others are often conditioned by what others do, and often it is these beliefs about the beliefs of others, and not what they do, that explain why we do what we do.

Beliefs about the beliefs of others are also important when individuals need to coordinate their actions. Take the seemingly simple example in which you and I try to meet without having decided in advance where to meet, and without being able to contact one another. In such a situation, I will go to **A** if I want to meet you and if I believe that you will also go to **A**. I believe that you will also go to **A** if I believe that you want to meet me and if I believe that you believe that I will go to **A**. And so on (see figure 3.4).

---

[21] Sometimes individuals who are aware of how this mechanism operates deliberately use it to serve their own interests. Restaurant owners, for example, often place guests near the front window to give the impression that the restaurant is more crowded and popular than it actually is. The most glaring example of its use, or abuse, occurred in the mid-1990s when the authors of *The Discipline of Market Leaders* purchased 50,000 copies of their own book. They targeted bookstores whose sales were monitored by the *New York Times* bestseller list, and their strategy was successful. Despite rather poor initial reviews, the book made the bestseller list, and this generated huge additional sales because being on the bestseller list influenced others' beliefs about the value of the book and thereby their purchasing decisions (Bikhchandani, Hirshleifer and Welch 1998).

[22] Ibsen often portrayed social interactions of this kind. In a scene in *Ghosts*, for example, Pastor Manders tries to explain to Mrs Alving why he condemns her reading books that he has not read himself: 'My dear lady, there are many occasions in life when one must rely on others. That's the way of the world, and things are best that way. How else would society manage?' (Ibsen 1981: 102). Pastor Manders was correct that this type of behaviour is common, but it is doubtful whether 'things are best that way'. Trusting the judgement of others may indeed economize on decision costs, but it also produces fads and can 'lock in' inefficient, oppressive and entirely arbitrary behavioural patterns.

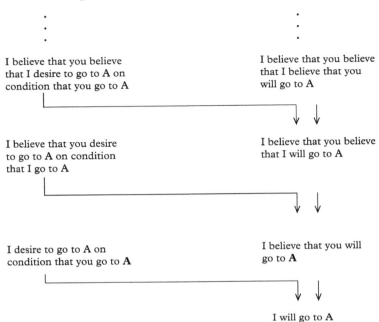

Figure 3.4. Belief-mediated interactions in coordination problems (adopted from Lewis 1969).

Situations such as these may seem to lead to an infinite regress, but there are often natural 'focal points' (Schelling 1960) that allow people to coordinate their beliefs and actions. If many individuals start to act in a certain way, perhaps for entirely arbitrary reasons or because the action has some salient features that make it a natural focal point, it may become a self-reinforcing convention that no one then has any reason to deviate from (Lewis 1969; Young 1996; Chwe 2001).[23] To explain why individuals do what they do in situations such as these, one would need to explicate the belief–action history that led to the establishment of the convention and how the existence of the convention compels individuals to do what they do.[24]

---

[23] Schelling (1960) exposed a group of individuals to the following coordination problem. Each individual had to choose a time and place in New York City for meeting another person. The problem seemed hopeless given the vast number of places to meet, but it turned out that more than half of the individuals chose Grand Central Station at 12 noon. Grand Central Station and 12 noon were thus salient focal points that enabled these individuals to spontaneously coordinate their actions.

[24] Unless, of course, the convention itself is sufficiently obvious and well recognized and therefore in need of no explanation. To explain why I now drive on the left side of the

Festinger's (1957) theory of cognitive dissonance also identifies important mechanisms of a non-intentional kind that help to explain how the beliefs of one person come to be influenced by the actions of others. The core of his theory can be summarized in the following way:[25]

1 Cognitive dissonance is a state of psychological discomfort that occurs whenever an individual holds or is exposed to two psychologically inconsistent cognitions (beliefs, desires, attitudes, opinions and so on).

2 Two cognitive elements are dissonant if the obverse of one element would follow from the other, and the magnitude of the dissonance depends upon the importance of the elements to the person.

3 Dissonance gives rise to pressures to reduce the dissonance, and the strength of the pressure is a function of the magnitude of the dissonance.

For example, if I believe p but the people I interact with do not, this may cause strong dissonance, particularly if the belief is important to me and I value my relationship with these people. One way to eliminate the dissonance would be to persuade them of the correctness of p.[26] Another, and often easier, way to reduce the dissonance would be to 'persuade' oneself that the belief was unwarranted.[27] This would then be an example of a belief-mediated interaction because the actions of others cause the dissonance I experience, and in order to reduce its magnitude I gather information that brings my beliefs closer to theirs, and this will subsequently lead me to act in different ways than I otherwise would. But whenever a belief revision is part of the dissonance reduction, in order for it to be effective it must operate behind the back of the actor. Consciously deciding to believe in something simply because the belief is desirable is an incoherent and unpersuasive project that would not reduce the dissonance.

---

road while earlier I drove on the right side it is not necessary to bring into the picture the historical background of driving conventions in Britain and Sweden. In order to explain why I do what I do, it seems sufficient to point to the existence of these conventions, that I have moved from Sweden to England, and to the fact that there are compelling reasons for me to follow them.

[25] Festinger's original formulation of the theory has been modified several times, but the core of the theory has survived the extensive empirical tests that it has been subjected to. See Harmon-Jones and Mills (1999) for an overview.

[26] As pointed out by Festinger, this strategy has a paradoxical and somewhat disturbing implication. If those who are most in doubt about the correctness of their beliefs are those who experience the greatest magnitude of dissonance, it follows that those who most vigorously try to persuade others about the correctness of their own position are often those who are most in doubt.

[27] If I did not value my relationship with these individuals sufficiently strongly, another possibility would be to change my circle of friends in such a way that my new friends share my belief in p.

Desire-mediated social interactions

When discussing desire-based interactions it is useful to make a distinction between primary and secondary desires. For example, if I desire p, and I believe that p if and only if q, it seems reasonable to say that this specific constellation of beliefs and desires causes my desire for q. In this case I have a primary desire for p and a secondary desire for q. For example, if I want a $100 bill because it enables me to buy an item p that I desire, I have a primary desire for p and a secondary desire for the $100 bill. But if I want that $100 bill because I am a collector of $100 bills and this specific bill will become part of my collection, I have a primary desire for the $100 bill. Similarly, if p expresses an exclusively self-serving desire and I believe that p if and only if q, where q is to behave nicely to other people, I may appear to be an altruist, but I am not. What characterizes an altruist is a primary and not a secondary desire to behave nicely to other people.

With these distinctions in mind, three types of desire-mediated interactions can be distinguished. They can be represented by three different syllogisms:

1 Others do **A**.
Their doing **A** influences how strongly I desire **A**.
Therefore the likelihood that I will do **A** is altered by their doing **A**.

2 Others do **A**.
I desire to be like(or unlike) them.
Therefore the likelihood that I will do **A** is altered by their doing **A**.

3 Others do **A**.
I belive that doing the same as they do increases (or decreases) my chances of attaining **B**, which I desire.
Therefore the likelihood that I will do **A** is altered by their doing **A**.

In all these cases the basic premises ('Others do **A**') and the conclusions ('Therefore the likelihood that I will do **A** is altered by their doing **A**') are the same, but the mechanisms differ. In (1) the actions of others are a *cause* of my desires, while in (2) and (3) they are an *object* of my desires in the sense that I desire to act like them. In (2) I have a *primary* desire to act like others, whereas in (3) I have a *secondary* desire to act like others.[28]

---

[28] See Broome (1993) for a further discussion of the difference between causes and objects of desires.

As far as the type (1) pattern is concerned, one should distinguish between two rather different types of mechanisms. Others who do **A** can influence how strongly I desire **A** either

1.1 by influencing **A** in such a way that it become more (or less) desirable to me, or
1.2 by influencing my mental states(desires) in such a way that **A** appears more (or less) desirable to me.

Processes of the (1.1) type typically involve some form of path-dependent strategic complementarity. The usefulness of different items of consumption – a fax machine, for example – depends crucially upon how many others use them. When no one used a fax, it was not worth having one, but once others started to use them they became increasingly useful and desirable.[29]

Although the examples I discuss are all of the positive feedback kind, where an increase in others' doing **A** *increases* my propensity to do **A**, it should be remembered that negative feedback is just as important. For example, Bourdieu (1979) argues that the value of a cultural taste, its distinction, is reduced when more people acquire it. Competition and crowding likewise are likely to result in negative feedback processes. To the extent that both positive and negative feedback processes are at work at the same time, we have a 'micro ecology' which is likely to operate according to similar principles as the 'macro ecology' analyzed by organizational ecologists such as Hannan and Freeman (1989) and Hannan and Carroll (1992).

Dissonance reduction processes similar to those discussed in the previous section are likely to generate the (1.2) pattern. If a focal actor's desires differ markedly from those of individuals with whom he or she interacts, dissonance is likely to arise. For example, if I have been brought up in a working-class environment, this is likely to have influenced my cultural preferences. If my friends and colleagues come from a more 'highbrow' cultural background, this may be socially and psychologically stressful for me, and may therefore set in motion dissonance-reduction processes that operate behind my back. If these processes are successful, my desires will change in the direction of those with whom I interact, and this would then be another way by which the actions of some can influence the desires and subsequent actions of others.[30]

---

[29] Such a positive feedback process has been used to explain not only market phenomena but also phenomena such as technological (e.g., David 1985) and institutional (e.g., Pierson 2000) change, or lack thereof.

[30] Personally I am always a bit surprised whenever it dawns on me that I have unreflectively adopted as my own someone else's desire. Although I am not a follower of fashion, or a

Processes of the (1.2) kind are likely to be an important reason why perceptions of what is 'normal' and acceptable are so often rooted in what is common and typical (see Opp 2004). For example, in his classic study of what money buys, Rainwater (1974) showed how perceptions of poverty and other economic states continuously adjust to the prevailing standard of living in society at large.

The type (2) pattern in which individuals act like others because they desire to be like them has been most vividly demonstrated in experiments on conformity pressures in small groups (e.g., Asch 1956; Deutsch and Gerard 1955). Although it is difficult to tell whether individuals conform to majority opinions because they desire to be like them or, for instance, because they believe that others are better informed, this is an important mechanism. In certain respects it can even be said to be a more fundamental mechanism than the (1.2) mechanism, at least insofar as the dissonance-based account of (1.2) is concerned. The reason for this is that the dissonance-based account presupposes and is founded upon the existence of conformist desires similar to those at the heart of (2). If it were not the case that individuals desire to be like others, it would be difficult to explain why they experience dissonance when there is a lack of overlap between their own desires and those of others. To the extent that fundamental conformist desires like these are what explain dissonance, they tend not to be consciously articulated by individuals, but belong to the unconscious processes operating behind their backs. It is, of course, open to discussion whether unconscious desires about desires should really be referred to as desires, but this is a semantic subtlety we need not concern ourselves with here.

The type (3) pattern describes situations where individuals do as others do because it helps them to obtain something they desire. In its disingenuous form, a person acting like this is what in Swedish is called 'a servant of the eye', that is, someone who publicly pretends to share the sentiments of the majority while in private being opposed to or even loathing them. In his book on private truths and public lies, Kuran (1995) explored in great detail the often surprising outcomes that tend to follow when many individuals act like this.

---

conformist, it happens rather often that a change in fashion, such as a change in the way jackets are cut, at first appears rather odd to me, but soon thereafter I notice the effect that others have had on me when I suddenly state a genuine preference for jackets being cut that way.

Opportunity-mediated social interactions

To conclude this discussion of the different types of social interactions, let me briefly mention something about opportunity-based interactions as well. The defining characteristic of such interaction is that the action of one actor influences the action of another by affecting the opportunities available to this actor. Variations in opportunity structures are at the core of many sociological explanations. Criminal acts are explained by reference to the opportunities for committing a crime (e.g., Cohen and Felson 1979). The emergence of social movements is explained by reference to variations in 'political opportunity structures' (e.g., Tarrow 1998). Differences in social mobility rates between different nations or between different points in time are explained by reference to differences in mobility opportunities due to differences in occupational or class distributions (e.g., Goldthorpe, Llewellyn and Payne 1980). Many other examples could be mentioned.

Although opportunities play such a vital role in many sociological explanations, in most cases the variations in the opportunities themselves are not theorized but are assumed to be exogenously given. For many purposes this is perfectly fine, of course, but here we are interested in opportunity-mediated interactions, and then the dynamic interplay between the actions of some and the opportunities of others is central.

Harrison White's *Chains of Opportunity* (1970) was published more than thirty years ago, but it still represents something of an ideal as far as theories based on opportunity-mediated interactions are concerned. White's focus was on job mobility within organizations, but the logic of the explanation he proposed applies to many other areas as well. His theory has been used in a wide array of substantive fields to explain phenomena as diverse as the movement of hermit crabs and the dynamics of career processes (see Chase 1991 for an overview).

An important feature of job mobility within organizations, captured in White's analysis, is that individuals' opportunities are directly constrained by the number of vacant jobs. Vacancies are created either when individuals leave their organizations or when new positions are created, and the rate at which this occurs becomes a key to understanding the mobility process. If no vacancies were created, no opportunities for mobility would exist and no mobility would be observed. When an individual fills a vacancy, a new vacancy is created in that person's old job, and this represents a mobility opportunity to others. One of these people will get the job and the vacancy will disappear, but a new vacancy has now been created in this person's old job. Individuals and vacancies thus move in different directions, and the mobility process is governed by these chains of opportunity. Opportunity-mediated interactions thus create social interdependencies that can be of crucial explanatory importance.[31]

In social settings characterized by a clear distinction between persons and positions, opportunity-mediated interactions are likely to be highly important for the dynamics being observed. Actions are then interdependent, and one individual's action will directly influence the opportunities available to others, and thereby, in many cases, their actions as well.

Concatenations of mechanisms

As suggested by Gambetta (1998), it is often necessary to consider several mechanisms simultaneously in order to make sense of a specific social phenomenon, and these mechanisms may interact with one another in complex ways. When one considers such concatenations of mechanisms, a decision tree like the one in figure 3.5 is a useful point of reference.

Figure 3.5 describes the situation facing an actor who has two alternative courses of action to choose from, here labelled **A1** and **A2**. p and $1-p$ indicate the strength of the actor's belief in the possible outcomes following action **A1** (and they can be thought of as subjective probabilities that reflect the estimated probabilities and the actor's belief in the correctness of the estimate), and d_1 to d_3 index how desirable the actor finds the outcomes to be.

We can use a simple and stylized example to illustrate how the concatenation of some of the mechanisms discussed so far can influence the outcomes being analyzed. Assume that the decision tree in figure 3.5 describes the situation facing an individual who is to decide whether or not to commit a crime. If our hypothetical individual chooses not to commit the crime (**A2**), she knows for sure what will happen, and the value of this is equal to d_3. If she instead decides to commit the crime (**A1**), two things can happen. If she gets away with it, and this she believes will happen with probability p, she obtains the most valued outcome (d_1). If she is caught, and this she believes will happen with probability $1-p$, the value of the outcome is equal to d_2, and this is less desirable than not committing the crime ($d_2 < d_3$). As suggested by Kahan (1997), the criminal activities of others are likely to influence the likely consequences of committing a crime. To the extent that law

---

[31] See Sørensen (1977), Stewman and Konda (1983) and Hedström (1992) for some applications and extensions of White's model.

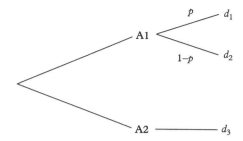

Figure 3.5. Decision tree illustrating a hypothetical choice situation consisting of two possible courses of action, **A1** and **A2**.

enforcement resources are more or less fixed, which they are likely to be at least in the short run, the probability of being caught is likely to decrease with the number of other individuals committing crimes. The law enforcement agencies are then too busy dealing with other crimes to be able to properly attend to the crime our hypothetical individual is considering committing. This means that the expected value of committing a crime ($p \times d_1 + (1-p) \times d_2$) is likely to increase with the number of others committing crimes, and in this way the actions of others may make our individual do something she otherwise would not have done.

In a situation like this other mechanisms are likely to be at work as well. The strength of the norm against stealing, for instance, is likely to be inversely proportional to the number of individuals breaking the norm. From the perspective of our focal individual, a reduction in the strength of this norm is equivalent to an increase in the value of the criminal alternative. Thus, an increase in the number of individuals committing crimes will increase the desirability of the criminal alternative and decrease the probability of detection, and this dual effect means that the actions of others can come to exercise a substantial influence on our hypothetical individual's choice of action. Concatenations of mechanisms like these appear to be central to explaining explosive outbursts of criminal activity that are sometimes observed during riots. The anonymity that one has in a crowd translates into a low probability of being caught, and the normative pressure against committing a crime is largely removed in a crowd of other law-breaking individuals.

When mechanisms like these are at work, an (apparent) Pareto-improving change, that is, a change leading to someone becoming better off without anyone becoming worse off, can trigger a process that eventually makes most people end up in a worse situation than they were in before the 'improvement'. An example related to the labour market and the decison tree in figure 3.5 can illustrate the point. Assume that the number of individuals who can attain the most desired type of job is fixed and equal to n_1. The probability of attaining such a job will then be equal to n_1/n, where n is the number of individuals who try to get the job. If the salaries of these jobs (d_1) were increased and the salaries of the other jobs remained the same, this would increase the expected value of trying to get the job, and this may induce more individuals to give it a try. The desire-mediated and belief-mediated interactions discussed above may act as reinforcers, making it appear even more desirable than it is, thereby further increasing the number trying to get the job. Since the number who can attain such a job is fixed and equal to n_1, however, this will simply lead to more people attaining d_2, which is the least desirable outcome of them all.[32] Assuming that individuals base their actions on strict expected-value calculations, and using the terminology of figure 3.5, there will always exist a value of d_1 such that all individuals choose **A1**, and thereby make all but n_1 end up in the worst possible outcome. For this to happen the following inequality must hold: $d_1 > d_3(n/n_1) - d_2((n - n_1)/n_1)$. Boudon (1981) used an argument along these lines to explain the puzzling finding of Stouffer and colleagues (1949) that military personnel with fewer advancement opportunities were often more satisfied than those with greater opportunities.

When it comes to explaining other social phenomena, concatenations of other types of mechanisms may be relevant. Tocqueville's explanation for the rapid secularization that took place in France at the end of the eighteenth century, for instance, evokes a combination of desire-mediated mechanisms and belief-mediated mechanisms of the rational-imitation kind:

> Those who retained their belief in the doctrines of the Church became afraid of being alone in their allegiance and, dreading isolation more than the stigma of heresy, professed to share the sentiment of the majority. So what was in reality the opinion of only a part (though a large one) of the nation came to be regarded as the will of all and for this reason seemed irresistible even to those who had given it this false appearance. (Tocqueville 1856[1998]: 155)

The logic of his argument is as follows. Although an actor believes that one course of action is best, he can decide to do something else for opportunistic reasons. If this is observed by others, the rational-imitation logic may lead them to do the same. Eventually this may feed back on the first actor and bring about a dissonance-reducing change in his desires, that is, lead him to genuinely desire what he initially only pretended to desire.

---

[32] The difference between d_2 and d_3 can be thought of as the cost of trying to get the job: for example, the cost of training.

Table 3.1. *Summary of some of the action-related mechanisms discussed in chapter 3*

Entities and activities	Structural pattern	Comment
Mental states and actions of a single individual		Baseline: among the set of known alternatives, the actor chooses the action believed to bring about the desired outcome.
– " –		Wishful thinking (or dread): the actor believes (not) what she desires to be the case. See Davidson (1980)
– " –		Adaptive (or counter-adaptive) desire formation: The actor desires only what she believes (not) to be possible. See Elster (1983b)
Mental states, opportunities and actions of two or more individuals		Dissonance-driven desire formation: e.g., Festinger (1957)
– " –		Rational imitation: e.g., Hedström (1998)
– " –		Vacancy chain: e.g., White (1970)
– " –		Self-fulfilling prophecy: e.g., Merton (1968b)
– " –		The Tocqueville pattern: e.g., Tocqueville (1856 [1998])

Types of mechanisms

Table 3.1 gives some systematic order to the type of action mechanisms discussed in this chapter, and illustrates one of the core ideas behind the mechanism approach: outcomes (in this case actions) depend upon the way in which the basic entities and activities of a mechanism are linked to one another. The letters B, D, O and A refer to the beliefs, desires, opportunities and actions of the indexed actors.

The table underscores that the same entities and activities, strung together in different ways, represent very different mechanisms. In chapter 4 the focus is on social-level phenomena, and I examine there in detail how mechanisms like these influence the social outcomes that groups of interacting actors are likely to bring about.

On the instrumentalism of rational-choice theorizing

Rational-choice-inspired theorizing has a long tradition in sociology, but it was not until the 1980s that a group of rational-choice sociologists emerged who defined themselves as such. The growth of rational-choice sociology has been inspired by advances made through the application of rational-choice theory within the neighbouring disciplines of economics and political science, as well as by widespread dissatisfaction with the current state of sociological theory (see Coleman 1990). Although the use of rational-choice assumptions is still somewhat controversial, and according to some sociologists represents a violation of a 'disciplinary taboo' (Baron and Hannan 1994), rational-choice sociology has made important contributions to several subfields of the discipline.[33]

My own initially highly positive attitude towards rational-choice sociology has gradually been tempered by what I consider to be an unfortunate instrumentalist tendency among many of its practitioners. Theoretical assumptions are often defended on entirely instrumentalist grounds, and this, I believe, threatens the explanatory value of the analyses and the long-term viability of the approach.

As mentioned above, rational-choice explanations have many traits in common with the approach advocated in this book. Most importantly, both approaches seek explanations that are abstract, precise and

---

[33] For rational-choice inspired analyses of norms, see Coleman (1990); for religion, see Stark and Iannaccone (1994); for education, see Morgan (2002); for comparative-historical development, see Kiser and Hechter (1991); for stratification, see Breen and Goldthorpe (1997); for revolutions, see Lindenberg (1989); and for collective behaviour, see Raub and Weesie (1990) and Heckathorn (1996). Many more examples could have been mentioned.

action-based. DBO theory makes no assumption that actors act rationally, however; it only assumes that they act reasonably and with intention. DBO theory is, for example, perfectly compatible with a selectionist trial-and-error account of action, and it recognizes the importance of various cognitive biases. DBO theory does not exclude the possibility that actors in sufficiently transparent environments may act according to the canons of rationality, but such situations are rare, and it therefore seems inappropriate to use rational-choice theory as the general point of departure. As there are numerous definitions of what it means to act 'rationally', and consequently also what a 'rational-choice explanation' entails, I will start by briefly defining how these terms are used here.

At the most fundamental level, a rational-choice explanation is an explanation that assumes that actors, when faced with a choice between different courses of action, will choose the course of action that is optimal with respect to their preferences or desires. In real-world settings it is difficult to tell what the optimal course of action may be, and this is particularly true when the actors are not perfectly informed about the available alternatives and their effects. As Elster (1986) has emphasized, once we allow that actors are imperfectly informed, and in most real-life situations this is surely something we must allow for, to act rationally imposes considerable demands on an actor. Not only must the action be optimal given the actor's beliefs about possible courses of action, but the beliefs themselves must be optimal, given the currently available information. In other words, actions based on beliefs that are not well founded in the available evidence cannot be considered rational. Furthermore, the amount of information a rational actor needs to gather before deciding what to do should also be optimal given the actor's preferences and prior beliefs. To endlessly collect pointless information, or to systematically ignore relevant information, appear to be obvious signs of irrational behaviour, but it is far from trivial to decide *ex ante* what the optimal amount of information is. One often needs to have access to the information one seeks to acquire in order to know what is optimal. The difficulties involved are dramatically increased once we allow for the fact that beliefs, desires, opportunities and outcomes are often brought about through interaction with others.

For these reasons it would seem to me rather obvious that such a theory is largely useful for normative purposes only, since the gap between the informational and computational assumptions of the theory and the decision-making capabilities of real actors is simply too wide for the theory to be of much explanatory use. Despite these rather obvious and frequently voiced objections to rational-choice-based explanations, the approach is endorsed by some of the best minds in the discipline. In order to justify intellectually the use of rational-choice theory, one must somehow be able to reduce the 'dissonance' caused by this gap between theory and reality, and these rational-choice sociologists seem to have followed two different 'dissonance reduction strategies'. Either they have redefined the notion of rationality in such a way that the gap between the canons of their revised notion of rationality and the everyday behaviour that they seek to explain is removed or reduced, or they have argued that the plausibility or realism of a theory's assumptions is of little or no importance. While I do not have any objections in principle to the redefining strategy – I simply find it rather pointless from an explanatory point of view – I have strong objections to the instrumentalist position, and this is the one that I focus upon here.

Instrumentalism is an important part of the theoretical heritage of rational-choice-based analyses, and it comes in two varieties: (1) predictability-motivated instrumentalism, and (2) tractability-motivated instrumentalism. These two varieties have an instrumentalist stance in common, but they differ on the principles that they suggest should replace realism as the guiding notion behind theory construction.

The classic arguments for the predictability-motivated form of instru-mentalism were presented by Friedman (1953). According to him, the idea of realistic assumptions is an illusion and therefore, he argued, the choice of theoretical assumptions should not be guided by how realistic they are, but by how accurate the predictions they generate are:

Truly important and significant hypotheses will be found to have 'assump-tions' that are widely inaccurate descriptive representations of reality, and, in general, the more significant the theory, the more unrealistic the assumptions (in this sense). The reason is simple. A hypothesis is important if it 'explains' much by little, that is, if it abstracts the common and crucial elements from the mass of complex and detailed circumstances surrounding the phenomena to be explained and permits valid predictions on the basis of them alone. To be important, therefore, a hypothesis must be descriptively false in its assumptions. (Friedman 1953: 14)

As pointed out by Sen (1980), Friedman's argument fails to convince, particularly because he obliterates the important distinction between descriptively false and descriptively incomplete statements, or between fictionalism and analytical realism (to use the terminology introduced in chapter 1). The distinction can be described in the following way.[34] If we have a set A = {a, b, c, d} and we assume that A = {e, f}, our assumption

---

[34] Sen never defined the terms, but these definitions seem to capture what he had in mind (or, in any event, they capture what I think he should have had in mind).

would be descriptively false and fictional, while if we assume that A = {a, d}, our assumption would be descriptively incomplete. In the former case we ascribe to A characteristics which it does not have, while in the latter case we assume A to be what it is only in part, that is, we accentuate certain aspects by ignoring others. While descriptive incompleteness appears to be a defining characteristic of all theories because they always focus on limited aspects of complex totalities, there cannot be any advantage in basing theories on fictitious assumptions, as Friedman implies. Although reasoning based on false premises can sometimes lead to correct conclusions, such reasoning has the obvious disadvantage, in comparison with reasoning based on correct premises, that it frequently leads to incorrect conclusions as well.

Instrumentalism is rarely advocated as explicitly as in the case of Friedman,[35] but his lack of concern for realism is something he shares with most of his rational-choice colleagues. Most rational-choice theorists are not instrumentalists in the same sense as Friedman, however. They justify the choice of theoretical assumptions neither on the basis of what appears to be realistic nor upon what generates good predictions. Rather, their choice of theoretical assumptions is, at least in part, dictated by their preference for parsimonious models with clear analytical solutions. This form of instrumentalism, in which assumptions are seen as instruments that can be freely tinkered with until one arrives at simple and elegant models, is widespread among mathematically oriented economists, but is also common among mathematically oriented rational-choice sociologists. One example is Coleman's (1990) analysis of school grades in which, without any real justification, he simply assumed that the relationship between a teacher and his or her students is similar to that which exists between buyers and sellers in a perfect neoclassical market. Introducing these assumptions allowed him to use mathematical models developed by economists and to perform analyses that he otherwise would not have been able to perform, but it also meant that his analysis came to be based on clearly false premises. No matter how elegant the resulting model was, the explanations and results derived from it must be called into question because the mechanisms and processes assumed in the model had little or nothing to do with the actual processes through which the grades he was trying to explain had been brought about.

Knowingly using false assumptions because they lead to tractable and elegant solutions reminds me of the man who was crawling under a lamp-post looking for his lost key. When asked what he was doing he

---

[35] However, see Jasso (1988) and Kanazawa (1998) for examples of contemporary sociologists advocating instrumentalist positions similar to those of Friedman.

answered, 'I am trying to find a key that I lost over there.' 'But if you lost your key on the other side of the street, why on earth are you looking over here?' With a surprised look on his face the man answered, 'Why should I waste my time looking over there? The light is so bad that I'd never find anything there!' As we all recognize, no matter how easy the light makes the search, it will not help the man to find his key. We seem to have a much more difficult time recognizing that the situation is similar as far as explanations are concerned. No matter how much easier the introduction of knowingly false assumptions makes the analysis, it will not help us to find the correct explanation because the resultant theory then 'looks' for answers in the wrong places.[36]

Being a social scientist can often be frustrating because our subject matter is such that we are rarely able to specify theories that are as precise and mathematically elegant as we would like them to be. But the temptation to invent entirely fictional worlds because in such worlds we can formulate more elegant theories is something that should be resisted. We should always aim for precision, but not for excessive precision if that simply entails fictional accounts or assumptions. Consider the following three statements:

1 Individuals are intentional beings.
2 Individuals are intentional beings whose beliefs, desires and opportunities influence their actions.
3 Individuals are intentional beings whose beliefs, desires, and opportunities influence their actions. Their beliefs are optimal in the light of the best information available, and in order to decide what to do they reason through sequences of potential actions by themselves and others and use backward induction to single out what is best to do at the moment.

The precision of the statements gradually increases by progressively more detailed specifications of how individuals decide what to do in a given situation. The third statement is a case of excessive precision, however, because although it is more precise than the first two it is entirely fictional (or at least I have not seen any evidence suggesting that individuals normally behave like this in real-world settings).[37] A

---

[36] Goldthorpe (2004: 101) has referred to this tendency as a form of 'sociological dandy-ism', by which he means 'a preoccupation with models, whether statistical or theoretical, on account more of their intrinsic elegance, refinement and subtlety than of what can be shown to follow from their sociological use that is of major substantive relevance, whether from the standpoint of pure or applied interests'.

[37] It should be noted that although this assumption appears to be without empirical support, it is empirically a rather more plausible assumption than many others routinely

statement such as this indicates that the theorist has precise ideas about a possible logic of action, but such logics are found only in worlds much different from our own. Therefore such stories are fictional and non-explanatory in our world.[38]

Rather than seeking excessively precise fictions, we should aim for theoretical assumptions known to be at least roughly correct in the real-world settings that we are analyzing. Such a modest and realist strategy characterizes some of the best theoretical work in the discipline. Take Merton and his notion of self-fulfilling prophecies as an example (Merton 1968b). At the core of this elegant and highly influential piece of work is the assumption that the actions of others influence individuals' beliefs and subsequent actions, but Merton never specified any precise model of the decision calculus. Doing so would be possible, but would it add any insights to those found in Merton's own analysis? As will be discussed in chapter 4, formalization often is required for explaining social phenomena but, if the model does not properly describe action principles observed in the real world, such formalizations are of little explanatory use. What appears important is to base the analysis on clear and empirically plausible assumptions about the actions and interactions of individuals, as Merton did, and then on this basis to develop theoretical models that allow us to get a handle on the social outcomes that the actors are likely to bring about. Such analyses either generate tendency statements about patterns likely to be observed, or suggest plausible processes through which the phenomena to be explained could have been brought about. More precision might be desirable, but not excessive precision that simply amounts to precisely stating and assuming to be true what is known to be untrue.[39] Theories of action should be based

---

used by rational-choice theorists, such as the mixed-strategy assumption so frequently evoked in dynamic analyses.

[38] See Elster (2000) for a critical discussion of different forms of excessive ambition that characterize many rational-choice-based analyses.

[39] One caveat needs to be added to this rather negative conclusion. Predictability-motivated instrumentalism seems justifiable if one is *exclusively* interested in *predicting* collective outcomes. If unrealistic actor models are successful in anticipating the actions of the individuals that constitute the collective unit, they can form the basis of such collective outcome predictions. Predicting the actions of real-life individuals has never been a strength of rational-choice theory, however (Green and Shapiro 1994). If one is concerned with that, one would seem better advised to look for theoretically more eclectic and empirically more grounded approaches. This conclusion runs counter to a frequently voiced argument in favour of rational-choice theory, which says that a micro-theory does not have to be particularly successful in predicting the actions of single individuals in order for it to properly predict macro-level outcomes (Stinchcombe 1968). The basic idea is that errors in micro-level theory tend to cancel themselves out, and one can therefore get more or less unbiased predictions of central tendencies, even with substantial individual-level errors. While there is some truth to this, I do not

on empirically grounded knowledge, not on optimality assumptions. As Tukey (1962: 15–16) once put it, 'far better an approximate solution to the *right* question than . . . an exact answer to the *wrong* question'.

Summary

Let me close this chapter by gathering the various threads in the form a brief synopsis. I started by noting that theories of action and interaction provide the foundation for explanatory sociological theories. I then suggested that the DBO theory, an action theory that explains action in terms of actors' desires, beliefs and opportunities, is an appropriate action theory for the type of sociological theories considered in this book. DBO theory is psychologically plausible, it is simple and it explains action in meaningful intentional terms.

I then continued by discussing social interaction from the perspective of DBO theory. Social interactions are at the core of most sociological theories for the simple reason that an individual's actions often cannot be explained unless they are related to the actions of others. When the actions or behaviours of some actors influence the actions of others, the DBO theory suggests that this influence must be mediated via the mental states (beliefs or desires) or the action opportunities of the latter actors. I introduced a distinction between belief-mediated, desire-mediated and opportunity-mediated interactions, and discussed at some length various examples of and reasons for the existence of such interaction effects.

I concluded the chapter by briefly discussing rational-choice theory and what I consider to be an unfortunate instrumentalist tendency among many of its practitioners. Knowingly accepting false assumptions because they lead to better predictions or to more elegant models threatens the explanatory value and the long-term viability of the rational-choice approach. While theories are by their nature always descriptively incomplete, descriptively false theories cannot be endorsed, because they give incorrect answers to why we observe what we observe.

---

think the argument holds up under closer scrutiny, because it presupposes that actors act independently of one another. Once interaction is allowed for, errors are not independent of one another, and then it will be evident that even rather small micro-level deviations from the canons of rationality can be echoed throughout the system and lead to aggregate predictions that are widely off-target. Furthermore, the argument rests on the questionable notion that correctly predicting central tendencies is what sociological theory should be about.

4   Social interaction and social change

In chapter 3 I focused on how the actions of individuals can be explained by reference to their beliefs, desires and opportunities, and how these mental states and action opportunities are, in turn, influenced by the actions and behaviours of others. This chapter builds upon and extends this foundation. The explanatory focus is no longer on individual actions, however, but on the macro-level or social phenomena that these actions bring about.[1]

As mentioned in chapter 1, the types of social phenomena I focus on are collective properties that are not definable for a single member of the collectivity.[2] Examples of different types of social phenomena and some associated why-questions include:

- *Typical actions, beliefs or desires*   Why have some racial prejudices changed over time? Why are some communities more conformist than others?
- *Distributions and aggregate patterns*   Why are some cities more ethnically segregated than others? Why are some societies more unequal than others?
- *Topologies of networks*   Why are social networks more tightly knit in some communities than in others? Why are some networks highly clustered while others are not?
- *Informal rules or social norms*   Why are norms of reciprocity common in some groups but not in others? Why are work norms stronger in some societies than in others?

In all of these cases, the entity to be explained concerns a social phenomenon that characterizes a collectivity of actors. Influential

---

[1] See Cherkaoui (2001) for a brief but most useful overview of various approaches that have been used for addressing this issue.

[2] The fact that a social property is not definable for a single actor does not imply that it cannot be explained in terms of the actions of individuals. I return to this issue later in this chapter.

sociological analyses that exemplify this focus on social phenomena include Durkheim's (Durkheim 1897 [1951]) analysis of suicide rates, Weber's (Weber 1904 [2002]) analysis of why modern capitalism emerged in the western world and Coleman's analysis of the diffusion of a new drug (Coleman, Katz and Menzel 1957). In all of these analyses the entities to be explained were social phenomena, and so were the main explanatory factors. In Durkheim's case, the main explanatory factor was the extent of social cohesion; in Weber's case it was the existence of a religious norm ('the Protestant ethic'); and in Coleman's case it was the topology of a network. The fact that both the explanans and the explanandum were social phenomena in these foundational studies is not a coincidence. It could be argued, but I will not do so here, that the combination of a social explanans and a social explanandum is a defining characteristic of sociology as a scientific discipline.[3]

From an explanatory point of view it is not sufficient simply to postulate that one social phenomenon causes another. Nor is it sufficient just to point to a correlation between a presumed cause and its effect. One must also open up the 'black box' to reveal the social mechanisms that are believed to be at work. Both Weber and Coleman were careful in detailing such mechanisms. They showed how properties of the social settings in which actors were embedded influenced their actions, and how these actions, in turn, brought about the social phenomena they sought to explain. As is well known, clarity about mechanisms was not Durkheim's strong suit, and he often gave the impression of subscribing to a rather obscure holistic ontology according to which social phenomena could directly cause each other.[4]

Despite the key explanatory importance of the link between the individual and the social, we are far from any comprehensive understanding of the ways in which they are interrelated. It is still common for theorists as well as empirical researchers to treat either the individual or the social as epiphenomenal, although, at least from a mechanism-based perspective, it seems obvious that one should seek explanations that explicate

---

[3] To avoid any misunderstandings, it should noted that explaining social change includes as one of its subsets the explanation of social stability. See Hernes (1976) for a discussion of this point.

[4] One typical and telling statement is the following: 'The sufficient cause of a social fact should always be sought among preceding social facts' (Durkheim 1895 [1978]: 191). However, as is also well known, Durkheim did not always follow his own methodological rules, and in his empirical studies he often explained social phenomena in terms of the actions that brought them about.

how the social and the individual mutually influence one another over time.[5] As discussed below, this unsatisfactory state of affairs can, at least in part, be traced to two common misconceptions: first, a tendency to reify and to treat as real purely analytical distinctions between different levels of reality; and second, a tendency to underestimate the analytical complexities involved in assessing the mutual interrelationships between the individual and the social.

The chapter is organized as follows. In the first section I discuss the unfortunate tendency of some sociologists to treat social reality as if it were stratified into different ontological levels that can be causally analyzed independently of each other. This sort of reification obscures rather than clarifies, and typically leads to rather superficial causal accounts and explanations. In the second section I discuss the complexities involved in developing precise explanatory theories that explicitly consider the interrelationship between the individual and the social. Social phenomena are emergent phenomena brought about by social processes that are difficult to comprehend without the aid of formal analytical tools. In the third and fourth sections I illustrate how one must proceed if one is to develop theories that explicitly consider the dynamic interplay between the individual and the social. In the third section I use the DBO theory as elaborated in chapter 3 as the foundation for a so-called agent-based simulation analysis. The analysis focuses on the social patterns of desires, beliefs and actions that are likely to emerge when large numbers of individuals act on the basis of the principles discussed in chapter 3. The analysis can be said to give a mechanism-based account of Marx's (1973: 146) important insight that 'The tradition of the dead generations weighs like a nightmare on the minds of the living'. In the fourth section I focus on how the structure of interaction within and between different groups is likely to influence the way individuals act. An important result of the analyses presented in the third and fourth sections is that small and seemingly trivial changes at the level of individual action can often lead to large and unexpected changes at the level of the social. The section that closes the chapter discusses the implications that such non-linearities have for sociological analyses more generally.

---

[5] See Alexander et al. (1987) for a useful overview of different approaches to addressing the micro–macro relationship. See Archer (1995) for an interesting discussion of the tendency of many sociologists to commit what she refers to as the fallacies of upwards and downwards conflation, that is, the failure to consider the mutual influence of the individual and the social on one another.

The individual and the social: ontological and methodological distinctions

The mechanism approach implies that all proper explanations of social phenomena must specify the mechanisms by which they were brought about. This implies that one should seek to explain how the social and the individual mutually influence each other over time, and close attention must be given to how actors in interaction with one another bring about social outcomes that in turn influence actions at later points in time. Social phenomena, as here defined, refer to properties of groups of individuals. Examples include typical actions among the set of individuals that belong to a certain collectivity or the properties of the networks that link the individuals to one another. These social phenomena are the result of individuals' actions, but they also causually influence individuals' actions. As discussed in chapter 3, individuals not only interact with other individuals; they also 'interact' with and are influenced by the properties of social aggregates. To repeat Schelling's clarifying everyday example (1998: 33), 'I interact with an individual if I change lanes when his front bumper approaches within five feet of my rear bumper; I interact with a social aggregate when I adjust my speed to the average speed on the highway.' For these reasons, whenever we seek to explain a social outcome, it is essential to examine the dynamic interplay between individual actions and social outcomes.

These explanatory principles are not subscribed to by those who believe that the social world is ontologically stratified in such a way that different 'levels of reality' are irreducible to one another. Within contemporary social theory, such positions are most clearly articulated by 'critical realists' such as Bhaskar (1998) and Archer (1995).[6] The key notion here is a particular form of 'emergence' which, according to the critical realists, makes entities, properties and/or mechanisms at one level in some sense unique and autonomous in relation to those at lower levels. Collier (1994:116) summarizes the main idea as follows:

Laws of human behaviour and of social processes will be distinct, and it will not be possible to reduce one or to predict one from the other. Each level is autonomous in the sense of having its own irreducible set of mechanisms.

Archer expresses similar ideas when discussing the core premises of her so-called morphogenetic approach to sociological analysis: '[I]t

---

[6] In addition to this social stratification of reality, critical theorists assume that the world is stratified into three different 'domains': the real, the actual, and the empirical. These are problematic distinctions, but they need not concern us here.

depends upon an ontological view of the social world as stratified, such that the emergent properties of structures and agents are irreducible to one another, meaning that in principle they are analytically separable.' According to Archer (1995: 66), structure and agency are 'neither co-extensive nor co-variant through time, because each possesses autonomous emergent properties which are thus capable of independent variation and therefore of being out of phase with one another in time'. 'Once emergence has taken place the powers and properties defining and distinguishing strata have relative autonomy from one another. Such autonomous properties exert independent causal influence in their own right' (1995: 14).[7]

Brante (2001) discusses some implications of these ideas for sociological research more generally. Like Archer and Bhaskar, he believes that reality is stratified and that there are 'non-reductive causal mechanisms' that operate at each level. Using a Bhaskar-like argument, he takes scientific practice as his point of departure and argues that current sociological practice suggests that one should distinguish between the following levels: (1) the international, (2) the national, (3) the institutional, (4) the inter-individual, and (5) the individual. Recognizing the relative autonomy of the various levels, Brante argues, will allow sociologists of different theoretical persuasions to get on with their explanatory work instead of being bogged down in meta-theoretical discussions. According to Brante (2001: 186), sociological theorists tend to be too preoccupied with philosophical niceties; there is a risk that 'we end up like Freud's patient who always polished his glasses but never put them on'.

I do not want to enter into a discussion of the advantages and disadvantages of Brante's proposal,[8] but it should be noted that arguments that are based exclusively on scientific practice have a strong inductivist and conservative bias. In essence, Brante says that sociologists should continue to do what they do because sociologists would not do what they do unless they had good reasons to do so. Obviously he has much more faith that sociology is on the right track than I have.

If social reality were ontologically stratified, and if the social had the causal powers that critical realists attribute to it, then their conclusions would be warranted. The individual and the social would be 'analytically

---

[7] Although the notion of emergence is at the very core of Archer's approach, she is rather ambiguous about its meaning and how different levels are interrelated. In certain parts of her 1995 book she emphasizes (correctly, in my view) that one must always examine the dynamic interplay between actors and structures, but in other parts of the book she maintains that emergent structures are autonomous and have their own 'causal powers'.

[8] See Aspers (1997) for a thoughtful critique of this rather arbitrary level ontology and the so-called miracle argument that it is based upon.

separable' and a division of labour like the one suggested by Brante would be perfectly reasonable. But why should we believe in these propositions about the ontological status of the social and about its causal powers?

Most of us agree that individuals exist and that they have causal powers that enable them to bring about change and to transcend social expectations. The critical realists believe that this also holds true for *society* and *structure*. Since *society* cannot be observed as such, a perceptual criterion of ontological existence cannot be used. Instead, Bhaskar and colleagues rely on a causal criterion of existence and argue that society and/or different social strata have a real ontological existence to the extent that they are causally efficacious; 'their *causal power* establishes their *reality*' (Bhaskar 1998: 25).

The arguments of Bhaskar and colleagues are not particularly convincing, however. The causal criterion of existence is a perfectly reasonable criterion, but it is difficult to rely upon (1) when an entity can have a causal power without exercising it — a government may, for example, have the causal power to more equitably distribute wealth, but may not exercise it — and (2) when an exercised causal power may be empirically unobservable because its effect is emasculated by other social processes. When this occurs — and most critical realists seem to agree that these conditions generally pertain — the claim to ontological existence and causal power hinges on the existence of empirically unobservable effects of an empirically unobservable entity.

Convincing the unconvinced about the autonomous ontological existence and causal powers of such social entities requires more than grand proclamations or references to sociological practice. What is needed is a reliable *method* by which such causal effects can be identified. I doubt that such methods can ever be devised and, given that no such methods exist today, one wonders why the critical realists seem so uncritically to believe in invisible powers of invisible entities. It should be noted that this criticism of the core ideas of critical realism is not founded on any positivist dogma about the privileged role of observables. Unobservables are essential for theorizing, but we cannot make them up at will if we want to remain realist. As far as I can see, the critical realists have no convincing arguments about the causal efficacy of social entities, nor are there any perceptual reasons for believing in their existence. Without reliable methods for establishing the causal powers of unobservable social entities, the claims that are advanced by the critical realists remain vacuous.[9]

---

[9] As Archer (1995: 28) so correctly observed, 'An ontology without a methodology is deaf and dumb.'

What this brief discussion suggests is that critical realists and other theorists who try to avoid the mysticisms of traditional holistic ontologies when they assign autonomous existence and causal power to social entities end up not much better off than the traditional holists.[10] For this reason I do not believe that ontological collectivism, in whatever form or shape, has anything to offer sociological theory. Some sociologists endorse a collectivist position not on ontological but on methodological grounds, however, and such arguments have more to offer, at least in principle. The strongest arguments along these lines are those based on the idea of 'supervenience'.

Ideas about supervenience have their roots in the philosophy of mind literature, where they have been used to characterize the relationship between the physical and the mental (e.g., Jackson 1996). The same ideas have also been used to describe the relation between the individual and the social (e.g., Kincaid 1996; Sawyer 2001; 2004). Briefly, a social property, S, is said to supervene on a set of individual-level properties, I, if identity in I necessarily implies identity in S. If the social is supervenient on the individual, as the mechanism-based account would insist, it means that, if the individual-level properties of two collectivities are identical, then their social properties also will be identical. It also implies that two collectivities that differ in their social properties will necessarily differ in their individual properties as well. But it does *not* imply that two collectivities with an identical social property will necessarily have identical individual-level properties, and the reason for this is that identical social properties can be brought about in different ways. If social properties are brought about in widely disjunctive ways, as Sawyer (2001) claims, one can conceive of a situation in which we observe a constant conjunction at the social level such that one type of social property always tends to be followed by another type of social property, without there existing any similar law-like relation at the individual level. Although social properties are always individually based, orderliness and predictability would then exist only at the social level. If these conditions pertained, one could argue, as Sawyer does, that the only reasonable position is to be an ontological individualist *and* a methodological collectivist. That is to say, although each token causal sequence is based on an individual-level process, the explanation would then, of necessity, have to be couched in terms of social-level factors only.

Although one must certainly allow for the possibility that situations like these may exist, I do not believe that they are at all as common as Sawyer seems to suggest, and Sawyer presents no arguments or

[10] Phillips (1976) is still a most readable exposition of these difficulties.

empirical data in support of his thesis. Furthermore, if the social level is not ontologically autonomous but depends on individual-level properties and relations, as is implied by the supervenience thesis, I fail to see how the social could have any causal powers of its own, as Sawyer seems to think. Instead, the supervenience thesis implies that a social property can causally influence another social property only by influencing its supervenience base (Kim 1984). From a causal point of view, a correlation between two social phenomena will therefore always be epiphenomenal and, in this sense, spurious. The alternative to causal explanations couched in terms of individual-level processes is not 'social laws', as Sawyer implies, but statements about correlations at the level of the social. Examples of such research range from Donald Black's form of 'pure sociology' (e.g., Black 2000) to the aggregate inductivism of comparative historical sociologists such as Theda Skocpol (e.g., Skocpol 1984). Aggregate correlational or inductive analysis may in certain circumstances be all we can hope for, but it is certainly nothing to strive for, and should be seen only as a very last resort.

Instead of making ontological distinctions between different levels of reality, it appears more useful and certainly much less problematic to view level distinctions as purely methodological. Thus, rather than assuming that the social world is ontologically stratified, one makes a methodological distinction between different 'mechanism levels'. Following Craver (2001), an item X can then be said to be at a lower mechanistic level than an item Y if X is one of the entities or activities of the mechanism that regularly bring about the type of Y-related outcome being considered. Given this notion of mechanism levels, beliefs and desires are at a lower mechanistic level than actions, according to the DBO theory developed in chapter 3. It also means that individual actions are at a lower level than the type of social phenomena discussed in the present chapter. But it also means, somewhat more counterintuitively, that social phenomena can be said to be at a lower level than actions or beliefs if such phenomena are components of the mechanism for these actions or beliefs. Notions of levels, as they are used here, are always relative to the mechanism under consideration.

Similarly, it seems far less problematic and more correct to view social emergence as an epistemological rather than an ontological problem. From an epistemological point of view, social emergence refers to social properties that cannot, in practice, be predicted by knowing everything there is to know about the pre-emergent properties of the parts. It is in this epistemological sense that the concept of emergence is used here.[11]

---

[11] See O'Connor and Wong (2002) for a discussion of different notions of 'emergence'.

The complexity of the link between the individual and the social

While critical realists can be said to attribute unwarranted causal powers to the social, another common fallacy is to give too little attention to the social. In much quantitative sociological research, for example, individuals are treated as if they were social atoms. Individuals are randomly selected and uprooted from their social environments, and research proceeds on the assumption that the whole — the social — can be understood by studying the individual parts in isolation from one another. However, as in all emergent systems, knowing the behaviour of the isolated parts leaves us a long way from knowing the whole (J. H. Holland 1998). In order to understand emergent social phenomena — and by 'emergent phenomena' I mean not any mystical holistic entities but simply to social phenomena, possibly complex social phenomena, that are brought about by the actions of individuals — we have to study the interactions as well as the parts.

Social outcomes, like other emergent phenomena, are difficult to anticipate because the outcome depends to such a high degree on how the individual parts are interrelated. As is shown later in this chapter, small and seemingly unimportant changes in the way actors are interrelated can have profound consequences for the social outcomes that are likely to emerge. For this reason, social outcomes cannot simply be 'read off' from the properties of the individuals that generate them. Schelling's (1971) analyses of segregation processes clearly illustrate this point. Even in very small groups in which actors act on the basis of highly simplified and known action logics, we often fail to anticipate the social outcomes they are likely to bring about. Granovetter (1973: 1360) has made a similar observation: 'At the micro level, a large and increasing body of data and theory offers useful and illuminating ideas about what transpires within the confines of the small group. But how interaction in small groups aggregates to form large-scale patterns eludes us in most cases.'

This unsatisfactory state of affairs is undoubtedly related to the complex nature of the problem. Explaining how individuals in interaction with one another bring about various social phenomena is usually too complex for us to handle without the use of formal analytical tools. Without such tools we can state our problems but we cannot solve them. We can specify action logics and patterns of interaction, but we cannot derive their social implications. In order to understand the complex relationships that exist between action, interaction and social emergence, the abstract logic of the process must be expressed in a suitable formalism.

The reason that I insist that social interactions must be part of sociological explanations is not simply that I want to remain within the core of the sociological tradition, but that social interactions are essential if we are to understand why we observe the social phenomena we observe. Similarly, I do not insist on the importance of formal analytical tools because I believe that formalization or model building is intrinsically valuable. The value of formalization lies exclusively in the fact that it allows us to explain problems that we otherwise would not have been capable of expaining. Without the appropriate analytical tools we would not be able to comprehend most forms of social emergence. As seen in the previous section, lacking such tools we can easily be led to believe that the social has emergent properties that cannot be derived from its individual-level bases.[12]

Social patterns in desires, beliefs and actions

Agent-based computational modelling is a formalism designed for analyzing the relationship between individual-level and social-level phenomena, whatever these phenomena may be. The core idea is to use computer simulations to assess the social outcomes that groups of virtual actors are likely to bring about. The best-known agent-based analysis in the social sciences is no doubt Schelling's (1971) analysis of segregation processes, but more recently a range of large-scale agent-based analyses have been published, such as Epstein's and Axtell's so-called Sugerscape model (1996).[13]

In this section, agent-based models are used to examine the social phenomena likely to emerge when actors act on the basis of the DBO theory discussed in chapter 3. It is important to recognize that such a focus does not imply a disregard of the potential importance of social relations and other forms of social phenomena. As has, one hopes, been made clear in previous chapters, social relations, social interactions and various types of social phenomena are at the very core of the social mechanisms approach. The reason for focusing on mental states and

---

[12] An important qualification should be added. Formalization is a necessary but not sufficient condition for arriving at a better understanding of the link between the individual and the social. If mathematics is simply used to define static properties of a system, as is often the case in the sociological network literature, it will not be of much help. The type of formalization I have in mind here is one that enables us to analyze how a complex system changes over time.

[13] See also Hägerstrand (1965) for an early and influential example of agent-based analysis, and Macy and Willer (2002) for a general overview of the field.

action opportunities is that they are the 'media' through which social phenomena exert whatever effects they may have.

By way of introducing these analyses, it is also important to emphasize that the relationship between the individual and the social revealed in agent-based analyses should not be interpreted as empirical predictions or as literal statements about empirical reality. As emphasized by the critical realists, and as discussed in chapter 2, societies are 'open systems' in which many different social processes coexist and influence each other. Analytically removing these processes from the theoretical analysis does not mean that they are removed from the empirical realm. The results of an agent-based analysis should therefore always be understood as referring to causal tendencies or, equivalently, to patterns likely to hold if the system were closed and behaved according to the logics stipulated in the model.

As discussed in chapter 3, the cause of an action can be seen as a constellation of desires, beliefs and opportunities in the light of which the action appears reasonable. Desires and beliefs have a motivational force that influences how individuals act. If we simplify the notion of desires and beliefs in such a way that they can be said either to be or not to be to hand, the possible patterns of desires, beliefs, opportunities and actions can be described as in Table 4.1. A 1 here indicates the presence of the relevant belief, desire, opportunity or action. The third pattern, for instance, represents a situation where an actor desires a certain outcome and has the opportunity to perform the relevant action, but does not believe that the action will bring about the desired outcome, and therefore decides not to act.

Of these eight possible DBO patterns, only the first one will bring about an action, because only in this situation does the actor have the opportunity to act in a way that (s)he believes will bring about the

Table 4.1. *DBO patterns and associated courses of action*

Pattern	Desire	Belief	Opportunity	Action
(1)	1	1	1	1
(2)	0	1	1	0
(3)	1	0	1	0
(4)	0	0	1	0
(5)	1	1	0	0
(6)	0	1	0	0
(7)	1	0	0	0
(8)	0	0	0	0

desired outcome. With respect to these DBO patterns, the importance of the *intra-individual* mechanisms discussed in chapter 3 is that they represent common ways through which pattern (1) is transformed into one of the other patterns, and vice versa. For example, the dissonance-driven desire formation mechanism discussed in chapter 3 may transform pattern (2) into pattern (1), and wishful thinking may transform pattern (3) into pattern (1). In both cases the presence of the intra-individual mechanism makes the actor perform an action (s)he otherwise would not have performed.

In order to simplify the presentation I will focus exclusively on the first four patterns in table 4.1, that is, I will assume that all actors have the opportunity to act. Although it would be interesting to allow for variations in the opportunity structure as well, this is not necessary in order to make the points I wish to make in this chapter. The analysis focuses on the desires, beliefs and actions of 2,500 virtual actors. At each point in time the relevant aspects of an actor can be described in terms of a desire-belief-action triplet, $<D,B,A>$. If the first two entries of the triplet are both equal to one, then the third entry will also become equal to one because actors act when they believe that the action will bring about the desired outcome; otherwise it will be equal to zero. If the first entry of the triplet is equal to 1, the actor is said to have a 'positive' desire, and if the second entry is equal to 1, the actor is said to have a 'positive' belief.[14] Since an actor's desires and beliefs are influenced by the beliefs and desires of those with whom the actor interacts, the content of the DBA triplets will change over time until the system reaches some form of steady state (which could be a stable cyclical pattern).

The agent-based simulation thus seeks to model an historical or temporal process. In the analyses presented below, the actors' beliefs and desires exhibit no social patterning whatsoever at the outset; they are entirely random. As history evolves, distinct social patterns start to emerge, however, because the actors interact and influence each other. The way in which these actors interact with one another is most easily imagined if we think of the actors as being placed on a square lattice consisting of fifty times fifty cells. A typical initial pattern of desires, beliefs and actions then looks like the pattern in figure 4.1. Squares identify actors with positive desires, that is, those with a 1 in the first entry of the DBA triplet. Circles identify actors with positive beliefs (a 1 in the second entry of the triplet). Black dots identify actors who have

---

[14] A positive belief thus means that the actor believes that the action is a good, efficient and/or appropriate means of attaining the desired result.

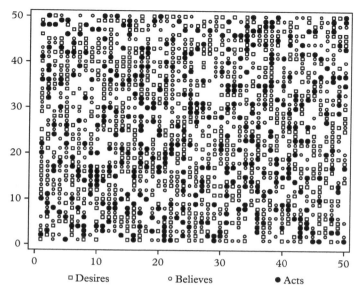

Figure 4.1. Initial patterns of beliefs, desires and actions in a population of 2,500 virtual actors. Each cell describes the current state of an actor's DBA triplet.

positive desires *and* positive beliefs. They are the ones who will act because they believe that the action will bring about the desired outcome. Consequently their triplets will be equal to <*1,1,1*>. The white areas of the graph consist of actors with DBA triplets equal to <*0,0,0*>, that is, they neither believe in the efficacy of the action nor desire the result, and therefore they do not act. In figure 4.1, 40 per cent of the actors have positive desires, 40 per cent have positive beliefs, and accordingly about 16 per cent act because they are the ones who have positive beliefs *and* positive desires.

To begin, it will be assumed that each actor directly interacts with the four neighbours described in figure 4.2.[15] If a majority of these neighbours have a different belief from that of the focal actor, the focal actor's belief will change. Otherwise it will remain the same. The desires of the actors evolve according to the same logic.[16] Thus, there will be two

[15] This type of interaction structure is often referred to as a von Neumann neighbourhood of range 1.

[16] The lattice used here is a so-called torus, that is, a lattice which is wrapped around itself in such a way that actors positioned at the borders of the lattice have neighbours on the

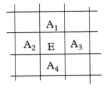

Figure 4.2. The structure of social interaction between Ego and Alters.

parallel contagion processes at work, one operating on the beliefs of the actors and the other on their desires, and actions are the joint result of these two processes. This simple setup emulates a type of process that is at the core of many sociological problems in that it captures the mutual interrelationships that exist between the individual and the social. Individuals' beliefs, desires and actions are causally influenced by social phenomena — in this case typical desires and beliefs of the significant others — and changes in the focal individual's desires, beliefs and actions in turn change the social environment of others.

Although our point of departure is the random social pattern of figure 4.1, interaction processes quickly lead to a lock-in on a highly clustered and segregated pattern. Figure 4.3 is a typical example of the type of pattern that emerges.[17] This pattern is typical in that it contains islands of desires and islands of beliefs that occasionally overlap and then lead to actions.

The composition of real-life groups typically changes over time because some individuals leave the groups and others enter, and such changes may alter the type of pattern observed in figure 4.3. One way of introducing such changes into the analysis is to randomly remove certain actors and replace them with new actors who hold different beliefs and desires from those that they replace. The results of this can be seen in table 4.2.

Each cell of the table presents averages based on 500 different simulations. The basic simulation columns refer to the type of setup discussed so far, the first column focusing on actions and the second on deprivation. The point of departure is a random assignment of desires and beliefs to 40 per cent of the actors, and this results in 16 per cent of the actors acting. Since a minority of the actors hold positive beliefs and

---

other side of the lattice. Hence all actors have the same number of neighbours. In the analyses all actors update their desires and beliefs at the same time.

[17] This pattern is the one that emerges from the random pattern in figure 4.1, when the actors have interacted for twenty rounds according to the rules just described.

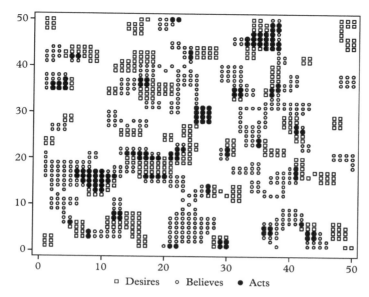

Figure 4.3. Typical patterns of beliefs, desires and actions in a population of 2,500 actors who socially interact with four neighbours.

desires, the interaction process will further reduce these proportions. After the actors have interacted and influenced each other for twenty rounds, only 5 per cent of the actors act. At that point, 20 per cent of the actors are replaced with new actors who hold the opposite beliefs and desires to those that they replace. This 'shock' to the system leads to a temporary increase in actions, but the interaction process quickly brings the new actors into line with the old ones, and the level of action more or less returns to what it was before they entered. Such social outcomes thus seem rather resilient to even rather abrupt 'generational' changes. It was these results I had in mind when near the beginning of the present chapter I referred to Marx's remark that, although men make their own history, the past is important because actors make their history under conditions transmitted from the past.

The same patterns can be observed in the second column, which focuses on the extent of deprivation. In terms of DBA triplets, deprivation is defined by the $<1,0,0>$ pattern, that is, an actor is considered to be deprived if (s)he fails to perform an action because (s)he believes that it will not bring about the desired outcome. Approximately one actor out of four is deprived at the outset, but the interaction process substantially

Table 4.2. *Summary of simulation results*
Each cell is an average based on 500 simulations.

	Basic simulation		Wishful thinking		Sour grapes		Wishful thinking and sour grapes	
	Action	Deprivation	Action	Deprivation	Action	Deprivation	Action	Deprivation
Initial	.16	.24	.16	.24	.16	.24	.16	.24
After social interaction	.05	.17	.10	.11	.04	.09	.07	.06
After entry of new actors	.11	.22	.14	.19	.09	.18	.11	.16
After additional social interaction	.04	.16	.10	.10	.03	.06	.06	.04

reduces the extent of deprivation. The entry of new actors more or less makes the deprivation level return to its initial level, but once again the 'force of history' makes the new actors fall into line and the extent of deprivation falls again.

The rest of table 4.2 focuses on two of the intra-individual mechanisms discussed in chapter 3, wishful thinking and the sour-grapes syndrome. The computational model that generated these results is the same as before, with the exception that 20 per cent of the actors are now exposed to wishful thinking and to the sour-grapes syndrome.

Wishful thinking, as the term is used here, denotes a causal connection from an actor's desires to his/her beliefs that makes the actor believe what (s)he desires to be the case. In terms of DBA triplets, this means that a $<1,0,0>$ triplet will be transformed into a $<1,1,0>$ triplet. But since actors act when they believe that an action will bring about a desired outcome, this pattern is not stable, but will be further transformed into a $<1,1,1>$ triplet. As can be seen from the table, wishful thinking leads to considerably more action and less deprivation than would otherwise have been the case. The effects of social interaction and the entry of new actors are similar to those found in the first two columns, but at each stage more actors act and fewer are deprived.

The sour-grapes syndrome is a causal connection from an actor's beliefs to his/her desires, which makes the actor desire only what (s)he believes (s)he can get. In terms of DBA triplets, this means that a $<1,0,0>$ pattern will always be transformed into a $<0,0,0>$ pattern. These simulation results reveal that the sour-grapes mechanism has a rather marginal effect on action but a considerable effect on deprivation.

At first sight it may seem surprising that the sour-grapes mechanism has any effects whatsoever on action, since the change from $<1,0,0>$ to $<0,0,0>$ does not represent any change in action — the third entry of the triplet is equal to zero in both cases. The change in the actor's desires brought about by the sour-grapes mechanism may, however, influence the desires of those with whom the actor interacts and thereby alter *their* actions. In this respect there is an important difference between the wishful-thinking and the sour-grapes mechanisms. While the former mechanism has a direct effect on the focal actor's actions and an indirect effect on the actions of others, the latter mechanism has only an indirect effect on the actions of others. In these simulations, this indirect effect is not particularly strong, but it is nonetheless clearly visible in the table.

The last two columns of table 4.2 describe the outcomes that are brought about when 20 per cent of the actors are wishful thinkers and

20 per cent are under the influence of the sour-grapes mechanism.[18] In terms of actions, the two mechanisms more or less cancel each other out, but they have a most profound effect on the deprivation level: jointly they reduce the deprivation level to a quarter of its initial size.

The results presented so far thus show that social interaction processes can have a profound impact on the social patterns we observe, and that intra-individual mechanisms can be of considerable importance for the social phenomena that emerge. All the results presented so far have assumed that the structure of interaction is the one depicted in figure 4.2. That is to say, throughout these analyses the structure of interaction has been held constant. As emphasized above, however, emergent properties to a large extent depend on how the individual parts, that is, the actors, are interrelated. To examine whether this is indeed the case, a small change in the structure of social interaction will be introduced, and agent-based analyses will be used to examine the extent to which this change influences how individuals act.

The structural change to be introduced may appear rather insignificant: one of the four neighbours with whom an actor interacts will be replaced by a randomly selected actor.[19] Thus, instead of interacting with four neighbours, each actor will interact with three neighbours and a randomly selected actor. The point of departure is, once again, the random desires and beliefs of figure 4.1, and, as previously, the actors will be allowed to interact and influence each other for twenty rounds. The social pattern that emerges under these slightly altered conditions is shown in figure 4.4.

The difference between figure 4.3 and figure 4.4 is rather striking, particularly when one considers the similarities between the processes that generated them. In the previous simulation, a large number of actors ended up with positive beliefs and/or desires, and about one actor out of twenty acted. In this simulation, however, only a few actors end up with positive beliefs or desires, and no one acts.[20] These differences in social outcomes are exclusively the result of the change in the structure of interaction, since everything else is held constant, including the sequence of random numbers. The reason why this change in the structure of interaction has such a profound effect should be sought in the fact that

[18] Since the assignments of beliefs and of desires are independent of one another, one should expect that this, on average, leads to 4 per cent having positive beliefs *and* positive desires.

[19] The actor being replaced is the actor to the left of the focal actor, and the actor interacts with the same randomly selected Alter throughout the analysis.

[20] Had we allowed the simulation to run for a few additional rounds, the isolates with positive beliefs and desires in the middle of the graph would also have become zeros.

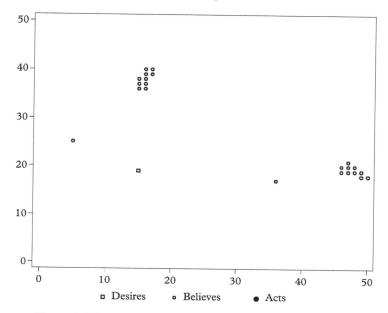

Figure 4.4. Typical patterns of beliefs, desires and actions in a population of 2,500 virtual actors who interact socially with three neighbours and one randomly selected actor.

local belief and desire clusters are much less likely to survive when the actors, through their randomly selected significant other, are exposed to influences from outside their own immediate sphere.

In order to make sure that these differences between the two interaction regimes were genuine, a large number of simulations were run with different initial values. The results are summarized in figure 4.5.[21]

The graphs in figure 4.5 show how the two interaction regimes influence actions. The graphs relate the proportion that acts at the (random) outset to the proportion that acts after the actors have interacted with one another. The 'line of no effect' indicates when the initial proportion is identical to the proportion that eventually acts.

---

[21] Figure 4.5 summarizes the results of 7,500 simulations. These simulations are based on the same set up as before, that is, 2,500 actors who are placed on a lattice with fifty times fifty cells. Their actions were recorded after they had interacted and influenced one another's beliefs and desires for twenty rounds. Normally a steady state was reached much earlier; however, typically beliefs and desires locked in on a stable pattern after about ten iterations. In these analyses there is neither wishful thinking nor sour grapes, and no new actors enter the analysis.

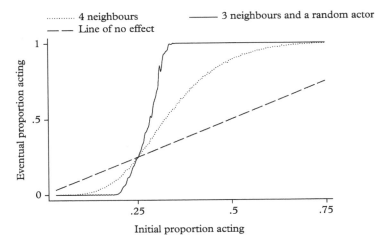

Figure 4.5. Effects on typical actions of two different structures of social interaction.

As expected, in both cases the proportion that eventually acts is a positive function of the initial proportion, but there are marked differences between the two interaction regimes. While the four-neighbour structure results in a smooth and gradual relationship between the initial conditions and the final outcome, the three-neighbour structure results in a sharp step-like relationship. In this latter case, the analyses show that no one is likely to act if the initial proportion is below 20 per cent, and that everyone is likely to act if it is above 35 per cent. This means that the two interaction regimes lead to dramatically different outcomes in certain circumstances. If the first interaction regime obtains, the interaction process will lead slightly more than half of the actors to act if one-third of the actors acted at the outset. But under the other regime, that is, when one of the four neighbours is replaced with a randomly selected actor, identical initial conditions will cause more than nine actors out of ten to act. These results thus show that there are genuine differences between these two interaction regimes in terms of how they affect actions. If we are to explain differences in the way actors in different groups act, we must pay close attention to the structure of interaction. Even if there are marked differences in how individuals in different groups act, this may simply be due to a small but systematic difference in the structure of interaction.[22]

---

[22] Another notable result is that both graphs intersect the line of no effect from below when the initial proportion acting is equal to 0.25. This means that, if fewer than 25 per cent of

The main purpose of this section has been to illustrate how one can proceed, in a theoretically coherent fashion from the level of individual desires, beliefs and actions to large-scale social outcomes. As a by-product, some interesting results have been produced. Most importantly, even if we knew everything there was to know about the properties of the actors (including their action logics), we would be a long way from knowing the 'social wholes' they would be likely to bring about. In order to explain social outcomes, we must focus not only on the properties of the actors, but also on the way in which the actors interact and influence one another.

Social outcomes and group affiliations

It seems rather clear to me that agent-based modelling is destined to become the dominant type of theoretical formalism in sociology. The flexibility of the approach means that it can be used to derive the social consequences of basically any type of interaction structure and action logic.[23] The main alternative to agent-based models is to use difference or differential-equation models to analyze the overall dynamics of the system of interaction. The types of problems that can usefully be analyzed with such models are somewhat restricted, however, because they are based on assumptions that are not always fulfilled. But when such models are appropriate, they have certain advantages over agent-based models, in that they are more straightforward to use and easier to link to

the actors act at the outset, the interaction process works like a negative spiral that reduces the number of actors who eventually act. Above 25 per cent, there will be a corresponding positive spiral increasing the number who act. The reason the turning point is 0.25 is that the underlying beliefs and desires are then such that half of the actors hold positive beliefs and half hold positive desires (in these simulations the initial proportions with D=1 and B=1 are always the same). If more than 25 per cent act at the outset, it means that the proportions with positive beliefs and desires are greater than 0.5. When this is the case, the contagion process will spread the belief and the desire to even more actors, and will thereby bring about an increase in the proportion who eventually act. If fewer than 25 per cent act at the outset, the proportion with positive beliefs and desires will be below 0.5 and then the opposite development will take place. If we had used a more behaviouristic approach in which actions were assumed to directly influence actions, which is rather common among agent-based modellers, the turning point would have been twice as high and equal to 0.5.

[23] The flexibility of the approach also has a minor downside, however. Since there are hardly any constraints on the analyses that can be performed, it sometimes leads analysts to specify simulation models that are almost as complex and difficult to comprehend as the real-life processes that they are supposed to help us understand. To be useful, a model must be realistic yet sufficiently simple and transparent to further our understanding of the key mechanisms at work. If it is not, then we may as well use real data and simply describe the patterns observed in them.

empirical data. In this section I use such models to analyze how patterns of interaction within and between different groups are likely to influence how individuals act – and for this type of problem, differential-equation models are highly useful.

By far the best-known sociological models of this kind were those used by Coleman, Katz and Menzel (1957) to analyze the adoption of a new drug by a group of physicians (see also Coleman 1964; Coleman, Katz and Menzel 1966). They recorded the time at which different physicians started to prescribe the new drug and they asked the following question: what are the likely social processes that intervened between the initial trials of the drug undertaken by a few physicians and its final use by virtually the entire medical community? They posited two alternative explanations for the patterns they observed: the pattern could be due either to an 'individual process' or to a 'snowball process'. In the first case, the adoption of the new drug is based on atomistic decisions by each individual doctor. In the second case, doctors who have adopted the drug influence the decisions of those who have not yet done so.

To examine the likely macro-level patterns to be observed under these two scenarios, Coleman, Katz and Menzel specified two differential equation models:

$$\frac{dI}{dt} = S(t) \times \alpha$$

and

$$\frac{dI}{dt} = I(t) \times S(t) \times \beta$$

The first equation expresses the individual-process hypothesis that the number of doctors who introduce the drug at each point in time is a constant percentage, α, of those who have not already adopted the drug, $S(t)$. The second equation expresses the snowball hypothesis that the adoption of the new drug is spread through social interaction; at each point in time there are $I(t) \times S(t)$ possible pairwise contacts between 'susceptible' and 'infected' individuals, and a constant percentage, β, of those contacts result in a new doctor adopting the drug. Figure 4.6 shows the macro-level patterns one would expect under these two ideal-typical scenarios.[24] As can be seen, the snowballing process generates an

---

[24] In both scenarios it is assumed that a single doctor adopted the drug at the first point in time. In the snowball process β is equal to 0.0005 and in the individual process α is equal to 0.05.

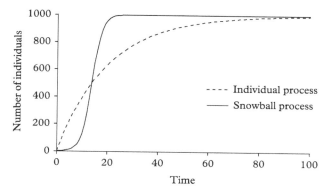

Figure 4.6. Macro-level patterns to be expected under atomistic and non-atomistic decision-making, according to Coleman, Katz and Menzel (1957).

S-shaped development over time, while the individual process generates a growth path gradually approaching its upper limit.

In order to identify the micro-level process likely to have explained the diffusion of the new drug, Coleman, Katz and Menzel compared these theoretically expected patterns with those found among different groups of physicians. On the basis of such comparisons they drew the conclusion that there were important differences between those doctors who were deeply embedded in professional networks and those who were not. In the former case the snowball process was important, but not in the latter:[25] 'The highly integrated doctors seem to have learned from one another, while the less integrated ones, it seems, had each to learn afresh from the journals, the detail man (drug salesman), and other media of information' (Coleman, Katz and Menzel 1957: 262).[26]

Although differential-equation models of aggregate dynamics such as those used by Coleman do not model each actor's behaviour, they are useful for analyzing the link between the individual and the social because they exactly describe the social patterns that follow from the individual-level assumptions upon which the model is based. That is to say, the differential-equation model will predict the same social outcomes as would a large-scale agent-based model based on the same micro-level

[25] Doctors were considered 'integrated' if they were named as 'friends' by three or more of their colleagues.

[26] Slightly modified versions of these types of models were later used to analyze such varied phenomena as race riots (Spilerman 1970), transitions into marriage (Diekmann 1989; Hernes 1972) and social change more generally (Hamblin et al. 1973).

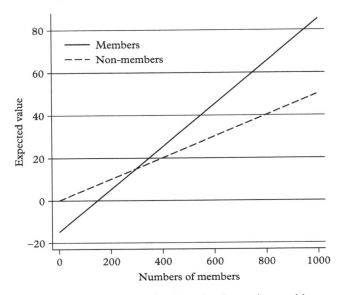

Figure 4.7. Decision situation in collective action problem, according to Åberg (2000).

assumptions as the differential-equation model. But as far as Coleman's models are concerned, some of the assumptions on which they are based are too unrealistic for the models to be of much explanatory use. Most importantly, they assume (1) a rather behaviouristic model of the actor, (2) that all actors interact with one another in an entirely random fashion, and (3) that all actors are equally influential and equally susceptible to influence. As shown below, these assumptions can be relaxed and then the models become more useful for explanatory purposes.

Åberg (2000) has shown how one can overcome the first of these problematic aspects of traditional differential-equation models. She took her point of departure from Schelling's (1978) work on binary decisions and tipping points, and specified a differential-equation model with a more reasonable micro-foundation. She used graphs like those in figure 4.7 to illustrate her core idea. The example described by the graph refers to the problem that individuals face when they need to decide whether or not to join a trade union.

The graph describes how the expected value of being or not being a member of a trade union depends upon the number of other individuals who have joined the union. When the union is small it is better not to be a member, but once the size of the union exceeds a critical threshold –

the tipping point – it becomes more advantageous to join the union than to remain outside it. The tipping point is where the two graphs intersect. If this point is reached, the union will succeed, since it then will be in the interests of all individuals to join the union. If the tipping point is never reached, the union will fail for analogous reasons.[27]

The Åberg model is perfectly general and applicable to the analysis of any situation characterized by a set of actors who are repeatedly confronted with a choice between two different courses of action. We may therefore think about the setup in figure 4.7 as referring to the decision between doing I and doing S, whatever I and S may be. If the actors' opportunity sets consist of these two alternative actions, if the value of doing one thing rather than another depends upon what others do, and if the speed at which individuals change action depends on how desirable each alternative is perceived to be,[28] then the social outcomes the actors are likely to bring about can be approximated with the following differential equation:[29]

$$\frac{dI}{dt} = \begin{cases} \left(u_I(t) - u_s(t)\right) \times S(t) = \left(\alpha + \beta \times I(t)\right) \times S(t) \text{ if } \alpha + \beta \times I(t) > 0 \\ \left(u_I(t) - u_s(t)\right) \times I(t) = \left(\alpha + \beta \times I(t)\right) \times I(t) \text{ if } \alpha + \beta \times I(t) \leq 0 \end{cases}$$

where

$I(t)$ = the proportion of individuals doing I at time t
$S(t)$ = the proportion of individuals doing S at time t
$u_I(t)$ = the expected value of doing I at time t, which is a function of the proportion doing I at t
$u_s(t)$ = the expected value of doing S at time t, which is a function of the proportion doing I at t [30]

and

---

[27] In order to simplify the presentation, I here assume that the pay-off schedules are linear, while Åberg assumed them to be curvilinear.

[28] As suggested by Åberg, it is not reasonable to assume that individuals will change their actions as soon as the expected value of the other alternative exceeds their currently chosen alternative, no matter how small this difference may be. The difference in expected values should rather be seen as influencing how *rapidly* an individual will change to the alternative course of action.

[29] For those unfamiliar with differential equations, simply think of the left-hand sides of the equals signs as describing the change in the proportion doing I, and the right-hand sides as a listing of the factors assumed to influence this change.

[30] The Åberg model assumes that the total number of actors is constant over time and that $S(t) + I(t) = 1.0$. Therefore, knowing the proportion doing I also means that we know the proportion doing S.

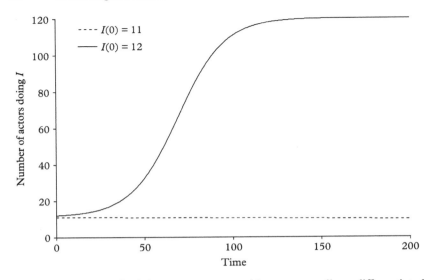

Figure 4.8. Social outcomes expected in a structurally undifferentiated setting.

$\alpha + \beta \times I(t) =$ the expected value of doing I minus the expected value of doing S at time t

By solving these equations one can see how a group of actors is likely to act at different points in time.[31] Figure 4.8 describes two possible time trajectories for a group of 120 actors.[32]

The figure illustrates the importance of the tipping point. If twelve actors coordinate their actions at the outset and start doing I, the tipping

[31] On the surface, this model looks quite different from the simple models used by Coleman, Katz and Menzel, but in fact they belong to the same family. This can readily be seen if, for instance, we assume that $u_I(t) = \beta \times I(t)$ and $u_s(t) = 0$. The Åberg model is then identical to Coleman's 'snowball model' where the rate of change is given by $\beta \times I(t) \times S(t)$. This identity underscores that one should always be wary about inferring micro-level processes from observed macro-level patterns. Coleman interpreted the model in belief or information-contagion terms, while Åberg's model refers to desires, that is, the value of performing an act increases with the number of others acting in the same way. The identity of the two models shows that in itself the existence of an S-shaped time trajectory says nothing about the importance of information diffusion, contrary to what Coleman believed. With reference to the medical innovation data used by Coleman, other interpretations have been suggested such as the structural equivalence hypothesis of Burt (1987) and the marketing hypothesis of Van den Bulte and Lilien (2001).

[32] These aggregate trajectories are brought about when $\alpha = -.95$ and $\beta = 10$. The value of α shows the difference in the value of doing I rather S when no one else does I, and the value of β shows how this difference changes when other individuals start to do I.

point will be reached and the endogenous process will then ensure that everyone will eventually start doing I. However, if one of those twelve actors instead decides to do S, the tipping point will not be reached, and then everyone will eventually cease doing I because doing S is then more advantageous. A fairly large part of the relevant population, 10 per cent, must thus coordinate their actions in order for action I to predominate.

As emphasized throughout this chapter, the structure of social inter-action can be of decisive importance in its own right for the social outcomes that are observed. In the agent-based analyses it was assumed that the pattern of interaction could be described as a local interaction network.[33] This is a plausible assumption when patterns of interaction are fairly stable over time, as is likely to be the case when strong ties are concerned.[34] Relations to family members and to close friends change over time, but the rate of change is sufficiently low to warrant the stability assumption. The situation can be rather different when we are dealing with interaction based on weak ties.

Let me take neighbourhood and workplace ties as examples, since outside the immediate family domain they are the chief interactional domains for most individuals. Being employed at a specific place or living in a specific neighbourhood provides weak ties to a large number of individuals. As much previous research suggests, not least Granovetter's (1974) study of how individuals get access to vacant jobs, weak ties can be of considerable importance. Individually, however, weak ties tend not to be invoked as frequently or as regularly as strong ties. Over a specific period of time, who one interacts with in the relevant weak-tie category may be more or less random. One day one runs into neighbour A on the way to work, and another day neighbour B. One day one talks to colleague C in the elevator, and another day to D. This means that the potentially relevant actor-to-actor network will be difficult to define *ex ante*, and, furthermore, that the causally efficacious network will vary considerably from one time point to another. In situations such as these, where the relevant actor-to-actor networks are unstable and difficult to pin down, it may be better to focus on a type of network that White (1965) referred to as a 'catnet', that is, a network connecting the social categories to which individuals belong. Following White, a category can

---

[33] See Wasserman and Faust (1994), Marsden (1990) and Marsden and Freidkin (1994) for a review of many of the ideas and models that have informed sociological network analysis. See Newman (2003) and Watts (2003) for reviews of more recent work on social networks, most of which has been done by physicists, applied mathematicians and other natural scientists.

[34] See Granovetter (1973) for the strong versus weak tie distinction.

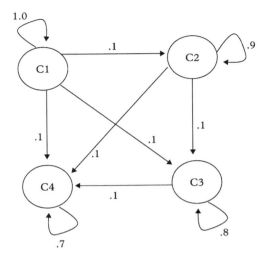

Figure 4.9. Graph of a hypothetical four-category catnet.

simply be defined as a 'bunch of people alike in some respect' (1965: 3), and a catnet as a network describing the relations that exist between such categories. The relevant catnet is often stable and possible to identify, even when the person-to-person network is neither. The percentage of my time devoted to interactions with people at work, for example, may be more or less stable over time, even though the specific people I interact with may vary a great deal from day to day. Similarly, the influence that people at work have on me may be more or less stable over extended periods of time, although the specific people who exercise this influence may vary from time to time.

The likely influence exerted by members of one category on members of another can be seen as a joint function of (1) how aware members of one category are of what those in other categories do, which partly, but only partly, depends upon the frequency of contacts between the categories; and (2) the probability that such awareness results in an individual in one category adopting the beliefs, desires or actions of an actor in the other category. If we categorize the actors in such a way that all actors who belong to a category have similar relations to the other categories, the resulting catnet can be described with a graph like the one in figure 4.9.[35]

---

[35] A network like this should perhaps be referred to as an influence-valued catnet, since a catnet, as originally defined by White, refers only to the patterns of interaction as such.

The values attached to the arcs signify the strength of the (relative) influence exerted by one category on another. The graph therefore provides a summary statement of the effective structure of social interaction. Some actors are more important than others – perhaps because they are more visible, have more power or are believed to be more knowledgeable than others – and this structural heterogeneity is captured by the catnet. Comparing categories C1 and C4, for example, we can see that those in C1 influence actors belonging to the other categories, while they themselves are immune from what others than those of their own kind are doing. In contrast, C4 consists of actors who are influenced by those in other categories and lack influence outside their own group.

By embedding the Åberg type of model into these sorts of catnets we can get a handle on how the group structure is likely to influence the social outcomes actors bring about.[36] One way of doing this is to examine what is likely to happen to the 120 actors of figure 4.8 if everything remained the same except that the actors were moved into a structurally differentiated setting consisting of the four groups described in figure 4.9. If ten of the actors then belonged to the first category, C1, twenty to the second, thirty to the third, and forty to the fourth, the social outcomes that they would bring about would be those set out in figure 4.10.[37]

Furthermore, since the similarities between the individuals are here defined on the basis of their ties to those in other categories, we could also have referred to the categories as *structurally equivalent blocks*, to use the terminology of White, Boorman and Breiger (1976).

[36] See Liljeros and Edling (2003) for a somewhat related approach to analyzing multigroup diffusion processes.

[37] The results reported in figure 4.10 are based on the following system of differential equations:

$$\frac{dI_i}{dt} = \begin{cases} \left(-.95 + 10 \times \sum_{j=1}^{4}(q_{ji} \times I(t)_j)\right) \times S(t)_i \text{, if } -.95 + 10 \times \sum_{j=1}^{4}(q_{ji} \times I(t)_j) > 0 \\ \left(-.95 + 10 \times \sum_{j=1}^{4}(q_{ji} \times I(t)_j)\right) \times I(t)_i \text{, if } -.95 + 10 \times \sum_{j=1}^{4}(q_{ji} \times I(t)_j) \leq 0 \end{cases}$$

where

q_{ji} = the effective influence of those in category j upon those in category i (that is, the influence values attached to the arcs in figure 4.8)

$I(t)_j$ = the proportion of category j doing I at time t
$S(t)_j$ = the proportion of category j doing S at time t and
$-.95 + 10 \times \sum_{j=1}^{4}(q_{ji} \times I(t)_j) = (u_{Ii}(t) - u_{Si}(t))$ = the difference in the expected value of doing I rather than S at time t for those in category i.

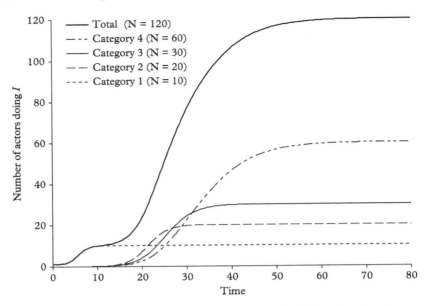

Figure 4.10. Social outcomes in a structurally differentiated setting.

There is an old Swedish saying that 'tiny tufts of grass often topple large loads of hay'. The sociological equivalent of this may be seen in figure 4.10. The graph describes the unfolding of a sequential tipping process set in motion by a single individual doing I (for example, joining an interest organization). While in a structurally undifferentiated setting as many as 10 per cent of the actors had to coordinate their actions for I to predominate (see figure 4.8), in this differentiated setting no coordination whatsoever is required. It is sufficient for a single actor in Category 1 to do I for everyone else to end up doing the same. Once this actor does I it becomes the best alternative for all the others in Category 1 as well. Although those in Category 1 do not have much influence on those in Category 2, once everyone in Category 1 is doing I their collective influence will be such that the tipping point in Category 2 is reached. Therefore everyone in Category 2 will also start doing I. The same pattern then occurs in Categories 3 and 4, and in the end all actors are doing I.

As they are applied to traditional collective action problems, these results lead to the seemingly paradoxical conclusion that particularism breeds universalism. In a social setting in which actors are socially divided and care more or less only about what those of their own kind are doing, large and all-encompassing organizations are more likely to emerge than in socially undifferentiated but otherwise identical settings. In his classic analysis of the logic of collective action, Olson (1965) emphasized that individuals who join interest organizations do so either for 'irrational' reasons or for reasons unrelated to the public good produced by the organizations. Olson reached this conclusion because he believed that in all but the smallest of groups a single individual's action will not have any impact on the likelihood that the collective good will be produced. What the above analysis reveals, however, is that a single individual's action can have a substantial impact in a large collectivity as well, if this collectivity is internally stratified. If individuals in Category 1 were aware of how their actions would influence others, there would be no conflict between individual and collective rationality. It would then be in their private interests to contribute to the collective good, to join the organization, for example, irrespective of what the others were doing. Once those in Category 1 have acted, the same conclusion holds for those in Category 2, then for those in Category 3, and so on.[38]

The stark contrast between the outcomes in these two structural settings is obviously no accident. In order to highlight the fact that the structural setting can have a dramatic influence in its own right, I chose a catnet structure that produced such a result. If the processes had instead unfolded in a four-category catnet with randomly assigned influence parameters, table 4.3 shows that the result would often have been different. Each column of the table is based on 10,000 simulations of processes like those underlying figure 4.10. In all of these analyses, everything but the structure of social interaction is held constant at their previous values.[39]

As can be seen from the first column of the table, the type of outcome seen in figure 4.10 is rarely observed. In only one case out of 10,000 did a single actor in Category 1 set in motion a cascade that eventually brought along all the others. But, as can be seen from the other columns, the probability of such an outcome increases rapidly with the number of actors who did I at the outset. If two actors did I at the outset, the probability of a global cascade was .29, and it increased to .68 with three actors and to .85 with four actors.

---

[38] See Sandell and Stern (1998), Hechter (1987) and Karklins and Petersen (1993) for related arguments. See also Kim and Bearman (1997).

[39] The variation in catnet structures resulted from randomly assigning q_{ji} parameters in the interval 0 to 1 from a uniform probability distribution. The parameters were then normalized in such a way that $\Sigma_{j=1}^{4} q_{ji} = 1.0$.

Table 4.3. *Probabilities (×100) of different social outcomes with randomly assigned catnet parameters and varying number of actors acting at the outset*

Number of actors eventually acting	Number acting at the outset			
	1	2	3	4
0	99.99	70.49	30.91	14.06
10	0	0.27	0.66	0.66
20	0	0	0.03	0.01
30	0	0	0.04	0.04
40	0	0	0.05	0.02
60	0	0	0.07	0.07
70	0	0	0.03	0.02
90	0	0	0.06	0.04
100	0	0.02	0.07	0.09
120	0.01	29.22	68.08	84.99

These results are interesting for a range of reasons. First, they suggest that an individual can substantially influence the likelihood of collective action, even in rather large groups, as long as the collectivity is internally stratified. Second, and more generally, they underscore how important the structure of interaction can be in its own right. If we observe that two groups act in different ways, this can simply be the result of a slight difference in the structure of interaction within the two groups. Third, and possibly of most general importance, they show that in a broad range of structural settings small and seemingly unimportant events can set in motion processes with profound long-term effects.

Summary and concluding discussion

I started this chapter by criticizing the critical realists for uncritically adopting many critical assumptions. Their arguments in support of their central claim about the causal autonomy and causal power of social entities were found to be unconvincing and implausible. Their thesis is also unfortunate in the sense that it directs attention away from what I would consider to be one of the most important tasks on the sociological agenda: detailed analyses of how actors who interact with each other under conditions inherited from the past bring about large-scale social phenomena.

I then presented various analyses focusing on the link between the individual and the social. Their main purpose was to illustrate how one can proceed from the type of action theories discussed in chapter 2 to large-scale social phenomena. For that purpose I used different agent-based and differential-equation models. Analyses using such models should be viewed as virtual laboratory experiments; they assume a closed social system in order to establish the causal tendencies of different social mechanisms. The results of these analyses lead to four important conclusions about the relationship between individual actions and social outcomes:

1 There is no necessary proportionality between the size of a cause and the size of its effect.
2 The structure of social interaction is of considerable explanatory importance in its own right for the social outcomes that emerge.
3 The effect a given action has on the social can be highly contingent upon the structural configuration in which the actor is embedded.
4 Aggregate patterns say very little about the micro-level processes that brought them about.

This means that the relationship between the individual and the social is not transparent and linear, but complex and precarious. If we fail to take these complexities into account, we are easily led astray. Almost half a century ago, Leon Festinger (1957: 233) made a similar point:

Mass phenomena are frequently so striking and dramatic in quality that one tends to think of them as exclusively so. There is also a tendency to seek explanations of these striking phenomena which match them in dramatic quality; that is, one looks for something unusual to explain the unusual result. It may be, however, that there is nothing more unusual about these phenomena than the relative rarity of the specific combination of ordinary circumstances that brings about their occurrence.

As the existence of notions such as Matthew effects (Merton 1968a), threshold effects (Granovetter 1978), tipping points (Schelling 1978), cumulative causality (Myrdal 1944) and path dependency (Arthur 1994) suggest, the interactive and endogenous nature of social processes has been a key concern of some of the very best social scientists. Nevertheless, I think it is fair to say that the insights of these writers have not fully penetrated the discipline, and that many sociologists still commit the type of linear exogeneity fallacy that Festinger referred to. The prevalence of this fallacy can, at least in part, be attributed to the informal character of most sociological theories. As discussed above, the social processes that link the individual and the social are usually so complex that outcomes become virtually unpredictable without the aid of some formal analytical tools. Without such tools it is difficult to recognize, and even more difficult to convince others, that the large-scale phenomena that are observed may simply be due to an uncommon combination of common events and circumstances. Sociology focuses on complex and difficult subject matters and, if the discipline is to be a rigorous science of the social, formal analytical tools are simply a necessity.

The results presented in this chapter also underscore the general importance of precision in theoretical analyses. At several points in this chapter it has been shown that small alterations in the structure of interaction – between actors as well as between different mental states – can have a profound impact on the social phenomena that emerge. If our concepts and theories are not sufficiently precise to pick up on such differences, they are not capable of explaining why we observe what we observe. If, for example, a theory simply states that 'agency' or 'structure' is important, this would not be incorrect, but it would be too blunt and imprecise to explain what is going on. For this reason precision and fine-grained distinctions are of crucial importance for the development of explanatory theory.

Let me end this chapter with a cautionary note about theories of the social. Theoretical analyses such as those presented in this chapter are important because they tell us whether a set of mechanisms can account for the type of phenomena that we seek to explain. As noted above, the relationship between the individual and the social is often precarious and easily altered by small changes in the logic of action or the structure of interaction. We also know that empirically observed phenomena are often the joint outcome of many different processes operating in tandem. This means that we should always be alert to the possibility that small events, external to the process focused upon, can result in very different outcomes from those the theory predicts in the absence of such events. This sort of discrepancy between theoretical predictions and empirical observations does not mean that the theory is wrong or falsified; it simply means that we must seek to further bridge the gap between the abstract theory and the concrete reality we seek to explain. In chapter 6 we will therefore introduce a type of model that we refer to as an *ECA model*, which combines agent-based models with quantitative statistical analyses.

5   On causal modelling

So far this book has been exclusively concerned with theory. Chapter 2 focused on theories of explanation, chapter 3 on theories of action and chapter 4 on theories linking individual action to social outcomes. This chapter and the next are concerned with the relationship between theory and empirical research. In this chapter I continue the discussion started in chapter 2 about statistical explanations; chapter 6 illustrates how one can establish a close link between the type of theory discussed in previous chapters and quantitative empirical analyses. As will be seen below, I have many objections to the way quantitative research is conducted today, but I nevertheless believe that quantitative research is essential for sociology. Although qualitative research can be important for the development of explanatory theory, it lacks the reliability and generalizability of quantitative research, and this is critical if sociology is to be a rigorous science of the social.

The chapter is organized as follows. In the next section I describe the main currents of causal modelling. I then spell out in some detail why I find these traditions wanting. The discussion centres on four topics, (1) the weak theoretical foundation of many causal models, (2) the excessive importance given to predictive accuracy, (3) the lack of attention given to the role of social interactions, and (4) the focus on individual rather than social outcomes.

The causal modelling tradition in sociology

The defining characteristic of causal modelling, as the term is used here, is the use of large-scale non-experimental data to estimate parameters of statistical models, which are then interpreted in causal terms. Goldthorpe (2000) makes a useful distinction between two main causal-modelling traditions: what he calls the 'robust dependence' and the 'consequential manipulation' traditions (see table 5.1).

Most of us are familiar with the robust dependence tradition from textbooks in quantitative methods. In this tradition, one seeks to establish

Table 5.1. *Main traditions of causal modeling*

Tradition	Key people[1]	Key focus
Causation as robust dependence	Lazarsfeld, Duncan	Statistical relations between variables
Causation as consequential manipulation	Neyman, Rubin	Statistical effects as displayed in quasi-experimental designs

[1] For representative work by these key people, see Lazarsfeld (1955), Duncan (1975) and Rubin (1974). See Freedman (1999) on the contributions of Neyman.

causal relations by partialling out the effects of confounding variables. If a significant relationship between two variables persists even after controlling for likely confounders, the relationship is interpreted as a 'causal relationship'. In the words of Lazarsfeld (1955: 124–5), 'If we have a relationship between x and y; and if for any antecedent test factor the partial relationships between x and y do not disappear, then the original relationship should be called a causal one.'

To illustrate the guiding principles behind this approach we can use a classic study within the tradition, Blau and Duncan's (1967) analysis of the status attainment process. Using data from a 1962 survey of American men, Blau and Duncan examined the relationship between the status of the respondents' own occupations and those of their fathers. They did this by estimating a series of regression models, and they presented their core findings using a diagram like the one in figure 5.1.

A straight line from one measured variable to another was assumed to represent the *direct causal effect* of one variable on another, and the strength of the effect was indexed by the size of the standardized regression coefficient. For example, the figure was meant to show that a father's occupation had a direct causal effect on a respondent's occupation because, even when one controlled for the respondent's own education and the status of the respondent's first job, a relationship did exist between the father's and the respondent's occupation. Similarly, Blau and Duncan found a relationship between a father's occupation and a respondent's education, even when controlling for the father's education, and therefore they concluded that the father's occupation had a direct causal effect on the respondent's education. This latter finding was interpreted as also implying that the father's occupation had an *indirect causal effect* on the respondent's own occupation via the respondent's own education.

Although analyses in this tradition later became more refined in terms of both statistical models and the type of data used, Blau and Duncan's

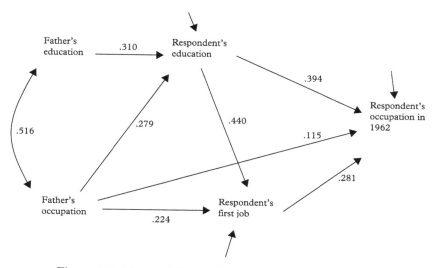

Figure 5.1. Blau and Duncan's (1967) path model of the process of stratification.

study has been one of the most influential in this tradition, and it illustrates well the general logic of the approach. The guiding principle is simply that a causal relationship between two variables can be established on the basis of a statistical analysis that controls for potentially confounding variables. If a statistical relationship between two variables persists after such controls, the relationship is interpreted as a causal relationship. Once the result of the statistical analysis is to hand, the explanation simply consists in referring to the variables that appear to be statistically relevant for the outcome or variable one seeks to explain. In other words, the respondent's education is 'causally explained' by the father's occupation, the respondent's own education and so on.

The second tradition identified by Goldthorpe, the consequential manipulation tradition, has a long history in statistics. It dates back to the works of Jerzy Neyman, and it is now entering sociology through the work of Rubin and other statisticians (e.g., P. Holland 1986; Rosenbaum 1984; Rubin 1974). This approach is a close cousin of the robust dependence approach, but it improves on the older approach in certain respects.

To use the vocabulary of experimentation (as most of those who work in this tradition do), the core idea is that a hypothesized causal effect can best be assessed by comparing the outcomes for individuals (or other relevant units) when they are 'treated' with those when they are not. An obvious difficulty with such an approach is that individuals are usually observed only in the treatment group or in the control group, but that the causal effect can be revealed only by comparing their outcomes in both groups. Rubin and colleagues believe that non-experimental data can be analyzed as if they derive from experiments, and they have developed methods for estimating *counterfactual effects*, that is, what the outcomes would have been for members of the treatment group had they been in the control group, and vice versa for those in the control group (for useful overviews of this literature, see Sobel 1998 and Winship and Morgan 1999).

Harding's (2003) analysis of neighbourhood effects on high school drop-out and teenage pregnancy rates in the United States shows how this counterfactual approach can be used in sociological research. Teenage pregnancies and school drop-out rates are more than twice as high in high-poverty neighbourhoods as in wealthier neighbourhoods, and Harding wanted to test whether the poverty rate in the neighbourhood one grew up in was a causally relevant factor. In order to do this, he compared drop-out and pregnancy rates among people who grew up in high-poverty neighbourhoods ('the treated') with those in a control group. Using so-called propensity score matching, he identified a control group consisting of individuals who did not grow up in high-poverty neighbourhoods but who were otherwise identical to the 'treatment' group in a range of observable characteristics. Using this approach, he found strong support for his hypotheses, because those who grew up in high-poverty neighbourhoods were considerably more likely to drop out of high school and to have teenage pregnancies than those in the 'control group', who grew up in wealthier neighbourhoods.

Although one can discuss the appropriateness of describing situations such as these in quasi-experimental terms since self-selection is of considerable importance for neighbourhood residence, the consequential manipulation tradition is in many respects conceptually more satisfactory than the robust dependence approach, and it also has some attractive statistical features. Nevertheless, the consequential manipulation tradition does not address what I would consider the most serious shortcomings of the causal modelling traditions. These problems are not related to a lack of statistical efficiency or to conceptual ambiguities, but to the substantive plausibility and theoretical relevance of the models being estimated. That is to say, their shortcomings have sociological rather than statistical roots.

Sociological theory and causal models

On one level it must be admitted that the ideas underlying these statistical approaches to causal analysis are rather appealing. They provide a ready-made recipe for how to explain virtually anything we may be interested in explaining. No matter how complex the processes that generate the outcomes we seek to explain may be, we can explain them without having to understand much about the processes as such. We simply need to collect relevant data, make sure that the causal ordering between the variables is plausible, and then let the statistical analysis take care of the rest.

Over the years, many quantitatively oriented sociologists have developed an almost superstitious belief in the saving grace of statistics. Many of the sharpest minds in the discipline have worked within these statistically oriented traditions. Yet the pay-offs in terms of established causal relations have been few, if any. Duncan, once the leading advocate of causal modelling in sociology, towards the end of his career disapprovingly referred to this approach to sociological analysis as a form of 'staticism'. By this he meant

the notion that computing is synonymous with doing research, the naïve faith that statistics is a complete or sufficient basis for scientific methodology, the superstition that statistical formulas exist for evaluating such things as the relative merits of different substantive theories or the 'importance' of the causes of a 'dependent variable'. (Duncan 1984: 226)

Although most causal modellers refer to sociological theories in their work, they rarely pay it any serious attention. More often than not, they simply use theories to justify the inclusion of certain variables taken from a data set that has often been collected for entirely different purposes than the one to hand. Theoretical statements have become synonymous with hypotheses about relationships between variables, and variables have replaced actors as the active subjects with causal powers. As suggested by Coleman (1986a: 1327–8) , much quantitative research has developed into an 'individualistic behaviorism' where behaviour is explained by reference to whatever individual or environmental variables can be measured: 'statistical association between variables has largely replaced meaningful connection between events as the basic tool of description and analysis'.[1]

Take quantitative labour market sociology as an example. In the 1970s and 1980s those working in this tradition sought to elaborate on the traditional status and income attainment analyses in the Blau and

---

[1] The affinity between behaviourism and structural equation modelling was also noted by Duncan: 'In [structural equation] models that purport to explain the behavior of individual persons, the coefficients [of the structural equation] could well take the form of units of response per unit of stimulus strength; the structural equation is, in effect, an S-R [stimulus-response] law' (Duncan 1975: 162–3).

Duncan tradition. They did this by including additional variables to those in figure 5.1 that measured various aspects of the social structure in which the individuals were embedded. Some of these studies included variables measuring individuals' class (e.g., Wright and Perrone 1977), while others included variables describing their labour market sector (e.g., Beck, Horan and Tolbert 1978), and yet others viewed themselves as 'multi-variate structuralists' (Kalleberg and Berg 1987) and sought to include a multitude of such variables in the analysis. The regression coefficients associated with these variables were then assumed to indicate whether or not the theories that had motivated the inclusion of the variables were important. If, for example, the regression coefficient associated with a class variable was statistically significant, this was seen as proof that class was an important causal factor explaining income differences between individuals. Interpreting the results of such a regression analysis, Wright (1979: 225) concluded that class 'represents one of the basic structural factors in the income determination process'.

In order for a statistical analysis to provide a reliable test of a causal hypothesis, the statistical model must represent reasonably well the process through which the outcome of interest was generated.[2] Consequently, whenever one estimates a specific statistical model and interprets the results in causal terms, one makes an implicit theoretical commitment because such an interpretation is valid only if one believes that the model represents reasonably well the process through which the outcome was generated. On grounds such as these, Sørensen (1998: 248) raised the important question of whether anyone really believes in the type of 'gas station' theory that regression models like those mentioned above imply:

This [regression] model [of earnings attainment], in fact, proposes a theory where each person receives x dollars from education, y dollars from family background, q dollars from gender, and z dollars from class. All of it adds up to the person's yearly earnings. We can imagine people walking around among pumps in a large gas station getting something from each of the pumps. The picture should be complemented by specifying hypotheses about how many dollars each pump provides, and this would give us some idea of the relative importance of the pumps that we could teach in courses on getting ahead in society.

Obviously, no one seriously believes in such a theory. Yet many causal modellers continue to estimate such models and interpret the results in causal terms. As Sørensen (1998: 254) correctly noted, 'we learn very little from such research'.

---

[2] See Freedman (1987) for an illuminating discussion of this.

In order for empirical research to have a bearing on the development of sociological theory, it must be closely linked with the theory in question. It is not sufficient to simply use theories to suggest what variables to include in a statistical analysis; theories must be taken much more seriously than that and guide the entire analysis, including the detailed specification of the model to be estimated. The wider the gap is between the data and the entities, relationships and activities of the core causal mechanisms, the less bearing the empirical research will have on theory development. Gas station regressions are not likely to have any impact on theory development because they are not sufficiently precise and finely tuned to say anything trustworthy about the specific mechanisms likely to be at work. Instead of estimating ad hoc regression models with lots of independent variables to try to control statistically for all possible confounders, empirical research should to a much higher degree be guided by careful realism and focus directly on the entities, relationships and activities that are believed to have brought about the outcome that one seeks to explain.

Is predictive accuracy all that matters?

As discussed in chapter 3, Friedman (1953) developed a powerful, but in my view seriously flawed, argument to the effect that the realism of a theory's assumptions is of little or no importance. What matters, according to Friedman, is predicting as well as possible with as few assumptions as possible. Jasso's (1988) arguments are reminiscent of Friedman's. She argues that sociologists should not be concerned with the plausibility or realism of a theory. According to her, it is sufficient if the assumptions are logically consistent with one another, and that they lead to accurate predictions. She summarizes her position in the form of a 'basic rule of empirical analysis' which states: 'test the predictions, never the postulates' (1988: 4).

Although the primacy of predictive accuracy is rarely as explicitly defended as in the case of Jasso, it is clearly given precedence over realism in most quantitative analyses. For example, although most sociologists would agree that social interactions are crucial for understanding individual actions, social interactions are largely ignored in most quantitative survey-based research (more on this below). As long as the individual-level outcomes that the analysis focuses on can be predicted reasonably well, such omissions seem to raise no eyebrows whatsoever.

The mechanism approach advocated in this book opposes instrumentalist positions such as that of Jasso. To explain is to provide an answer to the question of why we observe what we observe, and a proper answer to such a question details a mechanism through which the type of phenomenon one seeks to explain is typically brought about. Explanation is not synonymous with prediction. It is possible to predict well without explaining anything about what is going on – univariate forecasts of various macro-economic trends, for instance, can be highly accurate without giving the slightest clue as to why we observe what we observe. Theories based on fictitious assumptions, even if they predict well, give incorrect answers to the question of why we observe what we observe. Therefore, as discussed in some detail in chapter 3, theories, in order to be explanatory, must be based on plausible assumptions.[3]

As noted in chapter 2, a theoretical proposition about a social mechanism can be seen as an empirical commitment on the part of the theorist as to how a process would unfold if the assumptions upon which it rests were well founded. This conditional nature of mechanism-based explanations is important. Mechanisms should be seen as theoretical propositions about causal tendencies, not as statements about actualities. An explanation may be perfectly correct if understood as a proposition about a causal tendency, and yet it may be inadequate for predicting actual outcomes if other processes are also at work (see Gibson 1983). For example, in chapter 3 I discussed various mechanisms linking one person's actions to those of another, and made a distinction between belief-, desire- and opportunity-mediated mechanisms. If two or more such mechanisms are in operation simultaneously, they can cancel each other out and give the erroneous impression that they are irrelevant to the action to be explained.

Since it is the rule rather than the exception that concretely observed phenomena are influenced by several different processes, testing a theory by examining the accuracy of its predictions is likely to conflate the truth or relevance of the postulated mechanism with the importance of other processes, and this may lead us to mistakenly reject perfectly appropriate causal accounts. Thus, if one were to formulate a basic rule of empirical analysis in the spirit of Jasso, which one probably should not, it would be the opposite of hers and state: 'Test the postulates, never the predictions.'[4]

---

[3] As noted in earlier chapters, this does not imply that one should seek to describe all the various factors that are likely to be of relevance to a particular outcome. As suggested in chapter 1, analytical realism, in Parsons' (1937) sense of the term, seems to be the sensible position in that it recognizes the abstract and simplified nature of all theories without endorsing fictionalism.

[4] On the assumption, of course, that the set of postulates logically imply the outcome to be explained.

Causal modelling, social interactions and social outcomes

A core postulate of most sociological theories – not only those discussed in this book but also those of Weber, Coleman, Simmel and Goffman, to name a few — is that social interactions are important for explaining individual actions and social outcomes. That social interactions are at the core of the discipline can also be seen in most sociologists' strong and almost instinctive objection to neoclassical economic theory's assumption that individuals are like social atoms, not much influenced by the social structure in which they are embedded (e.g., Granovetter 1985). Given the importance attributed to social interactions in sociology, one would have expected causal modellers to be engaged in detailed analyses of its importance in different social contexts. But, as we all know, with the main exception of various diffusion studies, social interactions play as little a role in most sociologists' quantitative analyses as they do in economists' analyses.

One important reason for this glaring gap between sociological theory and quantitative research can, I believe, be traced to the frequent use of survey-based data. The widespread use of such data has much improved our ability to *describe* societal conditions, but such data are not particularly useful for testing interaction-based theories of the kind discussed in this book. The data collection design is generally such that one ends up with rich data on the attributes of individuals, but no data on the actions of those with whom these individuals interact. Individuals are randomly selected and thereby uprooted from their social environments, and research proceeds on the assumption that the whole — the social — can be understood by studying the individual parts in isolation from one another. However, as discussed in chapter 4, knowing the behaviour of the isolated parts leaves us a long way from knowing the whole that is likely to emerge. Empirical research based on survey data is likely to have a limited bearing on sociological theory simply because the relevant models cannot be estimated.

Even if such data were available, traditional quantitative approaches leave many questions unanswered. Assume, for example, that we were to analyze the type of data generated by the agent-based analyses described in chapter 4. The most natural way to approach such data would be to estimate some sort of logistic regression model that relates individuals' actions at one point in time to some variables that describe their properties at an earlier point in time. In addition, one may decide to include some contextual variables that describe typical actions or mental states among those with whom each individual interacts. If we use the data

Table 5.2. *Logistic regression model of the BDA data of figure 4.3*

	Parameter estimates (z-values in parentheses)
Initial desire	1.030
	(4.75)
Initial belief	1.006
	(4.67)
Initial action	1.115
	(3.73)
Neighbours' initial beliefs	0.957
	(12.12)
Neighbours' initial desires	1.059
	(13.02)
Constant	−4.684
	(−12.62)
Observations: 2,500	
−2LLR: 556.8	

upon which figure 4.3 was based and estimate such a model, we get the results in table 5.2.[5]

These types of analyses provide essential information, but — and this is important to recognize — they also fail to pick up important information contained in the data. Like most other regression-like models estimated on the basis of this type of data, this model describes how different factors are related to *individual* actions. That is to say, it shows how the propensity of an individual to do one thing rather than another is influenced by a set of independent variables. However, as discussed in chapter 4, much sociology is concerned with *social* phenomena such as spatial patterns, inequalities and the like. In order to derive the social-level implications of regression-based findings like these, they must be fed into some sort of *generative model*, that is, a model that formally represents the mechanisms through which the social outcomes are thought to have been brought about.[6]

---

[5] The 'neighbourhood' definition is the same as the one used in the analyses that generated figure 4.3, that is, a so-called von Neumann neighbourhood of range one. Instead of initial beliefs and desires, one could have used some lagged value of these variables and estimated the parameters of a panel model, but that would have been inconsequential for the argument developed here.

[6] A possible alternative would be to estimate a time-series model based on aggregate data. Such models cannot provide any useful information on the activities and entities that

Coleman touched upon these issues on several occasions. Although he never provided a satisfactory solution, he posed the right questions and pointed in the right directions. In his book on longitudinal analysis, for example, he made an important distinction between model testing and model calibration:

The general approach will be (1) to begin with the idea of a process, (2) to attempt to lay out the mathematical model that mirrors this process, and then (3) given particular kinds of data, to transform the mathematical model into a statistical model for estimating parameters of the process. In general the goal will not be one of testing hypotheses but rather one of estimating parameters in a mathematical model designed to mirror a substantive process . . . There is a distinct difference between the way I am proceeding and a more common way of proceeding in the analysis of data in the social sciences. The more common way can be termed *statistical data analysis*, in which the method of statistical analysis is designed for a particular form of data, and, in effect, determined by that data form. (Coleman 1981: 5)

The core idea of Coleman's approach thus is first to specify a *substantively* plausible model, and then to use the data to estimate the size of various unknown parameters of this model. The type of model that Coleman had in mind was a simple mathematical model of change, typically some form of differential equation model. This model was often elegant in its simplicity, but was a little too parsimonious and too variable-oriented. Although models of the rate of change in variables can have certain advantages over traditional variable-based models (see Sørensen 1998), the black-box problem remains the same. Just as in case of traditional variable-based models, variables rather than actors are assumed to be the active subjects with causal powers.

In this respect, Goldthorpe's (2000) proposal is more promising. Like Coleman and Sørensen, Goldthorpe finds the traditional causal modelling approaches wanting and argues for the importance of theoretically informed generative models. With reference to the work of Cox (1990; 1992), he argues that an appropriate generative model should be able to serve the function of a plausible simulation model. That is to say, the model should be able to generate the social regularities being observed in a way that is consistent with what we know about real-world processes, and this surely means that the model must be actor-based.

Although Goldthorpe did not discuss the emerging tradition of agent-based analyses in sociology,[7] his ideas about generative models are

generate social outcomes, however, because these entities and activities are not to be found at the aggregate social level with which time-series modelling is concerned.
[7] See Macy and Willer (2002) for a general overview of this literature.

closely in line with the core ideas of this tradition. Agent-based models make predictions about social outcomes, given different assumptions about the actions and interactions among actors. They provide the link between the individual and the social which, as Coleman so correctly observed, 'has proved the main intellectual hurdle both for empirical research and for theory' (Coleman 1986b). As discussed in the next chapter, closer links between agent-based analyses and quantitative sociological research are likely to be beneficial to both traditions, and will assign a much more important role to quantitative empirical research in the development of rigorous theories of the social.[8]

Boudon was an early proponent of the use of simulation models for making the transition from the level of the individual to the level of the social. In his book on education and inequality (Boudon 1974) he developed an empirically calibrated simulation model that he hoped would make intelligible a number of apparent paradoxes reported by empirical research on social mobility. Boudon viewed the mobility process as the result of a two-stage filtering process. The first stage of the process has to do with the mechanisms that influence individuals' move from a given social background to their attained educational level. The second stage of the process concerns mechanisms likely to influence their move from an achieved educational level to a social position in society at large. Although Boudon's model appears a little dated by today's standards, it was an important pioneering work that sought to develop a theoretically informed generative model of the mobility process.

Robert Hauser, one of the most vocal proponents of a strict statistical approach to sociological research, wrote a lengthy and rather ungenerous review of Boudon's book (see Hauser 1976). He suggested numerous changes to Boudon's model, many of them perfectly reasonable, but the main message of his review was a strong scepticism about the very idea that had motivated Boudon to write the book, that is, that an important distinction should be made between statistical models and substantive generative models. As he expressed it: 'Boudon dismisses several standard representations of the mobility process as "basically statistical". I can only guess what this means — perhaps that they are rich in formal properties or that sampling distributions of their parameters [sic] are known. Neither of these properties strikes me as undesirable' (Hauser 1976: 923).[9]

---

[8] One recent article that exemplifies the great potential of such an approach is Bearman, Moody and Stovel's (2004) study of adolescent sexual networks.

[9] Whatever desirable properties Hauser's statistical models may have, their *parameters* certainly do not have any sampling distributions: only estimates do.

In his response, Boudon (1976) expressed what I would consider to be the core idea of the mechanism-oriented approach to quantitative research. He noted that statistical models of the sort advocated by Hauser are useful for many purposes, but that their usefulness as causal explanations is considerably more restricted than Hauser and other causal modellers believed. As emphasized by Boudon, causal explanations are not achieved by simply estimating parameters of generic statistical models, but by developing evidence-based generative models that explicate the mechanisms at work.

Summary and conclusion

In this chapter I have focused on so-called causal modelling. The main message of the chapter has been that one must make a clear distinction between statistical analyses and sociological explanations. A statistical analysis is a test of an explanation, not the explanation itself. Another important point of the chapter was that quantitative research would be more useful for the development of explanatory theory if it focused directly on the entities, activities and relations of the social mechanisms assumed to be operative instead of on correlations between different social aggregates. Quantitative research would have a much more important role in theory development if it were to estimate parameters of theoretically grounded models of individuals' opportunities, mental states and actions. By producing statistical evidence on how such entities and activities are influenced by various individual and contextual factors, including the actions and mental states of those with whom they interact, quantitative research could come to have a much more direct bearing on the development of explanatory theories of the social. Chapter 6 illustrates how one can forge a tighter link between quantitative research and sociological theory by embedding the results of a statistical analysis in an agent-based model of the mechanisms believed to be at work.

6   Quantitative research, agent-based modelling and theories of the social (with Yvonne Åberg)

When discussing the relationship between sociological theory and empirical research, Merton always emphasized how each draws strength from the other (e.g., Merton 1968c). Without theory, empirical research often lacks wider significance, and without empirical research, sociological theory easily turns into fictitious storytelling. Although most of us recognize the importance of a symbiotic relationship between theory and research, the current division of labour within the discipline would suggest otherwise. Most theorists specialize in theory and have little or no contact with empirical research, while empirical researchers are rarely seriously interested in theory.

In an influential article, Goldthorpe (1996) discussed how one can bridge this gap between theory and empirical research by establishing a closer link between action-based theories and quantitative research. He argued that the contribution of quantitative research to sociology 'will be seriously limited unless it is allied in some way or other to accounts of social action' (1996: 111). For a variety of reasons Goldthorpe meant that rational-choice theory was particularly well suited to this purpose. Like Edling (2000), we have a somewhat mixed attitude towards some of the details in Goldthorpe's proposal. On the one hand his arguments for establishing close links between action-based theories and quantitative research are important and to the point. On the other hand his reasons for believing that rational-choice theory is uniquely suited to integrating quantitative research and sociological theory are not as persuasive.[1] What sociology seems to need is not to bind itself to one specific substantive theory. Rather, it needs a general methodology for more closely integrating theories of the social with the results of quantitative research. As shown in this chapter, empirically calibrated agent-based models, which we refer to as 'ECA models', can accomplish this integration without imposing any *a priori* constraints on the mechanisms

---

[1] See chapter 3, pages 60–66 for a discussion of why rational-choice theory cannot be considered a suitable foundation for sociological theory.

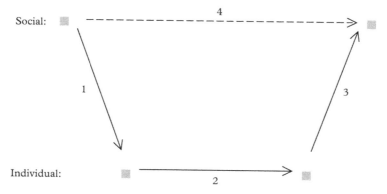

Figure 6.1. Coleman's micro-macro graph.

assumed to be operating, except, of course, that the mechanism in some way or other must be action-related. Unlike rational-choice theory, agent-based modelling is not a specific theory of action or interaction. It is a methodology for deriving the social outcomes that groups of interacting actors are likely to bring about whatever the action logics or interaction structures may be.

Coleman's (1986b) so-called micro-macro graph can be used for describing how quantitative research and agent-based modelling can complement one another (see figure 6.1). As emphasized in previous chapters, sociology is not a discipline concerned with explaining the actions or behaviours of single individuals. The focus is on larger-scale *social* phenomena characterizing groups of actors or collectivities. But the properties of these social phenomena and changes in them over time must always be explained with reference to individuals' actions, since it is individuals, not social entities, which are endowed with causal powers. Hence, even if we were exclusively interested in explaining the relationship between two social phenomena (arrow 4 in figure 6.1), a proper explanation would always entail showing how social phenomena influence individuals' actions at one point in time, and how these actions bring about the social outcomes we seek to explain at a later point in time.

As Coleman correctly pointed out, the link from the individual to the social (arrow 3) has been the main intellectual obstacle to the development of explanatory theories of the social. We know a great deal about how individuals' orientations to action, their desires, beliefs, opportunities and so forth are influenced by the social contexts in which they are embedded (arrow 1), and we also know a great deal about how their orientations to action influence their actions (arrow 2), but when it comes to the link between individual actions and social outcomes (arrow 3) we often resort to hand-waving. This unfortunate state of affairs is due, at least in part, to the lack of an appropriate methodology for addressing these types of questions. We have a large methodological toolbox for analyzing the first two types of relations in figure 6.1, but no appropriate methodology for the third and final stage of the analysis. It is as a general methodological tool for analyzing this link between individual actions and social outcomes that agent-based modelling in general, and ECA modelling in particular, is so important for sociology.

Agent-based modelling and quantitative research have not had much influence on one another. Quantitative researchers have analyzed the first two types of relations identified in the Coleman graph without paying much attention to what these results imply for the social. When they have considered such questions they have typically ignored social interactions and assumed that the social is a simple aggregate of the individual-level entities or actions. In addition, of course, many sociologists have used time-series analyses and various forms of aggregate comparisons to try to say something about the fourth arrow in the Coleman graph. As discussed in previous chapters, however, such approaches will have little to contribute to explanatory theory because they entirely ignore the micro-level mechanisms that explain why we observe a certain change (or lack thereof) at the level of the social.

Agent-based modellers similarly have ignored much of what quantitative researchers have done and have used agent-based modelling as an exclusively theoretical tool for assessing the social outcomes that different stylized action logics and interaction structures are likely to bring about. In this chapter we seek to demonstrate how these two traditions can fruitfully complement one another. The essence of the approach advocated here is to use large-scale quantitative data to analyze and to specify the details of the first two links in the Coleman graph, and then incorporate the results of these analyses into an agent-based model in order to assess the social outcomes that are likely to be brought about (arrow 3).[2] We use unemployment in Stockholm during the 1990s as a

---

[2] Coleman had some ideas of his own about how one could establish a direct link between quantitative research and action-based theories, which he referred to as 'linear systems analysis' (see Coleman 1990; Coleman and Hao 1989). However, for what we believe to be good reasons, this approach never captured the attention of the sociological community. It was simply too dependent on rather implausible assumptions about the logic of action and the structure of interaction to be a useful tool for sociology in general. As far as we know, Fong (1997) is the only sociologist (in addition to Coleman and Hao) to have used the approach so far.

case study to illustrate concretely how these ideas can be put into practice.

As mentioned above, sociologists almost exclusively use agent-based modelling for theoretical purposes. Macy and Willer, for example, describe agent-based modelling as 'a new tool for *theoretical* research' (2002: 161), and they argue that the core idea behind agent-based modelling is 'to perform *highly abstract thought experiments* that explore plausible mechanisms that may underlie observed patterns' (2002: 147, emphasis added). Given the purely theoretical orientation of this field, in the next section we briefly discuss why we believe that it is important to link quantitative research and agent-based modelling to one another. Thereafter we give a substantive background to our case study, which focuses on the role of social interactions in explaining spatial and temporal variations in youth unemployment. We then use a large-scale data set to empirically specify the first two links in the Coleman graph. We use this data to estimate how individuals' likelihood of leaving unemployment are influenced by various individual-level and social-level phenomena, including the unemployment level among those with whom the individuals interact. First we use some of the estimates from these analyses to inject some realism into the type of agent-based model analyzed in chapter 4. In order to predict how the probability of leaving unemployment affects the unemployment level, we thereafter develop the ECA model, and we use this model as a virtual laboratory to examine how various changes in the micro-level processes are likely to influence the level and spatial variation in unemployment. Social processes in which large numbers of heterogeneous actors influence one another through time are rather complex. As a result of this, some of the analyses reported below are also rather complex. This is an unfortunate but unavoidable consequence of the complexity of the subject matter.

Quantitative research and agent-based modelling

Computational modelling has changed a great deal over recent decades. Macy and Willer (2002) aptly describe the general trend as representing a change from factor-based to actor-based models (see also Gilbert and Troitzsch 1999). While social simulations used to be variable-based and sought to reproduce the aggregate dynamics of social systems, the trend has been towards actor-based models. These actor-based models first took the form of so-called micro-simulations, but during the last decade agent-based models have come to dominate (e.g., Carley 1991; Epstein and Axtell 1996; Macy 1991; Mark 1998). The distinguishing feature of an agent-based model is that it explains social phenomena from the bottom up, that is, social phenomena are analyzed as the outcomes of the actions of interacting actors.

While we consider this development towards actor-based models to be of fundamental importance for sociology as an explanatory science, it is important to recognize that this transition in most cases has also meant a change from empirically calibrated models to non-empirical models constructed by researchers to capture the logic of a particular theoretical mechanism. If we sought to derive the social-level consequences of a stylized theoretical mechanism, as was done in chapter 4 and as most agent-based modellers seek to do, this is exactly the type of model we should use. As noted above, however, agent-based modelling also is valuable for other reasons. Most importantly, it can be used for linking empirical research findings to their implied social-level consequences. When agent-based modelling is used for this latter purpose it is essential that the specification of the agent-based model is closely informed by the results of statistical analyses.

The results of such statistical analyses should influence both the ways in which the operative mechanisms are modelled and the set of confounding factors taken into account in the analysis. For example, instead of making up a rule for how actors' opinions or actions are influenced by the opinions or actions of others, as was done in chapter 4, one should use statistical analyses to arrive at a specification that as closely as possible mirrors how the relevant actors actually interacted and influenced one another. Similarly, and as discussed in chapter 4, societies are not closed systems. We must always allow for the possibility that various events or processes, external and unrelated to the processes we focus upon, may influence the outcomes we seek to explain. Not taking into account selection and environmental effects, for instance, may easily lead us astray.[3] Unless we are able to distinguish between these different types of processes, in the statistical as well as in the agent-based analyses, the usefulness of the approach advocated here is much reduced.

Establishing closer links between quantitative research and agent-based modelling thus promises to accomplish two different tasks. First, it provides a test of the agent-based model in the sense that it examines the extent to which it can bring about the social outcome it seeks to explain also for realistic parameter values. Second, it provides a

---

[3] See chapter 3, pages 45–47 for the distinctions between interaction, selection and environmental effects.

micro–macro link that allows us to derive the social-level implications of a set of quantitative research results.

We want to emphasize that we are not advocating a return to older system-level or micro-simulation techniques. The type of empirically calibrated agent-based model that we have in mind is a true agent-based model in the sense that it is a bottom-up model in which agents in interaction with one another bring about various social outcomes. But the model is calibrated with real data, and it takes into account various real-world events taking place during the course of the analysis. After giving a background to our case study and empirically assessing how important social interactions are for unemployment durations, we give precise content to these ideas by developing and analyzing an agent-based model that fulfils these requirements.

Social interactions and youth unemployment

During the 1990s unemployment figures rose sharply throughout the western world, particularly among young people. In Sweden, the focus of this empirical study, unemployment levels among young people had not been so high since the economic recessions of the 1930s. Our purpose here is not to try to explain why unemployment levels changed as they did. Instead, we focus on one specific type of mechanism that has not received sufficient attention in the literature but which nevertheless is likely to have been of considerable importance. We focus on social interactions and their potential importance in explaining temporal and spatial variations in unemployment.

Social interactions can influence unemployed individuals' actions for a variety of reasons, and in order to understand better why we observe what we observe it is essential to try to distinguish between them. As suggested in chapter 3, one should at least try to distinguish between three broad types of social interactions: opportunity-based, belief-based and desire-based. Consider the case where the focal actor is an un-employed individual and the action focused upon is one that increases the likelihood of the individual leaving the unemployed state. How can this action be influenced by the unemployment level among the individual's peers? The general answer is that this can occur in three distinct ways: (1) the unemployment level among peers can influence the focal individual's opportunities and thereby his or her choice of action; (2) it can influence the focal individual's beliefs and thereby his or her choice of action; and (3) it can influence the focal individual's desires and thereby his or her choice of action.

As observed by Granovetter (1974) and others, many individuals obtain their jobs via informal social contacts with friends and acquaintances, who pass on information about jobs to prospective job candidates and information about potential job candidates to employers. If the unemployment rate is high among friends and acquaintances, the quality of this information network is lowered and information about vacant jobs will not reach the focal actor to the same extent as if friends and acquaintances were employed. Therefore, the focal actor's probability of finding a job will be negatively influenced by the unemployment level among friends and acquaintances. This is an example of an opportunity-based interaction effect.

The individual's likelihood of leaving the unemployed state is also likely to be influenced by his or her beliefs about the jobs that he or she can expect to get. Traditional decision and search theory would suggest that those who expect to get a job, particularly a high-paying one, would invest more time and energy in a job search than those with bleaker prospects. To the extent that these beliefs are partly influenced by the experiences of friends, acquaintances or neighbours, we have an example of a belief-based interaction effect. One example of belief-based interaction is the so-called *discouraged worker effect*, that is, that a high unemployment rate may discourage individuals from looking for work because they do not expect to find any (e.g., Schweitzer and Smith 1974). Another type of belief-based interaction occurs when other individuals serve as role models for the focal individual. One reason for Wilson's concern about the exodus of middle-class families from many ghetto neighbourhoods in the United States, for example, was the influence of precisely such belief-based interaction effects: 'the very presence of these families . . . provides mainstream role models that help keep alive the perception that education is meaningful, that steady employment is a viable alternative to welfare, and that family stability is the norm, not the exception' (Wilson 1987: 56). In both the discouraged-worker and the role-model cases, unemployment among others influences the focal individual's beliefs such that his or her chances of leaving the unemployed state are altered.

There are also reasons to believe that desire-based interactions are important in this context. One such reason is the existence of the social norm, which holds that one should earn one's income. Being unemployed usually means that one cannot live up to this norm, and this may bring about feelings of shame or embarrassment (Elster 1989a). Such feelings in large part can be attributed to deviations from what is normal or typical in the unemployed individual's reference groups (Sherif and Sherif 1964). Since reference groups vary among individuals, however, the normative pressure is not likely to be felt with equal intensity by everyone. In particular, the more common it is to be unemployed in a group, the weaker the normative pressure is likely to be, and the less likely it is that an unemployed individual will experience such emotions. Being the only unemployed individual, furthermore, is likely to be a rather lonelier and duller existence than one in which many of one's friends and acquaintances also are unemployed. Thus, for several different reasons, one can expect that an increase in unemployment among an individual's friends and acquaintances will reduce the social and psychological 'costs' of being unemployed.

Clark (2003) presents some evidence suggesting that the unemployment of others indeed influences an individual's unemployment experience. Based on data from the British Panel Household Study, he found that it was easier for individuals to cope with unemployment (as measured by an index of subjective well-being) if they lived in places where many people were unemployed, or if others in the household also were unemployed. He also found that those whose subjective well-being fell the most on entering unemployment were more likely to search for new jobs and were less likely to remain unemployed later (see also Clark and Oswald 1994).

Clark's findings about the effects of the psychological and social costs of unemployment are parallel to those found in studies of the economic consequences of unemployment. The weight of this evidence suggests that increased unemployment benefits cause longer periods of unemployment. The main reason for this seems to be that higher benefits allow the unemployed to be more discriminating with regard to which jobs they accept and it allows them to somewhat reduce the effort they invest in searching for new jobs (see Holmlund 1998 for an overview). It seems likely that the social and psychological costs of being unemployed will have at least as strong an effect on the actions of the unemployed as these purely economic ones. The reason for this is that the variation in the non-pecuniary aspects is likely to be greater than the variation in the pecuniary ones and, as will be discussed below, the non-pecuniary consequences are likely to be self-reinforcing.[4]

To the extent that the unemployment of others influences an unemployed individual's subjective well-being and this, in turn, influences the unemployed individual's behaviour such that his or her chances of leaving the unemployed state are altered, we have an example of a desire-based interaction effect. As part of the project upon which this research

---

[4] They are self-reinforcing in the same sense as a system of unemployment benefits that automatically became more generous when the unemployment level increased would be self-reinforcing. In both cases an increase in unemployment would set in motion processes that would generate more unemployment.

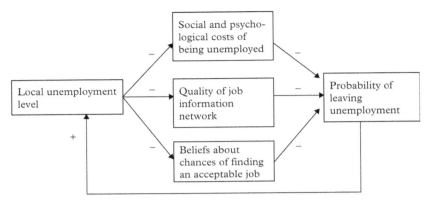

Figure 6.2. Unemployment as an endogenous process.

is based, we conducted a series of detailed interviews with unemployed youth in the Stockholm region. In these interviews, the importance of the unemployment of others was a recurrent theme, and one can find several examples that seem to indicate the importance of desire-based interactions. One interviewee said: 'If your friends are unemployed you do not think it is so bad to be unemployed since everyone else is. But if you are the only unemployed, you feel like an outsider.' And, he continued: 'If you do not have any unemployed friends, you don't have anything to do during the days. Then you would become restless and put more effort into finding a job.'

Figure 6.2 summarizes some of the discussion. An increase in the local unemployment level is likely to reduce the social and psychological costs of being unemployed (desire-based interactions), reduce the quality of the job information network (opportunity-based interactions) and reduce expectations about potential jobs (belief-based interactions). All these changes are likely to influence the unemployed individuals' behaviour in such a way that the probability of their leaving unemployment decreases, and this means that the local unemployment level will increase, everything else being the same.

If these types of social interaction effects are operating, one can expect endogenous processes to be important for changes in aggregate unemployment. A defining characteristic of an endogenous process is that the number of individuals who act in a certain way at a certain point in time in itself partly explains how many will adapt their behaviour at a later point in time. An exogenous event leading to a certain number of individuals becoming unemployed, then, can lead to many more individuals eventually becoming unemployed.

Transitions out of unemployment: statistical estimates

The discussion above thus suggests that there are good reasons to suspect that social interactions and endogenous processes play an important role in explaining temporal and spatial variations in unemployment. But whether or not they actually are important is still an open question. Answering this question is what we now seek to do.[5]

Data

The data set that we use contains information on all 20- to 24-year-olds who ever lived in the Stockholm metropolitan area during 1993–99.[6] For these individuals we have traditional socio-demographic information such as age, sex, education and ethnicity (obtained from various administrative registers). We know in what neighbourhood they resided at the end of each calendar year,[7] and for those who were ever unemployed we know the dates and exact lengths of all their unemployment spells.[8] During the period January 1993–December 1999 about 88,000 individuals out of a total of about 226,000 individuals in that age range had at least one unemployment spell during the period when they were 20 to 24 years old.

The reason for restricting the analysis to a single metropolitan area is that we wish to hold constant one of the most important contextual variables: the tightness of the local labour market. Given the excellent public transportation system in this area, for all practical purposes the Stockholm metropolitan area can be viewed as one and the same labour

---

[5] As far as we are aware, this is the first serious attempt to assess the importance of social interactions for unemployment durations. However, social interactions have been shown to be of importance for explaining other types of outcomes. See, for instance, Bertrand, Luttmer and Mullainathan (2000) and Mood (2004) for their role in explaining welfare use; Bearman and Brückner (2001) for their role in explaining the spread of virginity pledges; Glaeser, Sacerdote and Sheinkman (1996) for their role in explaining crime rates; Hedström (1994) and Hedström, Sandell and Stern (2000) for their role in explaining the diffusion of social movements; and Åberg (2003) for their role in explaining various demographic events.

[6] We here define the 'Stockholm metropolitan area' as consisting of the entire Stockholm county, except for the following municipalities, which are situated at the outskirts of the county: Norrtälje, Sigtuna, Upplands Bro, Södertälje, Nykvarn and Nynäshamn.

[7] The Stockholm metropolitan area is divided into 699 so-called SAMS areas, and these serve as our definition of neighbourhoods. The SAMS areas have been defined so as to contain socially homogeneous residential areas.

[8] The unemployment data has been obtained from the so-called Händel database. We focus on 'open' unemployment, which means that we do not count among the unemployed those engaged in labour market training programmes and the like.

market. Thus, by restricting the analysis to a single metropolitan area, we reduce the risk of mistaking environmental effects in the form of geographical variations in labour market conditions for interaction-based peer-group effects.

Following the tradition of Hägerstrand (1967), we will assume that the structure of social interaction in part reflects actors' spatial locations: the closer two actors are to one another, the more likely they are to be aware of and influence each other's behaviour. The spatial distribution of a population for these reasons is likely to influence the web of social ties linking actors to one another and thereby also the outcome of the interaction-based process being analyzed (see also Hedström 1994).

The reason for restricting the analysis to 20 to 24 year olds is that their significant others are to a large extent likely to be located in close geographical proximity. The processes we focus on are likely to be important for adults as well, but we then would have needed detailed information on the actual social networks linking the individuals to one another.

Neighbourhood variations

If social interactions are important then we should expect endogenous processes to generate differences in unemployment levels also between groups of interacting individuals who are similar to one another in terms of their labour-market-relevant characteristics. In order to examine whether or not this is the case, we examine the extent to which unemployment levels vary among neighbourhoods that are similar to one another in terms of their unemployment-relevant characteristics.

In order to identify neighbourhoods that resemble one another in terms of their unemployment-relevant characteristics, we estimated eighty-four logistic regression models, one for each month. We included only neighbourhoods with at least ten individuals in this age range. In the regression models the dependent variable indicated whether or not an individual was unemployed on the 15th of the month, and the independent variables measured the individual's age, sex, education, marital status, number of children, country of birth, whether or not (s)he was a student, and whether or not (s)he was a recent immigrant.[9] Using these

---

[9] We used sets of dummy variables to distinguish between the following educational levels: primary school only, vocational training school, high school degree and college degree; the following 'marital' statuses: living with parents, single household, and married or cohabiting; the following countries/regions of birth: Sweden, eastern Europe or former Soviet Union, Middle East or Africa, and the rest of the world. Being a 'recently' arrived

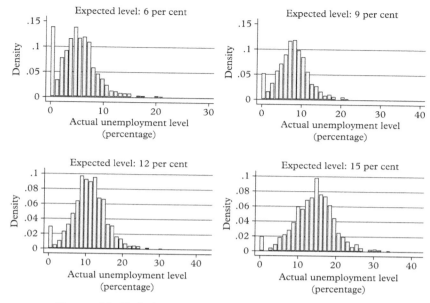

Figure 6.3. Variation in unemployment levels among neighbourhoods that are similar to one another in terms of their unemployment-relevant characteristics.

parameter estimates, we calculated each individual's predicted probability of being unemployed, and then we summarized these predicted probabilities for those within each neighbourhood. We thereby arrived at estimates of the unemployment level one would have expected to observe each month in a neighbourhood on the basis of the demographic characteristics of its members. Two neighbourhoods are similar to one another in their unemployment-relevant demographic characteristics if these expected unemployment levels are approximately the same.

Figure 6.3 compares four sets of neighbourhoods. In the first set the unemployment-relevant demographics were such that, on the basis of the results from the logistic analyses, one would have expected them to have an unemployment level of 6 per cent.[10] In the second set one would

immigrant was defined as having arrived in Sweden during the previous three years, and being a 'student' was defined on the basis of whether or not the individual had received student allowance ('studiebidrag') during the year.

[10] The expected levels are equal to the predicted levels rounded to the nearest integer value.

have expected an unemployment level of 9 per cent, and in the third and fourth sets 12 per cent and 15 per cent respectively.[11]

The results in figure 6.3 clearly show that unemployment levels vary more between neighbourhoods than one would expect them to do on the basis of their unemployment-relevant demographics. In approximately 50 per cent of these cases the actual unemployment level deviated by more than 25 per cent from the expected level.

As noted above, a likely reason for these 'excessive' differences between neighbourhoods is the existence of social interaction effects that set in motion endogenous social processes within certain neighbourhoods. But before we can endorse such an interpretation we need to examine whether the social interaction effect indeed is sufficiently strong to generate such a pattern.

Social interaction effects

In this subsection we seek to assess the extent to which individuals' unemployment-relevant actions are influenced by their peers. The ideas that have guided our analysis are displayed in the Coleman-like figure 6.4. We know that the chance that an unemployed individual will escape unemployment is influenced by his or her actions, for example, the extent and intensity of the individual's job search. We furthermore know that these actions vary among individuals with different attributes such as age, sex, education and ethnicity. As detailed above, there also are strong reasons to suspect that these actions are influenced by the unemployment level among their peers. Obviously their chances of leaving unemployment are not only due to their own actions but are also influenced by the tightness of the labour market (for example, by the number of vacant jobs in relation to the number of unemployed individuals) and by their attributes (reflecting employers' preferences for hiring individuals with certain characteristics). Finally, changes in the individual's probabilities of leaving unemployment will influence the unemployment level at the next point in time. However, this final stage of the analysis, which concerns the transition from the individual to the social, is not part of the statistical analysis. For that purpose the agent-based model will be used.

Since the process we analyze unfolds over time, and since the outcome variable we are interested in – leaving unemployment – is a discrete

---

[11] These four sets represented 29 per cent of all monthly neighbourhood observations and they appear representative of the others.

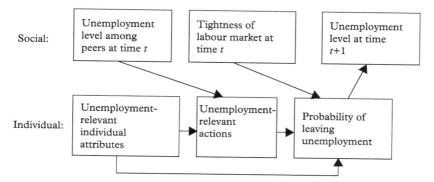

Figure 6.4. Social and individual components of the outflow from unemployment.

event, the statistical model we use is a so-called discrete-time-event history model (see Allison 1982). This essentially is a regular logistic regression model where the unit of analysis has been changed from persons to 'person weeks'. That is to say, before the parameters of the logistic model are estimated, the data is changed in such a way that each person contributes as many observations as the number of weeks that (s)he was at risk of leaving unemployment. An individual who was unemployed for two weeks thus contributes only two observations, while an individual who was unemployed for fifty weeks contributes fifty observations. The set of 87,924 individuals included in the analysis contributed a total of 2,463,079 person weeks.

Unfortunately, our data set does not include any information about what the unemployed individuals did to affect their chances of leaving unemployment. Therefore, we must estimate the parameters of a so-called reduced form model which directly relates an unemployed individual's probability of leaving unemployment to the tightness of the labour market, the attributes of the individual in question, and the unemployment level among his or her peers.

The first model in table 6.1 relates an individual's probability of leaving unemployment during a specific week to the unemployment level among his or her neighbourhood peers. The unemployment level among peers is calculated as the proportion of unemployed 20- to 24-year-olds in the neighbourhood at the end of the week preceding the week being analyzed. The logistic regression coefficient associated with this variable is less than zero, which means that the social interaction effect is in the expected direction. It suggests that the higher the unemployment level is among an unemployed individual's peers, the lower the likelihood is of

Table 6.1. *Logistic regression model of the probability of leaving unemployment: regression coefficients, with z statistics in parentheses*

	Model 1	Model 2
Unemployment level among peers (at the end of the preceding week)	−4.086 (82.99)	−2.087 (−33.59)
Woman		0.132 (25.98)
Age		−0.023 (−9.74)
Vocational training		0.027 (3.83)
High school education		0.137 (20.16)
College education		0.206 (21.71)
Immigrant from eastern Europe or former Soviet Union		−0.138 (−8.40)
Immigrant from Middle East or Africa		−0.192 (−18.84)
Immigrant from the rest of the world		−0.014 (−1.53)
Less than 3 years in Sweden		−0.455 (−27.64)
3–5 years in Sweden		−0.044 (−3.28)
Married		−0.034 (−2.76)
No. of children		−0.055 (−6.16)
Previous unemployment experiences (no. of weeks/10)		−0.019 (−19.12)
Number of unemployed per vacant job (at the beginning of the month)/100		−0.034 (−0.24)
Length of current unemployment spell (no. of weeks)/10		0.319 (65.40)
Square of the length of current unemployment spell		−0.045 (−51.26)
Constant	−2.085 (363.35)	−2.145 (33.69)
Annual and monthly dummy variables included	No	Yes
Log likelihood	−644312.97	−627468.57

him or her leaving unemployment. The value of −4.086 suggests a substantial social interaction 'effect'. To make an out-of-sample prediction, it suggests that, if everyone in the peer group were unemployed, the individual's probability of leaving unemployment would be only about 1.7 per cent of what it would have been had no one been unemployed.

Obviously, much of this so-called social interaction effect is likely to be due to individual heterogeneity across neighbourhoods, which we must control for. If we did not, we would seriously overestimate the extent to which individuals are influenced by others. In the second model, we therefore include variables to control for relevant individual-level differences: sex, age, education (highest degree), country of birth, number of years residing in Sweden, marital status, number of children and previous unemployment experiences measured as the total number of weeks the individual had been unemployed before the current unemployment period started. The variable measuring the extent of previous unemployment experiences has been included in order to control for unobserved and otherwise uncontrolled heterogeneity likely to influence the probability of an individual leaving unemployment (but it also may pick up so-called scarring effects of unemployment). We also control for the tightness of the labour market by including a set of yearly and monthly dummy variables and a variable measuring the number of unemployed per job vacancy at the beginning of each calendar month in the Stockholm county (according to statistics from the labour market authorities). The variable measuring the length of the current unemployment spell has been included to control for so-called duration dependence.

The most important result in model 2 is that the unemployment level among neighbourhood peers has a substantial effect on the probability of leaving unemployment even after we control for all these individual and labour market attributes. The logistic regression coefficient of –2.087 suggests that, if all the neighbourhood peers were unemployed, the individual's risk of leaving unemployment would be only about 12.4 per cent of what it would have been had no one been unemployed. But, once again, this is an out-of-sample prediction and should therefore be treated with some caution.

The effects of some of the other covariates are also interesting, but they are not our primary concern in this chapter. The results for these variables may be briefly summarized as follows. Everything else being the same, they suggest that women are more likely to leave unemployment than men; that the probability of leaving unemployment decreases with age; that those with higher education have better chances of leaving unemployment than those with lower education (the omitted reference category is those with compulsory schooling or less); that immigrants from eastern Europe and from the former Soviet Union have a more difficult time leaving unemployment than people born in Sweden, and that immigrants from the Middle East and Africa have even lower chances of leaving unemployment (though immigrants from the rest of the world do not differ from those born in Sweden); that being a recently arrived immigrant reduces the possibilities of leaving unemployment; that married persons have a smaller chance of leaving unemployment than single persons; that the more children a person has, the lower his or her chances of leaving unemployment are; and finally, that the more an individual has been unemployed in the past, the lower his or her

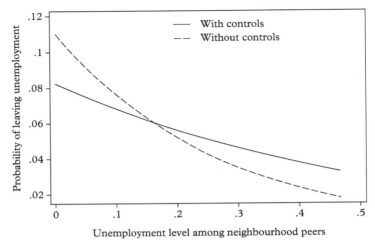

Figure 6.5. Estimated strength of social interaction effects for an average person.

chances of leaving the current unemployment spell are. The coefficients associated with the variables measuring the length of the current unemployment spell suggest that the probability of leaving unemployment gradually increases and reaches its peak when the individual has been unemployed for thirty-six weeks.

For an average individual these results imply the social interaction effects described in figure 6.5. The graphs show that the probability of an unemployed individual leaving unemployment is considerably influenced by the unemployment level among neighbourhood peers, also when all the covariates of table 6.1 are controlled.

Selection effects that we have not been able to control for may have led to an upward bias in these estimates. But our crude measure of the reference group variable is likely to have led to a bias in the opposite direction. It is unclear how these two sources of error jointly influence our estimates, but they should at least partly cancel one another out. A lower bound on the social interaction effect can be arrived at by a fixed-effect specification that controls for all time-invariant differences between the neighbourhoods. Using such a technique undoubtedly means that one introduces excessive controls and therefore biases the estimate downwards, but analyses not reported here show that, even with such excessive controls, with a 95 per cent confidence level the true logistic regression coefficient measuring the strength of the social interaction effect is to be found in the interval −3.24 to −1.50, with a point estimate as large as −2.37.[12]

All in all, these results strongly suggest that the unemployment level among neighbourhood peers has a considerable influence on the probability that an unemployed individual will leave unemployment. Although some of these social interaction effects are likely to be due to differences between the individuals that we have not been able to control for, it seems highly unlikely that such factors could wipe out these rather substantial peer-group effects.[13] In order to make the transition from the level of the individual to the level of the social, and to examine the implications of these results for the unemployment levels likely to be observed, we must incorporate the results into an agent-based model.

A simple agent-based model of unemployment

As mentioned above, the core idea of the approach advocated here is to use empirically calibrated agent-based models (ECA models) to derive the social-level implications of a set of quantitative research results. In order to convey what type of model we have in mind and how such models can be used for assessing the social outcomes implied by individual-level research findings, the empirical results of the previous section will be incorporated into an agent-based model. If this approach is used, quantitative research comes to have a direct bearing on the so-called micro–macro link discussed by Coleman and others (see arrow 3 in figure 6.1).

In order to illustrate the logic of the approach, we will proceed in the following manner. First, we inject some realism into the type of highly stylized agent-based model used in chapter 4. We use the logistic regression results of table 6.1 to arrive at a more plausible model of the ways in which the agents influence one another, and then examine the social outcomes they bring about under these more realistic conditions. Thereafter we develop the ECA model by replacing many of the simplified assumptions of this stylized agent-based model with information derived from the empirical analysis. The ECA model will be used as a virtual

[12] This estimate is based on a 5 per cent random sample of the unemployment spells, in total 121,727 person-weeks. For computational reasons it was not feasible to estimate the fixed-effect model on the total population.
[13] Results not reported here show that this conclusion remains the same when so-called fixed-effect specifications are used to control for all time-invariant differences between the individuals' neighbourhoods.

laboratory to examine how social outcomes are likely to be affected by various changes at the level of the individual.

The agent-based models of chapter 4 were used to analyze how social interactions among actors were likely to bring about changes in the actors' beliefs and desires, and thereby also in their actions. In those models it was assumed that actors' beliefs/desires changed if and only if a majority of their neighbours had beliefs/desires that were different from their own. This type of agent-based model can be made more realistic by implementing an evidence-based action rule. If we assume, as was done in chapter 4, that the actors' opportunities are such that they can be in only two states, the first regression model of table 6.1 says that the probability that an actor will change state/action at a specific point in time is given by the expression:

$$p_{jt} = \frac{1}{1 + e^{2.085 + 4.086 \times U_{jt-1}}}$$

where U_{jt-1} equals the proportion of the neighbours who were in the same state or acted in the same way as the focal actor at the previous point in time.[14] The equation says that the larger the proportion of the neighbours that acted in the same way as the focal actor, the less likely it was that the actor would change action.

In order to examine the social patterns that emerge when agents' actions are decided on the basis of this rule, we proceed in the same manner as in chapter 4. We assume that 2,500 actors are placed on a lattice (torus) with fifty rows and fifty columns. We start with an entirely random action pattern and then we examine the social patterns that emerge when the agents interact and influence one another. One important difference between these analyses and those in chapter 4 is that we now focus on the actions as such and not on the underlying beliefs and desires of the actors. It would have been desirable also to include beliefs and desires in the analysis, but we do not have any empirical information about them.

A typical initial action pattern looks like the upper-left graph of figure 6.6. Black areas identify actors who acted in one way (call their action a B-action), and white areas identify those who acted in the other way (call their action a W-action). In the simulation reported in figure 6.6, 40 per cent of the actors performed a B-action and 60 per cent performed a W-action at the outset of the analysis.

---

[14] The results of these analyses can be interpreted as either referring to the states in which the actors are or in terms of their actions. To simplify the presentation, hereafter the results are presented in action terms.

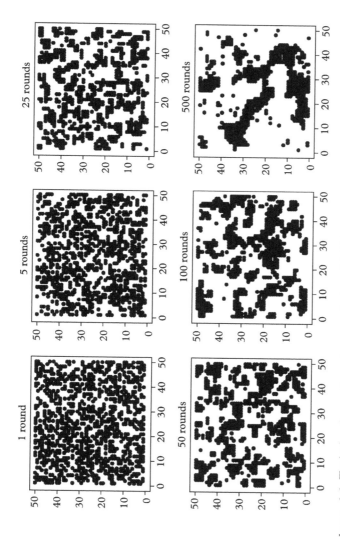

Figure 6.6. Typical action patterns in a population of 2,500 actors who socially interact with four neighbours on the basis of an empirically calibrated action rule.

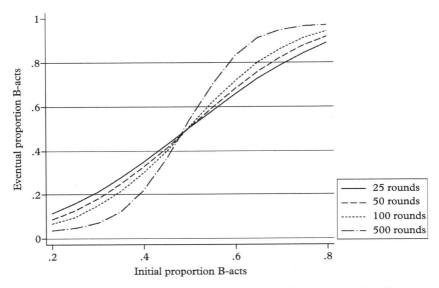

Figure 6.7. Summary of the results of 5,200 agent-based analyses in which 2,500 agents interact on a lattice (torus) with 50 rows and 50 columns on the basis of an empirically calibrated action rule.

We take social interactions into account by assuming that the actors are directly influenced by their four immediate neighbours (see Figure 4.2). These neighbours influence the focal actor's probability of changing his or her action in the manner described by the logistic regression equation. The social patterns that emerge under these conditions typically look like those in figure 6.6. Although we start with an entirely unstructured social pattern, a highly segregated pattern emerges rather quickly. Already when the actors have interacted and influenced one another over five rounds, segregated patterns start to emerge. As the interaction process proceeds, the extent of clustering and segregation increases. Thus it seems that social interaction processes can bring about highly segregated social patterns also when the agents act on the basis of plausible assumptions about the strength of social interaction.[15]

Figure 6.7 summarizes the results of a large number of agent-based analyses like these, and gives some additional insights into the social

[15] Bruch and Mare (2004) found that the use of plausible probabilistic decision rules in a traditional Schelling (1971) model of residential segregation did not generate the highly segregated patterns that Schelling models normally generate. They discussed whether their finding could be generalized to social-influence processes more generally. These results suggest that they cannot.

outcomes that these types of processes tend to generate. In addition to the clustering effects shown in figure 6.6, it seems that these types of processes also have important magnifying effects. If an action is common, the social interaction process makes it even more common, and if the action is uncommon, the interaction process makes it even less common. Figure 6.7 also shows that the longer or the more frequently the agents interact with one another, the stronger this magnifying effect is likely to be.

On a very abstract level, the patterns in figures 6.6 and 6.7 show some similarities with the unemployment patterns found above. Both types of pattern are highly segregated and they cannot be explained by reference to the attributes of the actors. Such similarities suggest that social interactions may have been important in generating the spatial variation in unemployment, but obviously the evidence is far from conclusive, and therefore we must carry out more detailed analyses.

Although the inclusion of the results of the logistic regression analysis into the agent-based model have reduced the gap between model and reality, the remaining gap is considerable by any measure. For this reason one can rightfully wonder whether or not this type of model can serve the intended purpose of being the micro–macro link that allows us to approximate the social outcomes implied by this set of micro-level statistical results. One obvious discrepancy between the model and reality is the assumed checkerboard structure, which shows little or no resemblance to real-world social structures. It is far from certain that a model based on such simplifying assumptions can accurately generate the social outcomes implied by the micro-level findings. Similarly, the agents of these analyses do not have much in common with real-world individuals. If we do not allow for real-world heterogeneity, it is likely that the social-level predictions derived from the model will be systematically biased. Finally, state-of-nature models such as these are always a little problematic. Most of the social phenomena that we seek to explain are the results of complex historical processes. As David Lewis once put it:

Any particular event that we might wish to explain stands at the end of a long and complicated causal history. We might imagine a world where causal histories are short and simple; but in the world as we know it, the only question is whether they are infinite or merely enormous. (Lewis 1983: 214)

Faced with a world consisting of causal histories of nearly infinite length, in practice we can hope only to provide reliable information on their most recent history. Instead of basing the analysis on models that start from a presocial random state, it seems safer to take certain social phenomena as given and incorporate them into the agent-based model.

The realism of the model is thereby enhanced, which gives us more faith in the results derived from it.

For all these reasons, highly stylized agent-based models are not likely to give a good approximation of the social outcomes implied by a set of statistical results. The model to be used must have more empirical texture than these models have in order to be useful for this purpose. Our strategy for arriving at such a model can be described as follows:

1 Hypothetical agents should be replaced with virtualized replicas of heterogeneous real agents.
2 The checkerboard structure should be replaced with real spatial or social structures.
3 The structure as well as the strength of social interaction should be estimated with real data.
4 Important real-world events known to influence the outcome to be explained should be incorporated into the model.

But – and this is at the heart of our approach – the logic of the analysis should remain the same as in traditional agent-based analyses. That is to say, it is the actions of and interactions between the agents that should generate the social patterns that emerge, and by altering various aspects of the simulation setup one ascertains what effects these changes may have on the outcomes.

An empirically calibrated agent-based model of unemployment

In order to construct an empirically calibrated agent-based (ECA) model of unemployment, instead of basing the analyses on 2,500 hypothetical actors we should use virtual replicas of the individuals who actually experienced unemployment during this period as our agents. Instead of assigning them positions on a checkerboard-like structure, we should assume that they resided where their real-world counterparts actually did and that they interacted with virtual replicas of their actual neighbourhood peers. And instead of just making assumptions about how agents' actions are influenced by the actions of others, we should use the results from the large-scale data analyses presented above to empirically specify what the functional relationships look like.

The agents of the ECA model thus are virtualized replicas of all the 20 to 24 year olds in the Stockholm metropolitan area who were ever unemployed during the period January 1993–December 1999. All in all, 87,924 agents are included in the analyses. These agents retain the true social and demographic characteristics of their real-world counterparts (see table 6.1 for a description of the characteristics we take into account). We also use information on the 20 to 24 year olds who did not experience any unemployment when we calculate the proportion of unemployed in the neighbourhoods, but the agents in our analyses are only those who experienced any unemployment. The agents interact with their true neighbourhood peers, and the extent to which they influence one another is given by the results of the empirical analysis.

In the analyses the agents become unemployed when their real-world counterparts actually became unemployed. They age, move and so forth just as their real-world counterparts did. The agents also exit from the analysis if their real-world counterparts move from the Stockholm metropolitan area, if they turn 25, or if they have been unemployed for more than 300 days (which is the maximum number of days that individuals in this age range could receive unemployment benefits).

Their probability of leaving unemployment is influenced by three sets of factors: (1) their own social and demographic characteristics, (2) the unemployment level among their neighbourhood peers, and (3) the tightness of the labour market. The ways in which these factors influence their probability of leaving unemployment are given by the second logistic regression equation in table 6.1.

The simulation model focuses on how changes in the rate at which the agents leave unemployment influence the level and spatial variation in the number of unemployed. The idea behind the virtual experiments is to introduce changes in the extent to which different factors influence the agents' exit probabilities. Such changes will have a direct effect on the expected number of unemployed agents but, since the agents interact and influence one another, it will also have an indirect social-multiplier effect on the unemployment level. The agents are interdependent because a change in the exit probability of some agents will change the level of unemployment in their neighbourhoods, and this will change the exit probabilities of others. At the end of each week the unemployment level in each neighbourhood is updated and allowed to influence exit probabilities during the following week. This will in turn influence unemployment levels at the end of that week, which will lead to further changes in exit probabilities, and so on, throughout the 364-week period from January 1993 to December 1999.

Figure 6.8 describes how the unemployment level developed during this period and the outcomes of some of the virtual experiments.[16] The

[16] In order to highlight general trends and differences, all seasonal variations have been removed from the graphs in figures 6.9–6.11 with a smoothing routine. All graphs report moving averages based on the 26-week periods before and after each date on the horizontal axes.

unemployment level was very high during 1993–95 but it fell rapidly thereafter (see the dash-dot line and use the right-hand axis). At its peak more than one young person out of ten was unemployed, and at its lowest point about one young person out of twenty-five was unemployed. The ECA simulations have a counterfactual purpose. We use them to assess how the unemployment level, overall as well as in different neighbourhoods, is likely to have differed if the social interaction effects had been different from what they actually were.

The baseline model in these analyses is a simulation based on the actual parameter estimates found in the second model of table 6.1. This baseline model serves two purposes. First, it allows us to examine the extent to which the agent-based model can bring about the social outcomes it was intended to explain. Second, it serves as a point of reference for the virtual experiments. As far as the first of these purposes is concerned, the results suggest that the model is fairly successful. The correlation between the actual unemployment level in the various neighbourhoods at different points in time and the unemployment levels brought about when we assume that the agents' actions are governed by the baseline parameters is as high as 0.84.

To simplify the comparisons between the baseline simulation and the various virtual experiments, the overall unemployment level brought about each week under the baseline regime is set equal to 100, and the unemployment levels brought about by the experimental regimes are expressed as a per centagé of the baseline level. The solid line in figure 6.8 is the baseline reference point, and the long-dashed line shows how the unemployment level would have changed if the social interaction effect (as measured by the logistic regression coefficient) was 50 per cent higher than it actually was but everything else remained the same. This increase in the extent to which the actors were influenced by others would have increased the number of unemployed by 8 per cent during an average week (from now on, use the left-hand axis). During the high unemployment period, the increase would have been as high as 10 per cent. It should be noted that these differences are entirely due to changes in the rate at which unemployed individuals leave unemployment. In both scenarios, the inflow of unemployed individuals is identical.

The medium-dashed line in figure 6.8 shows how the unemployment level would have changed if the social interaction effect was 50 per cent *lower* than it actually was (once again as measured by the size of the logistic regression coefficient). The results are similar, but in the opposite direction to those discussed in the previous paragraph. This change in

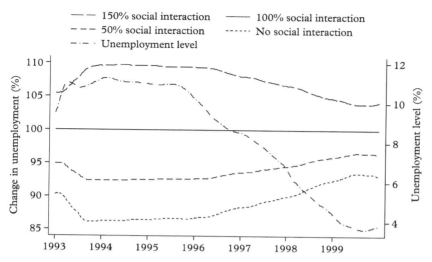

Figure 6.8. Actual and simulated unemployment levels in the Stockholm metropolitan area.

the extent to which the actors influence one another would have reduced the number of unemployed individuals by more than 5 per cent during the high employment period and by slightly less than 5 per cent during the latter half of the period.

The short-dashed line shows what would have happened if there were no social interaction effects at all, that is, if the probability of leaving unemployment were unaffected by the unemployment level among peers. Once again, the unemployment levels that the actors would bring about under these conditions differ considerably from those brought about in the baseline simulation. Under these conditions the unemployment levels would have been between 86 per cent and 93 per cent of what they were under the baseline set up. On average, the number of unemployed individuals would have been 89 per cent of what it was according to the baseline simulation had there been no social interaction effects.

In terms of economic as well as social costs, these differences are of considerable interest. These analyses suggest that on the average there would have been 990 fewer young people unemployed each week during the high unemployment years 1993–95 if there had not been any social interaction effect at all. This means that the social interaction generated about 51,000 additional unemployment weeks per year, which should be

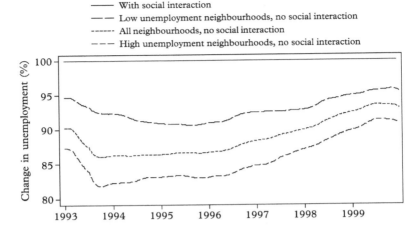

Figure 6.9. Unemployment levels and social interactions in low and high unemployment neighbourhoods in the Stockholm metropolitan area.

seen in relation to the fact that there were slightly fewer than 82,000 20 to 24 year olds who lived in the Stockholm metropolitan area during these years.

As can be seen from figure 6.9, social interactions are likely to influence not only the overall level of unemployment but also its spatial variation. Once again, to simplify the comparisons between the baseline and the various scenarios, the overall unemployment level brought about each week under the baseline regime is set equal to 100, and the unemployment levels brought about by the virtual experiments are expressed as a percentage of the baseline level. Figure 6.9 shows that social interactions tend to magnify the differences between low unemployment and high unemployment neighbourhoods.[17] That is, if the unemployment level is higher in certain neighbourhoods than in others, perhaps because of demographic differences between the individuals residing in the neighbourhoods, social interactions are likely to magnify these differences since the multiplier effect will be greater in the high unemployment areas. While the number of unemployed in the low unemployment areas would have been about 93 per cent of what it

---

[17] The 10 per cent neighbourhoods with the lowest average unemployment during 1993 were defined as 'low unemployment neighbourhoods' and the 10 per cent with the highest average unemployment as 'high unemployment neighbourhoods'.

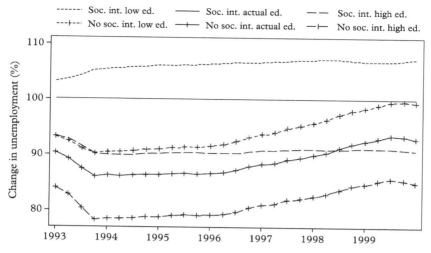

Figure 6.10. Effects of social interactions and education on the unemployment level in the Stockholm metropolitan area.

actually was had there been no social interaction effects, the corresponding figure for the high unemployment areas was 85 per cent.

Since data to examine social interaction effects are rarely available, it is difficult to have any intuitive sense of how the magnitude of these effects compares with the effects of factors usually considered in studies of unemployment. For this reason figure 6.10 compares the magnitude of the social interaction and the educational effects. As before, we assume that the agents base their actions on the results of the second logistic regression model in table 6.1, and we allow them to act and to influence one another week by week. The unemployment levels they then bring about are those shown in figure 6.10. The various outcomes shown in the figure are due to different experimental setups, that is, they are based on different assumptions about the strength of educational and social interaction effects. The solid lines describe outcomes brought about when the agents acted on the basis of their true educational levels, while dashed lines describe outcomes brought about when their educational levels had been altered.[18] Lines with vertical ticks describe outcomes the agents would have brought about had they not influenced one another,

[18] The straight solid line without vertical ticks thus is identical to the baseline in the previous figures.

while lines without vertical ticks describe outcomes brought about when they influence one another. Short-dashed lines report outcomes when all agents are assumed to have compulsory schooling or less, while long-dashed lines describe outcomes when all agents are assumed to have a college education.

A comparison of the various unemployment trajectories in figure 6.10 gives some insights into the relative importance of social interactions. First of all, these results suggest that a removal of the social interaction effect would have a greater influence on the unemployment level than a change in the educational levels of the unemployed. If all individuals had a college education or, expressed slightly differently, if all individuals were able to leave unemployment as fast as the college-educated could, these analyses suggest that the number of unemployed individuals during an average week would have been about 9 per cent lower than in the baseline scenario with actual education. This should be compared with what would have happened had the social interaction effect been eliminated. Such a change would have reduced the number of un-employed during an average week by approximately 11 per cent.[19] A similar conclusion can be drawn from the fact that the baseline setup generates higher unemployment levels than the setup which assumes atomistic agents with compulsory education or lower only.[20]

The results furthermore show that the combined educational and social interaction effects can be most substantial. The sharpest reduction in the unemployment level is brought about when the social interaction effects are eliminated *and* all individuals are able to leave unemployment as fast as the college-educated could (see the long-dashed line with vertical ticks). This experimental setup brings about 19 per cent fewer unemployed during an average week.

On the basis of these comparisons we therefore conclude that the social interaction effects are at least on a par with the educational effects.[21] Performing analyses like these allows us not only to state that

[19] That social interactions have a greater impact is indicated by the fact that the solid line with vertical ticks is below the long-dashed line without vertical ticks for most of the period.

[20] This can be seen by comparing the solid straight line with the short-dashed line with vertical ticks. During an average week, the number of unemployed was about 6 per cent lower in the latter scenario.

[21] It should also be noted that this way of assessing the magnitude of the educational effect somewhat overestimates its true unique effect. The effects we have reported combine a direct educational effect and an indirect social interaction effect. That is, changes in the educational effects lead to changes in unemployment levels and these lead to further changes in the unemployment level because of the social interaction effect. The experimental treatment which assumes that all agents have a college education will lead to 691

a social interaction process might have been of importance, but also to state with some confidence that such processes actually were at work and, in this case, that they most likely were of considerable importance for the social outcome we sought to explain. Being able to make such claims, we believe, is of utmost importance for the future of agent-based analyses in an empirically oriented discipline like sociology.

Concluding discussion

The lack of integration between sociological theory and sociological research that Merton so often brought to our attention still characterizes a large part of the discipline. Theorists who specialize in theory still have little or no contact with empirical research, and empirical researchers are often more concerned with statistical than with sociological theory. Coleman (1986b) argued that one important reason for this lack of integration is that we have neither a well-specified theory nor a dependable methodology for making the transition from the level of the individual to the level of the social. As a result, sociological theory and sociological research often appear mismatched. While most sociological theories focus on social phenomena, most quantitative research focuses on individual-level phenomena.

In this chapter we have advocated the use of so-called ECA models for arriving at a closer integration of theory and research. The modelling approach adopted here seeks to closely integrate mechanism-based theories and empirical research, and the core of the approach can be summarized in the following way:

1 Start with developing a stylized agent-based model that explicates the logic of the mechanism assumed to be operative. Simulate the model in order to examine *generative sufficiency* (Epstein and Axtell 1996), that is, make sure that the model can generate the type of social outcome to be explained. If the model exhibits generative sufficiency, we have a mechanism-based explanation of the outcome, but the explanation has not yet been empirically verified.
2 For empirical verification, use relevant data to examine the most important bits and pieces of the causal machinery in order to verify that the mechanism actually works as postulated.

fewer unemployed individuals during an average week if the agents interact and influence one another. Had they not interacted with one another, the corresponding figure would have been 551. The comparable figures for the set up where the agents have compulsory education or lower are 401 and 320.

3 Examine generative sufficiency when the agent-based model has been modified in the light of (2) and after controls for likely confounders have been introduced.

Only when our explanatory account has passed all of these three stages can we claim to have an empirically verified mechanism-based explanation of a social outcome.

7   Coda

In this book I have discussed some of the basic principles of analytical sociology and I have sought to clarify what a mechanism-based explanatory strategy looks like. In doing so, I have touched on a range of issues of fundamental importance for the discipline as a whole. Most importantly, I have discussed how one can forge tighter links between the micro and the macro on the one hand, and between theory and empirical research on the other. In this concluding chapter I draw attention to some areas that are destined to become core areas of analytical sociology and I briefly summarize the most important themes of the book.

The history of analytical sociology can be traced back to the works of Weber and Tocqueville. The analytical agenda was further developed by prominent mid-twentieth-century sociologists such as Parsons and Merton. Only in recent decades, however, has a clearly articulated analytical approach started to emerge. Scholars such as Boudon, Coleman, Elster and Schelling have demonstrated the possibility of developing precise, realistic and action-based explanations of various social phenomena of great sociological interest. Building upon the foundations laid by them, an analytical middle-range approach to sociological theory can be developed.

A cornerstone of the analytical approach is the principle that explanations of social phenomena should focus on the social mechanisms that brought them about. A social mechanism, as the concept is used in this book, is a constellation of entities and activities that is organized in such a way that it regularly brings about a particular type of outcome. A mechanism-based explanation of an observed outcome refers to the social mechanism by which such outcomes are regularly brought about. In one way or another these mechanisms are always about actors and the causes and consequences of their actions, because actors are the entities that bring about change in society.

When one analyzes the causes and consequences of actions, it is useful to make an analytical distinction between elementary intra-actor mechanisms, which focus on the proximate causes of actions, and molecular or inter-actor mechanisms, which focus on the structure of social inter-action. In this book all such mechanisms have been formulated in terms of the so-called DBO theory, which explains action in terms of an actor's desires, beliefs and opportunities. DBO theory is an appropriate foundation for analytical sociology, not least because it is a plausible theory from a phenomenological point of view and explains action in clearly articulated intentional terms.

From the perspective of DBO theory, desires and beliefs can be said to cause an action in the sense of providing reasons for the action. Desires and beliefs have a motivational force that allow us to understand and, in this respect, explain an action. The proximate cause of an action, therefore, is a constellation of desires, beliefs and opportunities in the light of which the action appears reasonable.

Elementary action mechanisms differ from one another in terms of how these entities and activities — desires (D), beliefs (B), opportunities (O) and actions (A) — are linked to one another. For example, the $D \rightarrow B \rightarrow A$ pattern describes a frequently observed causal sequence in which actors' desires influence their beliefs in such a way that they come to believe and act upon what they desire to be the case. Similarly, $B \rightarrow D \rightarrow A$ and $O \rightarrow D \rightarrow A$ patterns describe common causal sequences where actors' opportunities and/or beliefs causally influence their desires in such a way that they come to desire only what they believe they can get.[1]

Understanding the proximate causes of actions is only one piece in the larger sociological puzzle which seeks to understand change, or lack thereof, at the level of the social. Therefore we must not only specify the proximate causes of action but also seek to understand the causes of the (proximate) causes. Assuming that beliefs, desires and opportunities are fixed and exogenously given may be plausible in some very specific situations, but not in the general case. Beliefs, desires and opportunities vary in systematic ways between different groups; in order to get a better handle on how they are formed it is essential to consider various mechanisms focusing on the structure of social interaction and the resulting patterns of social influence.

From the perspective of DBO theory, social interactions are always mediated via the mental states (beliefs or desires) and/or the action opportunities of actors. Thus, if actors interact and influence one another, then it is possible to analytically distinguish between three types of

---

[1] See Davidson (1980) and Elster (1983b) for detailed discussions of these so-called wishful thinking and sour grapes mechanisms.

social interaction: belief-mediated interaction, desire-mediated inter-action and opportunity-mediated interaction. If, for instance, I do the same as you do because I believe that you are better informed or more able to decide on the appropriate course of action than I am, we have an example of a belief-mediated interaction ($A_j \rightarrow B_i \rightarrow A_i$). But if I do the same as you do because your actions influence my desires and thereby my subsequent actions, we have an example of a desire-mediated inter-action ($A_j \rightarrow D_i \rightarrow A_i$); and, if I do the same as you do because your actions enable me to do the same as you do, we have an example of an opportunity-meditated interaction ($A_j \rightarrow O_i \rightarrow A_i$).

Elementary and molecular mechanisms like these often operate in complex concatenated patterns. Once this is recognized and the com-plex totality has been dissected and decomposed into its elementary constituents, it becomes possible to understand and explain outcomes that otherwise would have been difficult to comprehend. One case in point is Tocqueville's explanation of the rapid secularization in France at the end of the eighteenth century, discussed in chapter 3, which referred to a complex combination of desire-mediated and belief-mediated mechanisms ($D_i \rightarrow A_i \rightarrow B_j \rightarrow A_j \rightarrow D'_i \rightarrow A_i$ where $D'_i \neq D_i$).

As emphasized by Coleman (1986b) and others, one of the main obstacles to the development of explanatory theories of the social has been the difficulty of linking individual actions to social outcomes. We know a great deal about how individuals' desires, beliefs, opportunities and so forth are influenced by the social contexts in which actors are embedded, and we also know a great deal about how desires, beliefs and opportunities influence actions, but how actors bring about various social outcomes in interaction with one another eludes us in most cases.

The link between individual actions and social outcomes is difficult to get a handle on because the outcome depends to a high degree on the details of the structure of social interactions. As was shown in chapter 4, small and seemingly unimportant changes in the networks that link actors to one another can have considerable consequences for the social outcomes they bring about. For this reason, social outcomes cannot simply be 'read off' from the properties of the actors that generate them. Even in very small groups in which actors act on the basis of known action logics, we often fail to anticipate the social outcomes they bring about (see Schelling 1978 for a range of examples). Anticipating and explaining the link between the individual and the social is simply too complex for us to handle without the use of some formal analytical tools. Sociology focuses on complex and difficult subject matters; and, if the discipline is to be a rigorous science of the social, the use of formal analytical tools is unavoidable.

When analyzing the link between the individual and the social, it is important not to fall into the trap of fictionalism or instrumentalism. Although explanatory accounts are always and by necessity descriptively incomplete, relying on descriptively *false* mechanisms must be avoided, because they will give incorrect answers to the question of why we observe what we observe.[2] We may, for instance, be able to tell a story that shows how a group of atomistic and rational individuals could have brought about the social outcome we seek to explain, but such an account would not explain why we observed what we observed unless the individuals acted and interacted as postulated by the theory (or at least approximately so). Basing the analysis on incorrect assumptions about the logic of action or interaction may allow us to formulate elegant and parsimonious models, but if such logics are found only in hypothetical worlds much different from our own, causal accounts based on such assumptions will be fictional and non-explanatory in our world. In order to find an explanation we must refer to mechanisms known to be operative in the real-world settings that we are analysing.

Until fairly recently the most readily available formalism for addressing the link between the individual and the social was some sort of mathematical model, not seldom an equilibrium model imported from economics (see Edling 2002 for an overview). One fundamental problem with many of these models is that they force the analyst to introduce knowingly false assumptions because otherwise the model cannot be solved, and a mathematical model that cannot be solved is not of much use. As discussed in chapter 3, this is a dilemma that mathematically oriented rational-choice theorists must often face. Although no one believes that actors behave as these models assume they do, heroic actor assumptions are routinely invoked because they allow for clean and tractable analytical solutions. These models can be extremely elegant and sometimes represent remarkable intellectual achievements, but it is questionable whether they can be said to explain anything in the real world. As a consequence such models often have more in common with Hermann Hesse's (1970) glass-bead game than with explanatory theories proper. Genuine explanations of social phenomena must always

---

[2] As discussed in chapter 3, the difference between descriptively false and descriptively incomplete statements can be defined as follows. If we have a set A = {a, b, c, d} and we assume that A = {e, f}, then our assumption would be descriptively false, while if we assume that A = {a, d}, then our assumption would be descriptively incomplete. In the former case we ascribe to A characteristics which it does not have, while in the latter case we assume A to be what it is only in part, that is, we accentuate certain aspects by ignoring others.

account for what happens, as it actually happens, not as it could have happened in a fictional world very different from our own.

This book has been guided by Tukey's (1962) motto that it is better to seek an approximate and possibly not so elegant solution to the *right* question than an exact and elegant answer to the *wrong* question. From such a vantage point, agent-based modelling is a more attractive type of formalism than traditional mathematical models for addressing the link between the individual and the social. Agent-based modelling uses computer simulations to assess the social outcomes that groups of virtual actors are likely to bring about (see Macy and Willer 2002 for an overview). Such models may lack the elegance and beauty of mathematical models, but they often have more explanatory power because they do not force the analyst to base the analysis on knowingly false assumptions.

In chapter 4 formal models were used to assess generic relationships between individual actions and social outcomes. These analyses taught us several important lessons. One such lesson was that the structure of social interaction can often be of considerable explanatory importance in its own right. Small and seemingly unimportant changes in the structure of social interaction can have a profound impact on the social outcomes that emerge. This also means that the effect a given action has on the social can be highly contingent upon the structural configuration in which the actor is embedded. In one structural context a given action can set in motion a cascade that eventually brings along all the other actors, while in a slightly different setting the same action may have no effect whatsoever on the actions of the others. All of this means that aggregate social patterns typically say very little about the micro-level processes that brought them about. If we want to explain why we observe certain social outcomes, and this is surely what most of us want to do, then there is no substitute for detailed examination of the action-level mechanisms that are likely to have been at work.

The relationship between networks and dynamic processes is destined to become a central area of analytical sociology. The reason that many of us are interested in the structure of social networks is that they are important for understanding the processes that take place upon them. If networks did not influence how people act or the outcomes of their actions, they would not be particularly important to sociology. Almost half a century ago Coleman, Katz and Menzel (1957) did some pioneering work relating the structure of social networks to the dynamic processes that unfold upon them. As discussed in chapter 4, they examined two different types of network. One was a hierarchical network in which each actor was tied to a central source of influence but had no contact with the other actors. The other was a non-hierarchical random network linking actors to one another. Coleman, Katz and Menzel examined how the social outcomes brought about would be likely to differ between these two types of network, and found that the networks left strikingly different dynamic imprints. In the random network the expected adoption trajectory was S-shaped, while in the hierarchical network it was smooth and gradual.

The Coleman, Katz and Menzel study is generally considered to be one of the classics of the social network tradition, yet social network analysts have been slow to adopt their model-based approach for analyzing the link between network structures and dynamic processes. Although there exist numerous other types of relevant networks in addition to those considered by Coleman, Katz and Menzel, and although the link between structure and process is at the core of many empirical network studies (see Strang and Soule 1998 for a review of some of the recent diffusion literature), model-based analyses of the relationship between network structure and social dynamics have not been common. In the last few years, however, physicists and applied mathematicians have started to pay attention to social networks. They have adopted similar analytical strategies to that of Coleman and colleagues, and have been concerned with the dynamic aspects of the networks, both the growth dynamics of the networks themselves and the dynamics of the processes that unfold upon them (see Newman 2003 and Watts 2003 for overviews of this literature). Examples include Watts' important work on diffusion processes in small-world networks (e.g., Watts 1999a; Watts 1999b; Watts and Strogatz 1998), and Barabasi's work on scale-free networks (e.g., Barabasi and Albert 1999; Barabasi and Bonabeau 2003).[3] Although this line of work still is in its infancy, it is of considerable interest because it suggests the possibility of a mechanism-based typology of different types of networks (see Amaral et al. 2000 for some initial efforts in this direction). Networks differ from one another in terms of properties such as the extent of clustering, the frequency distribution of ties and the extent of assortative mixing, and different combinations of these structural properties can be expected to bring about different types of social outcomes.[4]

When we are to explain a concretely observed phenomenon, as distinct from examining theoretically implied consequences of a specific

---

[3] See also Liljeros et al. (2001) for some additional empirical evidence on the potential real-world importance of scale-free networks.

[4] I wish to thank Fredrik Liljeros for suggesting these three properties as being of particularly importance.

mechanism, 'generative sufficiency' (Epstein and Axtell 1996) is not sufficient. The fact that a mechanism *can* explain an outcome does not mean that it *actually* explained it. Many different mechanisms can generate the same type of outcome, and somehow we must be able to identify the mechanisms that most likely do generate them. This is where empirical research enters the picture.

The currently most common type of quantitative empirical research uses large-scale non-experimental data, typically survey data, to estimate parameters of statistical models, which are then interpreted in causal terms. This type of research has not had much influence on the kind of explanatory theory advocated in this book. In part this is due to the use of survey data, which rarely contains any information about the interactions of the individuals surveyed. Therefore, this type of research has not produced much information about the structure of social interaction. Furthermore, much of this research is guided by an implicit quasi-behaviouristic action theory that explains actions by reference to various 'determinants' such as age, sex, education and class. How or through what mechanisms factors such as these exert their effects on action has typically not been a concern of this tradition. Intentions, for instance, play little or no role. From the perspective of DBO theory, such explanations appear shallow and ad hoc. In order for sociology to be a rigorous science of the social, it is important that empirical research comes to have a more direct bearing on theory development, and this requires a certain reorientation away from the atomistic and quasi-behaviouristic variable approach currently subscribed to by many quantitative empirical researchers.

Such a reorientation of empirical research can and should take many different forms. One type of empirical research that promises to be of considerable importance for analytical sociology is laboratory-based experimental research. Such research has a long tradition in sociology, but it has always been somewhat marginal to the main currents of the discipline. Yet recent developments in experimental economics have shown how important such work can be for core issues of the discipline. There has been an explosive growth of experimental work in economics, and much of this research has focused on sociologically highly important topics such as social norms (Fehr and Fischbacher 2004), discrimination (Fershtman and Gneezy 2001), social interactions (Falk and Fischbacher 2002) and network formation (Kosfeld 2004). It should only be a matter of time before a similar development takes place in sociology, because experimental research can address many questions about action logics and interaction structures that would be difficult or even impossible to address with traditional non-experimental designs.

The analyses of Fehr and his collaborators of the role of emotions in collective action exemplify a type of question that would have been difficult to address using non-experimental designs. At least since the publication of Mancur Olson's (1965) *The Logic of Collective Action*, the free-rider problem has been a puzzle: why do individuals join a collective action organization even when they can reap the benefits of the organization without being members of it? For a long time it has been recognized that punishment, or the threat thereof, could be the reason for the absence of free-riding; that is, individuals join such organizations out of fear of otherwise being punished or ostracized by the members. But this is not a satisfactory answer, since punishment in itself is a public good the voluntary contribution to which is just as puzzling as the first-order free-rider problem (see Heckathorn 1989 for a discussion of some of the issues involved). Fehr and Gächter (2002) show that emotions may prove the key to understanding the production and maintenance of collective action. Their experimental results suggest that free-riding causes strong negative emotions and a willingness to punish the free-riders because doing so is intrinsically rewarding.[5] Furthermore, their results suggest that most people expect others to react in this way, and this latent threat of punishment may explain why free-riding is not at all as common as traditional rational-choice accounts would seem to suggest.

External validity is always a concern with experiments, because we can never know for sure whether results obtained in the artificial setting of a laboratory can be generalized to the outside world. This type of research does, however, offer enormous possibilities for testing action theories that are not at hand in traditional non-experimental designs; and the problem with external validity can, at least in part, be overcome by repeating the same experiments in different social settings (as exemplified by Henrich et al. 2004). For these reasons I believe that experimental research is likely to become as important to analytical sociology as it already is to economics.

---

[5] The reasons why most of us react in this way should probably be sought in human evolution, and this reaction pattern is most likely hard-wired into our brains. In de Quervain et al. (2004), Fehr and his collaborators report some evidence in support for such a thesis. PET scans of the brain activities of experimental subjects show, just as the experimental results did, that punishment provides satisfaction to the punisher and activates reward-related regions of the brain.

In this book I have not reported any experimental results. Instead I have focused on quantitative research and advocated the use of so-called ECA models (empirically calibrated agent-based models) for arriving at a closer integration of sociological theory and research. This approach starts with the development of a stylized agent-based model that explicates the basic logic of the mechanism assumed to be operative. If this model generates the type of outcome to be explained, it may be the explanation we are looking for, but the explanation has not yet been empirically verified. Empirical verification examines whether the most important bits and pieces of the causal machinery operate as postulated, and whether the ECA model exhibits generative sufficiency also when possible confounders have been taken into account. If it passes the test, we have an empirically verified mechanism-based explanation of a social outcome, and the ECA model then can serve as a virtual laboratory to examine how social outcomes are likely to be altered by various changes at the level of individual action. I exemplified the approach by studying the role of social interactions in explaining youth unemployment in Stockholm during the 1990s.

Weber once described the core ideas of his 'interpretative' sociology as follows (quoted from Gerth and Mills 1958: 55):

Interpretative sociology considers the individual . . . and his action as the basic unit, its 'atom' . . . In this approach, the individual is also the upper limit and the sole carrier of meaningful conduct . . . In general, for sociology, such concepts as 'state', 'association', 'feudalism', and the like, designate categories of human interaction. Hence it is the task of sociology to reduce these concepts to 'understandable' action, that is, without exception, to the actions of participating individual men.

Similar principles have guided the analyses in this book. Instead of evoking categorical concepts such as 'class', 'culture' and 'institution', I have sought to express all mechanisms in terms that are appropriate at the level of 'understandable action'. One important reason for adopting this strategy is that concepts such as class and culture do not seem to add anything to the explanation of an action once we know the relevant entities and activities at the level of understandable action. That is, once we know the desires, beliefs, opportunities, past actions and social relations of the actors themselves and of their significant others, introducing notions such as class and culture does not give any new insights into why the actors act as they do. Concepts such as these may be useful as descriptive typologies; but, since they do not refer to entities with causal powers or identify any unique explanatory mechanisms at the level of action, they do not add any relevant information to what is already covered in the DBO explanation. For these reasons categorical concepts have been avoided as far as possible in this book.[6]

The usefulness of these specific categorical concepts is further reduced by the lack of agreement on their specific meanings. From the perspective of DBO theory, it would seem reasonable to define 'class' as a collectivity of actors with similar opportunities, 'culture' as a cluster of desires and beliefs shared by a collectivity, and 'institution' as a common way of acting or as a commonly held belief about the appropriate way of acting. Shorthand terms such as these can be extremely useful but only when there is agreement on what they refer to. Anyone who explains an action or other event by reference to 'class' or 'culture', for instance, is not being particularly informative since there are so many different and opposing definitions of the concepts. In order to understand what the person is uttering we must therefore examine in detail how the person defines the concept and what mechanisms he or she assumes to be operative. When this is required, much of the usefulness of the concept as shorthand has been lost. Instead of devoting time and energy to convincing others of the 'true' meaning of contested concepts such as these, it seems wiser to get on with the explanatory work. From an explanatory point of view, the labels we attach to entities and mechanisms are always of minor importance as long as their defining characteristics and operative logics are clearly articulated.

In concluding this book, let me emphasize the importance of not trivializing the idea of a mechanism-based approach to sociology. Over the last few years there has been a surge of interest in mechanism-based explanations, in sociology as well as in political science. Most of this work has been important and valuable in that it has sought to clarify the distinctiveness of the approach and to apply it empirically. But some of this work has been somewhat problematic in that it threatens to strip the approach of all its distinctive features. If a mechanism-based approach simply becomes synonymous with an approach that is attentive to

---

[6] The 'classes' or 'cultures' to which individuals belong can also be used as proxies for opportunities, desires, relations or other action-relevant factors. For instance, if we do not know how opportunities vary between different groups of actors, we can use information about their 'class' as a proxy. This may often be the best we can hope for in empirical research. However, one should not make a virtue out of necessity, but instead recognize that it represents an unfortunate proxy solution that reduces the precision of the analysis.

potential causes or to intervening variables, as some recent contributions seem to suggest, adopting a mechanism-based vocabulary simply contributes to an unnecessary proliferation of theoretical concepts. I have sought to clearly articulate the guiding principles behind the mechanism approach. This approach is abstract, realistic and precise, and it explains specific social phenomena on the basis of explicitly formulated theories of action and interaction.

References

Abbott, A. 1998. 'The Casual Devolution.' *Sociological Methods and Research* 27: 148–81.

1999. *Department and Discipline: Chicago Sociology at One Hundred.* Chicago: University of Chicago Press.

Abell, P. 2003. 'On the Prospects of a Unified Social Science: Economics and Sociology.' *Socio-Economic Review* 1: 1–26.

2004. 'Narrative Explanation: An Alternative to Variable-Centered Explanation?' *Annual Review of Sociology* 30: 287–310.

Åberg, Y. 2000. 'Individual Social Action and Macro Level Dynamics: A Formal Theoretical Model.' *Acta Sociologica* 43: 193–205.

2003. *Social Interactions: Studies of Contextual Effects and Endogenous Processes.* Stockholm: Stockholm University.

Ainslie, G. 2001. *Breakdown of Will.* Cambridge: Cambridge University Press.

Alexander, J. C. 1982. *Theoretical Logic in Sociology.* Vol. I. Berkeley: University of California Press.

Alexander, J. C., B. Giesen, R. Munch and N. J. Smelser (eds.). 1987. *The Micro-Macro Link.* Berkeley: University of California Press.

Allison, P. D. 1982. 'Discrete-Time Methods for the Analysis of Event Histories.' *Sociological Methodology*: 61–98.

Amaral, L. A. N., A. Scala, M. Barthélémy and H. E. Stanley. 2000. 'Classes of Small-World Networks.' *Proceedings of the National Academy of Sciences* 97: 11149–52.

Archer, M. S. 1995. *Realist Social Theory: The Morphogenetic Approach.* Cambridge: Cambridge University Press.

Archer, M. S. et al. (eds.). 1998. *Critical Realism: Essential Readings.* London: Routledge.

Arthur, W. B. 1994. 'Path Dependence, Self-Reinforcement, and Human Learning', in *Increasing Returns and Path Dependency in the Economy*, ed. W. B. Arthur. Ann Arbor: University of Michigan Press, pp. 135–58.

Asch, S. E. 1956. 'Studies of Independence and Conformity: A Minority of One Against a Unanimous Majority.' *Psychological Monographs* 70: 1–70.

Aspers, P. 1997. 'Vetenskaplig Realism.' *Sociologisk Forskning*: 73–80.

Bandura, A. 1977. *Social Learning Theory.* Englewood Cliffs, NJ: Prentice-Hall.

2001. 'Social Cognitive Theory: An Agentic Perspective.' *Annual Review of Psychology* 52: 1–26.

Barabasi, A. L., and R. Albert. 1999. 'Emergence of Scaling in Random Networks.' *Science* 286: 509–12.

Barabasi, A. L., and E. Bonabeau. 2003. 'Scale-Free Networks.' *Scientific American*: 50–9.

Barbera, F. 2004. *Meccanismi Sociali; Elementi di sociologia analitica.* Bologna: Il Mulino.

Baron, J. N. and M. T. Hannan. 1994. 'The Impact of Economics on Contemporary Sociology.' *Journal of Economic Literature* 32: 1111–46.

Bauman, Z. 2001. *The Individualized Society.* Cambridge: Polity Press.

Bearman, P. S., and H. Brückner. 2001. 'Promising the Future: Virginity Pledges and the Transition to First Intercourse.' *American Journal of Sociology* 106: 859–912.

Bearman, P. S., J. Moody and K. Stovel. 2004. 'Chains of Affection: The Structure of Adolescent Romatic and sexual Networks.' *American Journal of Sociology* 110: 44–91.

Beck E. M., P. M. Horan and C. M. Tolbert. 1978. 'Stratification in a Dual Economy: A Sectoral Model of Earnings Determination.' *American Sociological Review* 43: 704–20.

Beck, U., and M. Ritter. 1992. *Risk Society: Towards a New Modernity.* London: Sage.

Bershady, H. J. 1974. *Ideology and Social Knowledge.* Oxford: Basil Blackwell.

Bertrand, M., E. F. P. Luttmer and S. Mullainathan. 2000. 'Network Effects and Welfare Cultures.' *Quarterly Journal of Economics* 115: 1019–55.

Bhaskar, R. 1978. *A Realist Theory of Science.* Hassocks: Harvester Press.

1998. *The Possibility of Naturalism: A Philosophical Critique of the Contemporary Human Sciences.* London: Routledge.

Bikhchandani, S., D. Hirshleifer and I. Welch. 1998. 'Learning from the Behaviour of Others: Conformity, Fads, and Informational Cascades.' *Journal of Economic Perspectives* 12: 151–70.

Black, D. 1976. *The Behavior of Law.* New York: Academic Press.

1979. 'A Strategy for Pure Sociology', in *Theoretical Perspectives in Sociology,* ed. S. G. McNail. New York: St Martin's Press, pp. 149–56.

2000. 'Dreams of Pure Sociology.' *Sociological Theory* 18: 343–67.

Blau, P. M. 1970. 'A Formal Theory of Differentiation in Organizations.' *American Sociological Review* 35: 201–18.

1977. *Inequality and Heterogeneity: A Primitive Theory of Social Structure.* New York: Free Press.

1986. *Exchange and Power in Social Life.* New Brunswick: Transaction Books.

Blau, P. M., and O. D. Duncan. 1967. *The American Occupational Structure.* New York: John Wiley.

Boudon, R. 1974. *Education, Opportunity, and Social Inequality: Changing Prospects in Western Society.* New York: John Wiley.

1976. 'Comment on Hauser's "Review of Education, Opportunity, and Social Inequality".' *American Journal of Sociology* 81: 1175–87.

1979. 'Generating Models as a Research Strategy', in *Qualitative and Quantitative Social Research: Papers in Honor of Paul F. Lazarsfeld,* ed. P. H. Rossi. New York: Free Press, pp. 51–64.

1981. *The Logic of Social Action: An Introduction to Sociological Analysis.* London: Routledge & Kegan Paul.

1982. *The Unintended Consequences of Social Action.* London: Macmillan.

1986. *Theories of Social Change: A Critical Appraisal.* Cambridge: Polity Press.

1991. 'What Middle-Range Theories Are.' *Contemporary Sociology* 20: 519–22.

1994. *The Art of Self-Persuasion: The Social Explanation of False Beliefs.* Cambridge: Polity Press.

1998a. 'Social Mechanisms without Black Boxes', in *Social Mechanisms: An Analytical Approach to Social Theory,* ed. P. Hedström and R. Swedberg. Cambridge: Cambridge University Press, pp. 172–203.

1998b. 'Limitations of Rational Choice Theory.' *American Journal of Sociology* 104: 817–28.

2002. 'Sociology that Really Matters.' *European Sociological Review* 18: 371–8.

2003. 'Beyond Rational Choice Theory.' *Annual Review of Sociology* 29: 1–21.

Bourdieu, P. 1979. *La Distinction: critique sociale du judgement.* Paris: Editions de Minuit.

1990. *The Logic of Practice.* Cambridge: Polity Press.

Braddon-Mitchell, D., and F. Jackson. 1996. *Philosophy of Mind and Cognition.* Oxford: Blackwell.

Braithwaite, R. 1953. *Scientific Explanation: A Study of the Function of Theory, Probability and Law in Science.* Cambridge: Cambridge University Press.

Brante, T. 2001. 'Consequences of Realism for Sociological Theory-Building.' *Journal for the Theory of Social Behaviour* 31: 167–95.

Breen, R., and J. H. Goldthorpe. 1997. 'Explaining Educational Differentials: Towards a Formal Rational Action Theory.' *Rationality and Society* 9: 275–305.

Broome, J. 1993. 'A cause of preference is not an object of preference.' *Social Choice and Welfare* 10: 57–68.

Bruch, E. E., and R. D. Mare. 2004. 'Neighborhood Choice and Neighborhood Change.' *California Center for Population Research. On-Line Working Paper Series* no. 7.

Bunge, M. A. 1967. *Scientific Research.* Berlin and New York: Springer-Verlag.

1996. *Finding Philosophy in Social Science.* New Haven: Yale University Press.

1997. 'Mechanism and Explanation.' *Philosophy of the Social Sciences* 27: 410–65.

2004. 'How does it Work?: The Search for Explanatory Mechanisms.' *Philosophy of the Social Sciences* 34: 182–210.

Burger, T. 1977. 'Talcott Parsons, the Problem of Order in Society, and the Program of an Analytical Sociology.' *American Journal of Sociology* 83: 320–34.

Burt, R. S. 1987. 'Social Contagion and Innovation – Cohesion Versus Structural Equivalence.' *American Journal of Sociology* 92: 1287–335.

Calhoun, C. J. 1996. 'What Passes for Theory in Sociology?' *Sociological Theory* 14: 1–2.

Calhoun, C. J., M. W. Meyer and W. R. Scott (eds.). 1990. *Structures of Power and Constraint: Papers in Honor of Peter M. Blau.* Cambridge: Cambridge University Press.

Camic, C. 1987. 'The Making of a Method: A Historical Reinterpretation of the Early Parsons.' *American Journal of Sociology* 52: 421–39.

Carley, K. 1991. 'A Theory of Group Stability.' *American Sociological Review* 56: 331–54.

Carlsson, G. 1968. 'Change, Growth, and Irreversibility.' *American Journal of Sociology* 73: 706–14.

Castells, M. 2000. *The Rise of the Network Society*. Malden, MA: Blackwell.

Charon, J. M. 2001. *Symbolic Interactionism: An Introduction, an Interpretation, an Integration*. Englewood Cliffs, NJ: Prentice-Hall.

Chase, I. D. 1991. 'Vacancy Chains.' *Annual Review of Sociology* 17: 133–54.

Cherkaoui, M. 2001. 'Macrosociology-microsociology', in *International Encyclopedia of the Social and Behavioral Sciences*. Amsterdam: Elsevier Science, pp. 9117–22.

Churchland, P. 1981. 'Eliminative Materialism and the Propositional Attitudes.' *Journal of Philosophy* 78: 67–90.

Chwe, M. S-Y. 2001. *Rational Ritual: Culture, Coordination, and Common Knowledge*. Princeton: Princeton University Press.

Clark, A. E. 2003. 'Unemployment as a Social Norm.' *Journal of Labor Economics* 21: 323–51.

Clark, A. E., and A. J. Oswald. 1994. 'Unhappiness and Unemployment.' *Economic Journal* 104: 648–59.

Cohen, L. E., and M. Felson. 1979. 'Social Change and Crime Rate Trends: A Routine Activity Approach.' *American Sociological Review* 44: 588–608.

Coleman, J. S. 1964. *Introduction to Mathematical Sociology*. New York: Free Press of Glencoe.

1973. *The Mathematics of Collective Action*. Chicago: Aldine.

1981. *Longitudinal Data Analysis*. New York: Basic Books.

1986a. *Individual Interests and Collective Action: Selected Essays*. Cambridge: Cambridge University Press.

1986b. 'Social Theory, Social Research, and a Theory of Action.' *American Journal of Sociology* 91: 1309–35.

1990. *Foundations of Social Theory*. Cambridge, MA: Harvard University Press.

Coleman, J. S., E. Katz and H. Menzel. 1957. 'The Diffusion of an Innovation Among Physicians.' *Sociometry* 20: 253–70.

1966. *Medical Innovation: A Diffusion Study*. Indianapolis: Bobbs-Merrill.

Coleman, J. S., and L. Hao. 1989. 'Linear Systems Analysis: Macrolevel Analysis with Microlevel Data.' *Sociological Methodology* 19: 395–422.

Collier, A. 1994. *Critical Realism: An Introduction to Roy Bhaskar's Philosophy*. London: Verso.

Cox, D. R. 1990. 'Role of Models in Statistical Analysis.' *Statistical Science* 5: 169–74.

1992. 'Causality – Some Statistical Aspects.' *Journal of the Royal Statistical Society Series A – Statistics in Society* 155: 291–301.

Craver, C. F. 2001. 'Role Functions, Mechanisms, and Hierarchy.' *Philosophy of Science* 68: 53–74.

Dahrendorf, R. 1968. *Essays in the Theory of Society*. Stanford, CA: Stanford University Press.

David, P. 1985. 'Clio and the Economics of QWERTY.' *American Economic Review* 75: 332–7.

Davidson, D. 1980. *Essays on Actions and Events*. Oxford: Clarendon Press.

De Quervain, D., U. Fischbacher, V. Treyer, M. Schellhammer, U. Schnyder, A. Buck and E. Fehr. 2004. 'The Neural Basis of Altruistic Punishment.' *Science* 305: 1254–8.

Dennett, D. C. 1981. *Brainstorms: Philosophical Essays on Mind and Psychology*. Brighton: Harvester Press.

Deutsch, M., and H. B. Gerard. 1955. 'A Study of Normative and Informational Social Influences upon Individual Judgment.' *Journal of Abnormal and Social Psychology* 51: 629–63.

Diekmann, A. 1989. 'Diffusion and Survival Models for the Process of Entry into Marriage.' *Journal of Mathematical Sociology* 14: 31–44.

Duncan, O. D. 1975. *Introduction to Structural Equation Models*. New York: Academic Press.

1984. *Notes on Social Measurement: Historical and Critical*. New York: Russell Sage Foundation.

Durkheim, E. 1895 [1978]. *Sociologins Metodregler (The Rules of Sociological Method)*. Göteborg: Bokförlaget Korpen.

1897 [1951]. *Suicide: A Study in Sociology*. New York: Free Press.

Edling, C. 2000. 'Rational Choice Theory and Quantitative Analysis – A Comment on Goldthorpe's Sociological Alliance.' *European Sociological Review* 16: 1–8.

2002. 'Mathematics in Sociology.' *Annual Review of Sociology* 28: 197–202.

Elster, J. 1978. *Logic and Society: Contradictions and Possible Worlds*. Chichester: Wiley.

1979. *Ulysses and the Sirens: Studies in Rationality and Irrationality*. Cambridge: Cambridge University Press.

1983a. *Explaining Technical Change: A Case Study in the Philosophy of Science*. Cambridge: Cambridge University Press.

1983b. *Sour Grapes: Studies in the Subversion of Rationality*. Cambridge: Cambridge University Press.

1985. *Making Sense of Marx*. Cambridge: Cambridge University Press.

(ed.). 1986. *Rational Choice*. New York: New York University Press.

1989a. *The Cement of Society: A Study of Social Order*. Cambridge: Cambridge University Press.

1989b. *Nuts and Bolts for the Social Sciences*. Cambridge: Cambridge University Press.

1989c. 'Social Norms and Economic Theory.' *Journal of Economic Perspectives* 3: 99–117.

1991. 'Rationality and Social Norms.' *Archives Europeennes de Sociologie* 32: 109–29.

1993. *Political Psychology*. Cambridge: Cambridge University Press.

1994. 'Rationality, Emotions, and Social Norms.' *Synthese* 98: 21–49.

1996. 'Rationality and the Emotions.' *Economic Journal* 106: 1386–97.

1998a. 'Emotions and Economic Theory.' *Journal of Economic Literature* 36: 47–74.

1998b. 'A Plea for Mechanisms', in *Social Mechanisms: An Analytical Approach to Social Theory*, ed. P. Hedström and R. Swedberg. Cambridge: Cambridge University Press, pp. 45–73.

1999. *Alchemies of the Mind: Rationality and the Emotions*. Cambridge: Cambridge University Press.

2000. 'Rational Choice History: A Case of Excessive Ambition.' *American Political Science Review* 94: 685–95.

Epstein, J. M., and R. Axtell. 1996. *Growing Artificial Societies: Social Science from the Bottom Up*. Washington, DC: Brookings Institution Press.

Esping-Andersen, G. 1990. *The Three Worlds of Welfare Capitalism*. Princeton: Princeton University Press.

Falk, A., and U. Fischbacher. 2002. 'Crime in the Lab: Detecting Social Interaction.' *European Economic Review* 46: 858–69.

Fehr, E., and U. Fischbacher. 2004. 'Social Norms and Human Cooperation.' *Trends in Cognitive Science* 8: 185–90.

Fehr, E., and S. Gächter. 2002. 'Altruistic Punishment in Humans.' *Nature* 415: 137–40.

Fershtman, C., and U. Gneezy. 2001. 'Discrimination in a Segmented Society: An Experimental Approach.' *Quarterly Journal of Economics* 116: 351–77.

Festinger, L. 1957. *A Theory of Cognitive Dissonance*. Stanford: Stanford University Press.

Fiske, S. T., and S. E. Taylor. 1991. *Social Cognition*. New York: McGraw-Hill.

Fodor, J. A. 1988. *Psychosemantics: The Problem of Meaning in the Philosophy of Mind*. Cambridge, MA: MIT Press.

1994. 'Fodor, Jerry A.' in. *A Companion to the Philosophy of Mind*, ed. S. Guttenplan. Oxford: Blackwell, pp. 292–300.

Fong, E. 1997. 'A Systemic Approach to Racial Residential Patterns.' *Social Science Research* 26: 465–86.

Freedman, D. 1987. 'As others see us: A Case Study in Path Analysis.' *Journal of Educational Statistics* 12: 101–28.

1991. 'Statistical Models and Shoe Leather.' *Sociological Methodology*: 291–313.

1999. 'From Association to Causation: Some Remarks on the History of Statistics.' *Statistical Science* 14: 243–58.

Friedman, M. 1953. 'The Methodology of Positive Economics', in *Essays in Positive Economics*, ed. Milton Friedman. Chicago: University of Chicago Press, pp. 210–244.

Gambetta, D. 1998. 'Concatenations of Mechanisms', in *Social Mechanisms: An Analytical Approach to Social Theory*, ed. P. Hedström and R. Swedberg. Cambridge: Cambridge University Press, pp. 102–24.

Gerth, H. H., and C. W. Mills. 1958. *From Max Weber: Essays in Sociology*. Oxford: Oxford University Press.

Gibson, Q. 1983. 'Tendencies.' *Philosophy of Science* 50: 296–308.

Gilbert, N., and K. G. Troitzsch. 1999. *Simulation for the Social Scientist*. Maidenhead: Open University Press.

Glaeser, E. L., B. Sacerdote and J. A. Sheinkman. 1996. 'Crime and Social Interactions.' *Quarterly Journal of Economics*: 507–47.

Glennan, S. S. 1996. 'Mechanisms and the Nature of Causation.' *Erkenntnis* 44: 49–71.

Goldstone, J. A. 1998. 'Initial Conditions, General Laws, Path Dependence, and Explanation in Historical Sociology.' *American Journal of Sociology* 104: 829–45.

Goldthorpe, J. H. 1996. 'The Quantitative Analysis of Large-Scale Data-Sets and Rational Action Theory: For a Sociological Alliance.' *European Sociological Review* 12: 109–26.

2000. *On Sociology: Numbers, Narratives, and the Integration of Research and Theory.* Oxford: Oxford University Press.

2004. 'Sociology as Social Science and Cameral Sociology.' *European Sociological Review* 20: 97–105.

Goldthorpe, J. H., C. Llewellyn and C. Payne. 1980. *Social Mobility and Class Structure in Modern Britain.* Oxford: Clarendon Press.

Granovetter, M. S. 1973. 'The Strength of Weak Ties.' *American Journal of Sociology* 76: 1360–80.

1974. *Getting a Job: A Study of Contacts and Careers.* Cambridge, MA: Harvard University Press.

1978. 'Threshold Models of Collective Behavior.' *American Journal of Sociology* 83: 1420–43.

1985. 'Economic Action and Social Structure: The Problem of Embeddedness.' *American Journal of Sociology* 91: 481–510.

Green, D. P., and I. Shapiro. 1994. *Pathologies of Rational Choice Theory: A Critique of Applications in Political Science.* New Haven: Yale University Press.

Habermas, J. 1987. *The Theory of Communicative Action.* Boston: Beacon Press.

Hägerstrand, T. 1965. 'A Monte Carlo Approach to Diffusion.' *Archives Europeennes de Sociologie* 6: 43–57.

1967. *Innovation Diffusion as a Spatial Process.* Chicago: University of Chicago Press.

Hahn, R. A. 1973. 'Understanding Beliefs: An Essay on The Methodology of the Statement and Analysis of Belief Systems.' *Current Anthropology* 14: 207–29.

Hamblin, R. L., R. B. Jacobsen and J. L. L. Miller. 1973. *A Mathematical Theory of Social Change.* New York, Wiley.

Hannan, M. T. and J. Freeman. 1989. *Organizational Ecology.* Cambridge, MA: Harvard University Press.

Hannan, M. T. and G. R. Carroll. 1992. *Dynamics of Organizational Populations.* Oxford: Oxford University Press.

Harding, D. J. 2003. 'Counterfactual Models of Neighborhood Effects: The Effect of Neighborhood Poverty on Dropping Out and Teenage Pregnancy.' *American Journal of Sociology* 109: 676–719.

Harmon-Jones, E., and J. Mills (eds.). 1999. *Cognitive Dissonance: Progress on a Pivotal Theory in Social Psychology.* Washington DC: American Psychological Association.

Harré, R. 1985. *The Philosophies of Science: An Introductory Survey.* Oxford: Oxford University Press.

Hauser, R. M. 1976. 'Review Essay: On Boudon's Model of Social Mobility.' *American Journal of Sociology* 81: 911–28.

Hechter, M. 1987. *Principles of Group Solidarity*. Berkeley: University of California Press.

Heckathorn, D. D. 1989. 'Collective Action and the Second-Order Free-Rider Problem.' *Rationality and Society* 1: 78–100.

1996. 'The Dynamics and Dilemmas of Collective Action.' *American Sociological Review* 61: 250–77.

Hedström, P. 1992. 'Organizational Vacancy Chains and the Attainment Process.' *Journal of Mathematical Sociology* 17: 63–76.

1994. 'Contagious Collectivities – On the Spatial Diffusion of Swedish Trade-Unions, 1890–1940.' *American Journal of Sociology* 99: 1157–79.

1998. 'Rational Imitation', in *Social Mechanisms: An Analytical Approach to Social Theory*, ed. P. Hedström and R. Swedberg. Cambridge: Cambridge University Press, pp. 306–27.

Hedström, P., R. Sandell and C. Stern. 2000. 'Mesolevel Networks and the Diffusion of Social Movements: The Case of the Swedish Social Democratic Party.' *American Journal of Sociology* 106: 145–72.

Hedström, P., and R. Swedberg. 1996. 'Social Mechanisms.' *Acta Sociologica* 39: 281–308.

(eds.). 1998a. *Social Mechanisms: An Analytical Approach to Social Theory*. Cambridge: Cambridge University Press.

1998b. 'Social Mechanisms: An Introductory Essay', in *Social Mechanisms: An Analytical Approach to Social Theory*, ed. P. Hedström and R. Swedberg. Cambridge: Cambridge University Press, pp. 1–31.

Hempel, C. G. 1965. *Aspects of Scientific Explanation*. New York: Free Press.

Henrich, J., R. Boyd, S. Bowles, C. Camerer, E. Fehr and H. Gintis (eds.). 2004. *Foundations of Human Sociality:Economic Experiments and Ethnographic Evidence from Fifteen Small-Scale Societies*. Oxford: Oxford University Press.

Hernes, G. 1972. 'The Process of Entry into First Marriage.' *American Sociological Review* 37: 173–82.

1976. 'Structural Change in Social Processes.' *American Journal of Sociology* 82: 513–47.

1998. 'Real Virtuality', in *Social Mechanisms: An Analytical Approach to Social Theory*, ed. P. Hedström and R. Swedberg. Cambridge: Cambridge University Press, pp. 74–101.

Hesse, H. 1970. *Magister Ludi (The Glass Bead Game)*. New York: Bantam Books.

Holland, J. H. 1998. *Emergence: From Chaos to Order*. Cambridge, MA: Perseus Books.

Holland, P. 1986. 'Statistics and Causal Inference.' *Journal of the American Statistical Association* 81: 945–60.

Holmlund, B. 1998. 'Unemployment Insurance in Theory and Practice.' *Scandinavian Journal of Economics* 100: 113–41.

Ibsen, H. 1981. *Four Major Plays*. Oxford: Oxford University Press.

Jackson, F. 1996. 'Mental Causation.' *Mind* 105: 377–413.

Jackson, F., and P. Pettit. 1992a. 'In Defense of Explanatory Ecumenism.' *Economics and Philosophy* 8: 1–21.

1992b. 'Structural Explanation in Social Theory', in *Reduction, Explanation, and Realism*, ed. K. Lennon. Oxford: Clarendon Press, pp. 97–131.

Jasso, G. 1988. 'Principles of Theoretical Analysis.' *Sociological Theory* 6: 1–20.

Kahan, D. M. 1997. 'Social Influence, Social Meaning, and Deterrence.' *Virginia Law Review* 83: 349–95.

Kalleberg, A. L., and I. E. Berg. 1987. *Work and Industry: Structures, Markets, and Processes.* New York: Plenum Press.

Kanazawa, S. 1998. 'In Defense of Unrealistic Assumptions.' *Sociological Theory* 16: 193–204.

Karklins, R., and R. Petersen. 1993. 'Decision Calculus of Protesters and Regimes: Eastern Europe 1989.' *Journal of Politics* 55: 588–614.

Karlsson, G. 1958. *Social Mechanisms: Studies in Sociological Theory.* Stockholm: Almqvist & Wiksell.

Kim, H., and P. S. Bearman. 1997. 'The Structure and Dynamics of Movement Participation.' *American Sociological Review* 62: 70–93.

Kim, J. 1984. 'Supervenience and Supervenient Causation.' *Southern Journal of Philosophy* 22: 45–56.

Kincaid, H. 1996. *Philosophical Foundations of the Social Sciences: Analyzing Controversies in Social Research.* Cambridge: Cambridge University Press.

King, G., R. Keohane and S. Verba. 1994. *Designing Social Inquiry: Scientific Inference in Qualitative Reseach.* Princeton: Princeton University Press.

Kiser, E., and M. Hechter. 1991. 'The Role of General Theory in Comparative-Historical Sociology.' *American Journal of Sociology* 97: 1–30.

Kosfeld, M. 2004. 'Economic Networks in the Laboratory.' *Review of Network Economics* 3: 20–41.

Kuran, T. 1995. *Private Truths, Public Lies: The Social Consequences of Preference Falsification.* Cambridge, MA: Harvard University Press.

Latane, B. 1981. 'Psychology of Social Impact.' *American Psychologist* 36: 343–56.

Lazarsfeld, P. 1955. 'Interpretation of Statistical Relations as a Research Operation', in *The Language of Social Research*, ed. P. Lazarsfeld and M. Rosenberg, New York: Free Press, pp. 115–25.

Leibenstein, H. 1950. 'Bandwagon, Snob, and Veblen Effects in the Theory of Consumers' Demand.' *Quarterly Journal of Economics* 64: 183–207.

Lewis, D. K. 1969. *Convention: A Philosophical Study.* Cambridge, MA: Harvard University Press.

1973. *Counterfactuals.* Cambridge, MA: Harvard University Press.

1983. *Philosophical Papers.* Oxford: Oxford University Press.

1994. 'Reduction of Mind', in *A Companion to the Philosophy of Mind.* Oxford: Blackwell, pp. 413–31.

Liljeros, F., and C. Edling. 2003. 'Spatial Diffusion of Social Organizing.' *Advances in Strategic Management* 20: 267–90.

Liljeros, F., C. R. Edling, L. A. N. Amaral, H. E. Stanley and Y. Åberg. 2001. 'The Web of Human Sexual Contacts.' *Nature* 411: 907–8.

Lindenberg, S. 1989. 'Social Production Functions, Deficits, and Social Revolutions: Pre-Revolutionary France and Russia.' *Rationality and Society* 1: 51–77.

Little, D. 1991. *Varieties of Social Explanation: An Introduction to the Philosophy of Social Science.* Boulder, Co: Westview Press.

Loewenstein, G., and J. Elster (eds.). 1992. *Choice Over Time.* New York: Russell Sage Foundation.

Lombard, L. B. 1990. 'Causes, Enablers, and the Counterfactual Analysis.' *Philosophical Studies* 59: 195–211.

Machamer, P., L. Darden and C. F. Craver. 2000. 'Thinking About Mechanisms.' *Philosophy of Science* 67: 1–25.

Macy, M. W. 1991. 'Chains of Co-operation: Threshold Effects in Collective Action.' *American Sociological Review* 56: 730–47.

Macy, M. W., and R. Willer. 2002. 'From Factors to Actors: Computational Sociology and Agent-Based Modeling.' *Annual Review of Sociology* 28: 143–66.

Mahoney, J. 2001. 'Beyond Correlational Analysis: Recent Innovations in Theory and Method.' *Sociological Forum* 16: 575–93.

Manski, C. F. 2000. 'Economic Analysis of Social Interactions.' *Journal of Economic Perspectives* 14: 115–36.

Mark, N. 1998. 'Beyond Individual Differences: Social Differentiation from First Principles.' *American Sociological Review* 63: 309–30.

Marsden, P .V. 1990. 'Network Data and Measurement.' *Annual Review of Sociology* 16, pp. 435–63.

Marsden, P. V., and N. E. Freidkin. 1994. 'Network Studies of Social Influence', in *Advances in Social Network Analysis: Research in the Social and Behavioral Sciences*, ed. S. Wasserman and J. Galaskiewicz. Thousand Oaks, CA: Sage, pp. 3–25.

Marx, K. 1973. *Political Writings*. Vol. II, *Surveys from Exile*. Harmondsworth: Penguin.

Mayhew, B. H. 1980. 'Structuralism Versus Individualism: Part 1, Shadowboxing in the Dark.' *Social Forces* 59: 335–75.

1981. 'Structuralism Versus Individualism: Part II, Ideological and Other Obfuscations.' *Social Forces* 59: 627–48.

Mayntz, R. 2004. 'Mechanisms in the Analysis of Social Macro-Phenomena.' *Philosophy of the Social Sciences* 34: 237–59.

McAdam, D., S. Tarrow and C. Tilly. 2001. *Dynamics of Contention*. Cambridge: Cambridge University Press.

Merton, R. K. 1936. 'The Unanticipated Consequences of Purposive Social Action.' *American Sociological Review* 1: 894–904.

1967. 'On Sociological Theories of the Middle Range', in *On Theoretical Sociology*, ed. Robert K. Merton. New York: Free Press, pp. 39–72.

1968a. 'The Matthew Effect in Science.' *Science* 159: 56–63.

1968b. 'The Self-Fulfilling Prophecy', in *Social Theory and Social Structure*, ed. Robert K. Merton. New York: Free Press, pp. 475–90.

1968c. *Social Theory and Social Structure*. New York: Free Press.

Mill, J. S. 1844. 'On the Definition of Political Economy; and on the Method of Investigation Proper to It', in *Essays on Some Unsettled Questions of Political Economy*, ed. J. S. Mill. London: John W. Parker.

1874. *A System of Logic, Ratiocinative and Inductive, Being a Connected View of the Principles of Evidence and the Methods of Scientific Investigation*. New York: Harper & Bros.

Miller, R. W. 1987. *Fact and Method: Explanation, Confirmation and Reality in the Natural and the Social Sciences*. Princeton: Princeton University Press.

Mood, C. 2004. 'Social Influence Effects on Social Assistance Recipiency.' *Acta Sociologica* 47: 235–51.

Morgan, S. L. 2002. 'Modeling Preparatory Commitment and Non-Repeatable Decisions.' *Rationality and Society* 14: 387–430.

Myrdal, G. 1944. *An American Dilemma: The Negro Problem and Modern Democracy*. New York: Harper & Bros.

Nagel, E. 1961. *The Structure of Science: Problems in the Logic of Scientific Explanation*. London: Routledge & Kegan Paul.

Newman, M. E. J. 2003. 'The Structure and Function of Complex Networks.' *SIAM Review* 45: 167–256.

O'Connor, T., and H. Y. Wong. 2002. 'Emergent Properties', in *The Stanford Encyclopedia of Philosophy*. Winter 2002 edition, ed. Edward N. Zalta. http://www.plato.stanford.edu.

Olson, M. 1965. *The Logic of Collective Action: Public Goods and the Theory of Groups*. Cambridge, MA: Harvard University Press.

Opp, K. D. 2004. '"What is always becoming what ought to be." How Political Action Generates a Participation Norm.' *European Sociological Review* 20: 13–29.

Parsons, T. 1937. *The Structure of Social Action*. New York: Free Press.

Pawson, R. 2000. 'Middle-Range Realism.' *Archives Europeennes de Sociologie* 41: 283–325.

Pearce, J. R. 1994. *Analytical Sociology: Its Logical Foundations and Relevance to Theory and Empirical Research*. Lanham, MD: University Press of America.

Phillips, D. C. 1976. *Holistic Thought in Social Science*. Stanford: Stanford University Press.

Pierson, P. 2000. 'Increasing Returns, Path Dependence, and the Study of Politics.' *American Political Science Review* 94: 251–67.

Popper, K. R. 1961. *The Poverty of Historicism*. London: Routledge & Kegan Paul.

1994. 'Models, Instruments, and Truth: The Status of the Rationality Principle in the Social Sciences', in *The Myth of the Framework: In Defence of Science and Rationality*, ed. K. R. Popper. London: Routledge, pp. 154–84.

Rainwater, L. 1974. *What Money Buys: Inequality and the Social Meanings of Income*. New York: Basic Books.

Raub, W., and J. Weesie. 1990. 'Reputation and Efficiency in Social Interactions: An Example of Network Effects.' *American Journal of Sociology* 96: 626–54.

Ritzer, G. 1991. *Metatheorizing in Sociology*. Lexington, KT: Lexington Books.

Ritzer, G., and B. Smart (eds.). 2001. *Handbook of Social Theory*. London: Sage.

Rosenbaum, P. R. 1984. 'From Association to Causation in Observational Studies: The Role of Tests of Strongly Ignorable Treatment Assignment.' *Journal of the American Statistical Association* 79: 41–5.

Ross, L., and R. E. Nisbett. 1991. *The Person and the Situation: Perspectives of Socialy Psychology*. New York: McGraw-Hill.

Rubin, D. B. 1974. 'Estimating Causal Effects of Treatments in Randomized and Nonradomized Studies.' *Journal of Educational Psychology* 66: 688–701.

Rydgren, J. 2004. 'The Logic Of Xenophobia.' *Rationality and Society* 16: 123–48.

Salmon, W. C. 1971. *Statistical Explanation and Statistical Relevance*. Pittsburgh: University of Pittsburgh Press.

1984. *Scientific Explanation and the Causal Structure of the World*. Princeton: Princeton University Press.

Sandell, R., and C. Stern. 1998. 'Group Size and the Logic of Collective Action: A Network Analysis of a Swedish Temperance Movement 1896–1937.' *Rationality and Society* 10: 327–45.

Sawyer, R. K. 2001. 'Emergence in Sociology: Contemporary Philosophy of Mind and Some Implications for Sociological Theory.' *American Journal of Sociology* 107: 551–85.

2004. 'The Mechanisms of Emergence.' *Philosophy of the Social Sciences* 34: 260–82.

Schelling, T. C. 1960. *The Strategy of Conflict*. Cambridge, MA: Harvard University Press.

1971. 'Dynamic Models of Segregation.' *Journal of Mathematical Sociology* 1: 143–86.

1978. *Micromotives and Macrobehavior*. New York: W. W. Norton.

1984a. *Choice and Consequence: Perspectives of an Errant Economist*. Cambridge, MA: Harvard University Press.

1984b. 'The Mind as a Consuming Organ', in *Choice and Consequence: Perspectives of an Errant Economist*, ed. T. C. Schelling. Cambridge, MA: Harvard University Press, pp. 328–48.

1998. 'Social Mechanisms and Social Dynamics', in *Social Mechanisms: An Analytical Approach to Social Theory*, ed. P. Hedström and R. Swedberg. Cambridge: Cambridge University Press, pp. 32–44.

Schweitzer, A. O., and R. E. Smith. 1974. 'The Persistence of the Discouraged Worker Effect.' *Industrial and Labor Relations Review* 27: 249–60.

Sen, A. 1980. 'Description as Choice.' *Oxford Economic Papers* 32: 353–69.

Sherif, M., and C. W. Sherif. 1964. *Reference Groups. Explorations into Conformity and Deviance of Adolescents*. New York: Harper & Row.

Sica, A. (ed.). 1998. *What is Social Theory?: The Philosophical Debates*. Malden, MA: Blackwell.

Skocpol, T. 1979. *States and Social Revolutions: A Comparative Analysis of France, Russia and China*. Cambridge: Cambridge University Press.

1984. 'Emerging Agendas and Recurrent Strategies in Historical Sociology', in *Vision and Method in Historical Sociology*. Cambridge: Cambridge University Press, pp. 356–91.

Skog, O. J. 1988. 'Testing Causal Hypotheses about Correlated Trends: Pitfalls and Remedies.' *Contemporary Drug Problems* 15: 565–607.

Sobel, M. E. 1998. 'Causal Inference in Statistical Models of the Process of Socioeconomic Achievement: A Case Study.' *Sociological Methods and Research* 27: 318–48.

Sørensen, A. B. 1977. 'The Structure of Inequality and the Process of Attainment.' *American Sociological Review* 42: 965–78.

1998. 'Theoretical Mechanisms and the Empirical Study of Social Processes', in *Social Mechanisms: An Analytical Approach to Social Theory*, ed. P. Hedström and R. Swedberg. Cambridge: Cambridge University Press, pp. 238–66.

Spilerman, S. 1970. 'The Causes of Racial Disturbances: A Comparison of Alternative Explanations.' *American Sociological Review* 35: 627–49.

Stark, R., and L. R. Iannaccone. 1994. 'A Supply-Side Reinterpretation of the "Secularization" of Europe.' *Journal for the Scientific Study of Religion* 33: 230–52.

Stewman, S., and S. L. Konda. 1983. 'Careers and Organizational Labour Markets.' *American Journal of Sociology* 88: 637–85.

Stich, S., and I.Ravenscroft. 1994. 'What is Folk Psychology?' *Cognition* 50: 447–68.

Stinchcombe, A. L. 1968. *Constructing Social Theories*. New York: Harcourt Brace & World.

    1991. 'The Conditions of Fruitfulness of Theorizing About Mechanisms in Social-Science.' *Philosophy of the Social Sciences* 21: 367–88.

Stouffer, S. A. et al. 1949. *The American Soldier*. Princeton: Princeton University Press.

Strang, D., and S. A. Soule. 1998. 'Diffusion in Organizations and Social Movements: From Hybrid Corn to Poison Pills.' *Annual Review of Sociology* 24: 265–90.

Suppes, P. 1970. *A Probabilistic Theory of Causality*. Amsterdam: North Holland.

Swedberg, R. 1998. *Max Weber and the Idea of Economic Sociology*. Princeton: Princeton University Press.

Tarrow, S. 1998. *Power in Movement*. Cambridge: Cambridge University Press.

Therborn, G. 1995. *European Modernity and Beyond*. London: Sage.

Thomas, W. I., and D. S. Thomas. 1928. *The Child in America: Behavior Problems and Programs*. New York: Alfred Knopf.

Tocqueville, A. de. 1856[1998]. *The Old Regime and the Revolution*. New York: Anchor Books.

Tukey, J. M. 1962. 'The Future of Data Analysis.' *Annual of Mathematical Statistics* 33: 1–67.

Turner, B. S. (ed.). 1996. *The Blackwell Companion to Social Theory*. Oxford: Blackwell.

Turner, J. H. 1987a. 'Analytical Theorizing', in *Social Theory Today*, ed. J. H. Turner. Stanford: Stanford University Press, pp. 156–94.

    1987b. 'Toward a Sociological Theory of Motivation.' *American Sociological Review* 52: 15–27.

Turner, S. 1983. 'Weber on Action.' *American Sociological Review* 48: 506–19.

Udehn, L. 2001. *Methodological Individualism: Background, History and Meaning*. London: Routledge.

Van den Bulte, C., and G. L. Lilien. 2001. 'Medical Innovation Revisited: Social Contagion Versus Marketing.' *American Journal of Sociology* 106: 1409–35.

Wasserman, S., and K. Faust. 1994. *Social Network Analysis: Methods and Applications*. Cambridge: Cambridge University Press.

Watts, D. J. 1999a. 'Networks, Dynamics, and the Small-World Phenomenon.' *American Journal of Sociology* 105: 493–527.

    1999b. *Small Worlds: The Dynamics of Networks Between Order and Randomness*. Princeton: Princeton University Press.

    2003. 'The "New" Science of Networks.' *Annual Review of Sociology* 30: 243–70.

Watts, D . J., and S. H. Strogatz. 1998. 'Collective Dynamics of "Small World" Networks.' *Nature* 393: 440–2.

Weber, M. 1949. *Max Weber on the Methodology of the Social Sciences*. Glencoe, IL: Free Press.

1978. *Economy and Society*. Berkeley: University of California Press.

Weber, Max. 1904 [2002]. *The Protestant Ethic and the Spirit of Capitalism*. Oxford: Basil Blackwell.

White, H. C. 1965. 'Notes on the Constituents of Social Structure.' Unpublished manuscript, Department of Sociology, Harvard University.

1970. *Chains of Oppurtunity: System Models of Mobility in Organizations*. Cambridge, MA: Harvard University Press.

White, H., S. A. Boorman and R. L. Breiger. 1976. 'Social Structure from Multiple Networks. Blockmodels of Roels and Positions.' *American Journal of Sociology* 81: 730–80.

Whitehead, A. N. 1930. *Science and the Modern World: Lowell Lectures 1925*. Cambridge: Cambridge University Press.

Williams, B. 1973. *Problems of Self*. Cambridge: Cambridge University Press.

Wilson, W. J. 1987. *The Truly Disadvantaged: The Inner City, the Underclass, and Public Policy*. Chicago: University of Chicago Press.

Winship, C., and S. L. Morgan. 1999. 'The Estimation of Causal Effects from Observational Data.' *Annual Review of Sociology* 25: 659–706.

Von Wright, G. H. 1971. *Explanation and Understanding*. Ithaca, NY: Cornell University Press.

1989. 'A Reply to my Critics', in *The Philosophy of George Henrik von Wright*, ed. L. E. Hahn. La Salle, IL: Open Court.

Wright, E. O. 1979. *Class Structure and Income Determination*. New York: Academic Press.

1997. *Class Counts*. Cambridge: Cambridge University Press.

Wright, E. O., and L. Perrone. 1977. 'Marxist Class Categories and Income Inequality.' *American Sociological Review* 42: 32–55.

Wrong, D. H. 1961. 'The Over Socialized Conception of Man.' *American Sociological Review* 26: 183–93.

Young, H. P. 1996. 'The Economics of Convention.' *Journal of Economic Perspectives* 10: 105–22.

Index

Numbers in bold refer to figures or tables.

Abbott, A. 1, 33
Abell, P. 19, 45
Åberg, Yvonne 10, 47, **90**, 123
  model 90, 91, 92, 95
abstraction 2–3
accuracy, predictive 107–8
action 5–6, 26–27
  based explanation 28–29
  based theories 114–17, 116
  related mechanisms **59**
  collective **90**, 96–97, 152
  concept of 38
  patterns **133**
  'understandable' 153
  see also under belief
action and interaction 9, 34–66
  concatenations of mechanisms 56–58
  DBO theory 38–42
  instrumentalism of rational-choice
      theorizing 60–66
  social interaction 42–45
    belief-mediated 47–51
    desire-mediated 52–54
    opportunity-mediated 55–56
    related behavioural patterns 45–47
  types of mechanisms 58–60
  see also social interaction and social change
activities 25–27, 28
actors 26–27
  actor-based models 117–18
  ideal-typical actors 38
adaptive desire formation **59**
adaptive preferences 40
agent-based
  analyses 76–77, 93, 109, 111, 112, **134**
  computational modelling 76
  models 87–88, 100, 112, 116, 117–19, 149
    of unemployment 131–6, 136–43
  simulation 78
Ainslie, G. 42

Albert, R. 150
Alexander, J. C. 37, 69
Allison, P. D. 127
alternative mechanism definitions **25**
Amaral, L. A. N. 150
analytical tradition 10
  action 5–6
  clarity and precision 3–4
  dissection and abstraction 2–3
  explanation 1–2
  history of 145–6
  realism and 3, 62
Archer, M. S. 13, 69, 71, 72
  as critical realist 24, 70, 71
Arthur, W. B. 99
Asch, S. E. 54
Aspers, P. 71
assumptions, false 63–64
Axtell, R. 76, 117, 143, 151

Bandura, A. 38, 41
Barabasi, A. L. 150
Barbera, F. 6
Baron, J. N. 60
Bauman, Z. 12
Bearman, P. S. 97, 123
Beck, E. M. 106
Beck, U. 12
behaviour 38
  individualistic 105
  patterns 45–47
belief 38, 120
  based explanation 40
  based interaction 119, 122
  mediated interactions **50**
  mediated mechanisms 108
  mediated social interaction 47–52
  desires and actions (BDA) 76–87, 78–83,
      79, 81, 85, 110
    typical 67

desires and 18
see also DBO (desires, beliefs and
    opportunities) theory
Berg, I. E. 106
Bershady, H. J. 6
Bertrand, M. 123
Bhaskar, R. 24, 70, 71
    causal power and 72
Bikhchandani, S. 49
black boxes 19, 26, 27, 68, 111
Black, Donald 19, 27
    'pure sociology' and 18, 19, 74
Blau, Peter 19, 27, **103**
    law-like propositions and 18, 19
    organizational differentiation and 17,
        18, 32
    status-attainment process and 102, 105
Bonabeau, E. 150
Boorman, S. A. 95
Boudon, Raymond 1, 8, 23, 26, 58, 145
    analytical tradition and 6, 7
    Hauser and 112, 113
    micro–macro link and 7
    simulation models and 112
Bourdieu, Pierre 4, 53
Braddon-Mitchell, D. 41
Braithwaite, R. 15, 18
Brante, T. 29, 71, 72
Breen, R. 60
Breiger, R. L. 95
British Panel Household Study 121
Broome, J. 53
Bruch, E. E. 132
Brückner, H. 123
BSA (British Sociological Association) 12
Bunge, M. A. 17, 24
Burger, T. 6
Burt, R. S. 92

Calhoun, Craig J. 12, 17
Camic, C. 6
Carley, K. 117
Carlosson, G. 5
Carroll, G. R. 53
Castells, M. 12
catnet **93–95, 94,** 97
causal accounts 13–14
causal mechanisms 17
causal modelling 10, 101, 113
    interactions and social outcomes
        109–113
    predictive accuracy 107–8
    sociological theory and 104–7
    tradition **102,** 104
causal 'totality' 32
'causalism' 37

causality, cumulative 99
central tendencies 65–66
ceteris paribus clauses 32
Chains of Opportunity (White) 55
Charon, J. M. 13
Chase, I. D. 55
Cherkaoui, M. 67
Churchland, P. 41
Chwe, M. S-Y. 50
clarity and precision 3–4
Clark, A. E. 120, 121
cognitive dissonance 40, 51–52
Cohen, L. E. 55
Coleman, James S. 1, 6, 68, 89, 145, 147
    Åberg and 92
    action, interaction and 35, 60, 63
    causal modelling and 105, 109, 110,
        111, 112
    differential equation models and 88,
        89, 90
    linear systems analysis and 116
    micro–macro link and 8,
        [–9.122–], 89
        graph 115, 116, 117, 126, 132, 143
    quantitative research and 8
    social interaction, change and 68
    social networks and 149, 150
collective action 90, 96–97, 152
collectivism 73
Collier, A. 70
computational modelling 117
consequential manipulation 101, 104
contagion 87, 92
counteradaptive preferences 40
counterfactual effects 104
covering-law explanations 14, 15–20,
    19, **30–31**
Cox, D. R. 111
Craver, C. F. 25, 26, 74
critical realists 24, 70, 72–73, 75, 77
cumulative causality 99

Dahrendorf, R. G. 36
Darden, L. 25
David, P. 53
Davidson, D. 38, 39, 42, 146
DBA (desire-belief-action) triplets
    78–83, **56**
DBO (desires, beliefs and opportunities)
    theory 26, 66, 69, 146–7, 151, 154
    action, interaction and 37, 38–42,
        43, 44
    analytical tradition and 9, 10
    core components of **39**
    patterns 76, 77, 77–78
    rational choice and 61

De Quervai, D. 152
decision-making **56, 89, 90**
deductive-nomological model 20
Dennett, D. C. 37, 39
descriptions 12–13
    false statements 62–63, 66
    incomplete statements 62–63, 66
desire 38
    based explanation 40
    based interaction 119, 120–21
    belief-action triplet (DBA) 78–83, **79**
    mediated mechanisms 108
    mediated social interaction 52–54
    belief and 18
    formation **59**
        mechanism, dissonance-driven 78
    see also DBO (desires, beliefs and
        opportunities) theory
Deutsch, M. 54
Diekman, A. 89
differential equation models 89–92, 111
direct causal effect 102
dissection and abstraction 2–3
dissonance
    driven desire formation 78, **59**
    cognitive 40, 51–52
    reduction 43, 53–54, 62
distributions and aggregate patterns 67
Duncan, O. D. 102, 103, 105
    status attainment and 102, 105
Durkheim, Émile 3, 7, 43
    social interaction, change and 67, 68

ECA models (empirically calibrated
        agent-based models) 100, 114, 116,
        117, 131, 136–43, 153
Edling, C. 95, 148
education 141, 142–43
Ego and Alters social interaction **80**
Elster, Jon 120, 145, 146
    action, interaction and 36, 40, 42, 61, 65
    analytical tradition and 6, 7, 8
    social mechanisms and 24, 25, 31
emergence 70, 71, 74, 75
empirical analysis 107
empirical research 109, 112, 114, 118, 145,
        151–52, 154
empirically calibrated agent-based models
    see ECA models
entities 25–27, 28
environmental effect 46
Epstein, J. M. 76, 117, 143, 151
Esping-Andersen, G. 13
'establishing the facts' 21
events 14
experimental results 152–53

explanation 1–2, 108, 113, 144, 154
    action-based 28–29
    belief-based 40
    covering-law 14, 15–20, 19, **30–31**
    desire-based 40
    mechanism-based 24–30, 30–31
    opportunity-based 40
    programme 29–30, **29**
    statistical 14, 20–23, 30–31
    types of **14**
    see also social mechanisms and
        explanatory theory

Falk, A. 151
false assumptions 63–64
Faust, K. 93
Fehr, E. 151, 152
Felson, M. 55
Fershtman, C. 151
Festinger, Leon 59, 99
    dissonance and 51
fictionalism 62, 148
    accounts and 64
    temptations and 3
Fischbacher, U. 151
Fiske, S. T. 43
Fodor, Jerry 34, 41
'folk psychology' model 41
Fong, E. 116
formalism 75–76, 148–9
formalization 65, 76
Freedman, D. 23, 102, 106, 107
Free-rider problem 152
Freidkin, N. E. 93
Freud, Sigmund 71
Friedman, M. 107
    action, interaction and 39, 62, 63

Gächter, S. 152
Gambetta, D. 24, 56
generative models 110, 111–12, 113
generative sufficiency 143, 151
Gerard, H. B. 54
Gerth, H. H. 153
Gibson, Q. 32, 108
Gilbert, N. 117
Glaeser, E. L. 123
Glennan, S. S. 24
Gneezy, U. 151
Goffman, Erving 109
Goldstone, J. A. 19
Goldthorpe, J. H. 21, 114
    action, interaction and 55, 60, 64
    causal modelling and 101, 103, 111
Granovetter, Mark 37, 59, 109
    social interaction, change and 75, 93, 99

Green, D. P. 65
group
    affiliations 87–98
    uniformity 47

Habermas, J. 12
habitus 4
Hägerstrand, T. 76, 124
Hahn, R. A. 38
Hamblin, R. L. 89
Händel database 123
Hannan, M. T. 53, 60
Hao, L. 116
Harding, D. J. 104
Harmon-Jones, E. 51
Harré, R. 19
Hauser, Robert 112, 113
Hechter, M. 60, 97
Heckathorn, D. D. 60, 152
Hedström, P. 1, 59, 123, **124**
    action, interaction and 41, 47, 55
    social mechanisms and 23, 24, 25
Hempel, Carl 15
    Blau and 18
    covering-law model and 15, 16, 17
Henrich, J. 152
Hernes, G. 37, 68, 89
Hesse, Hermann 148
Hirshleifer, D. 49
Holland, J. H. 75
Holland, P. 103
Holmlund, B. 121
homo economicus 36
Horan, P. M. 106
Humean approach 27

Iannaccone, L. R. 60
ideal-typical actors 38
indirect causal effect 102
individual
    the social and 70–74, 75–76
'individualistic behaviorism' 105
inductive-probabilistic model 20
informal rules 67
instrumentalism 62–63, 65, 148
    attitudes 3
    positions of 107
    of rational-choice theorizing
        60–66
    tendencies to 66
interactions
    belief-mediated **50**
    see also action and interaction
interpretive sociology 153
interpretive tool 37
intra-individual mechanisms 78, 83

Jackson, F. 29, 41, 73
Jasso, G. 63, 107, 108
job mobility 56

Kahan, D. M. 56
Kalleberg, A. L. 106
Kanazawa, S. 63
Karklins, R. 97
Karlsson, G. 24
Katz, E. 8, 68, **89**, 92
    social networks and 149, 150
    social outcomes and 88, 89
Keohane, R. 27
Kim, H. 97
Kim, J. 74
Kincaid, H. 27, 73
King, G. 27
Kiser, E. 60
Konda, S. L. 55
Kosfeld, M. 151
Kuran, T. 54

Latane, B. 45
Lazarsfeld, P. 102
Leibenstein, H. 46
Lewis, David K. 13, 41, 50, 135
Lilien, G. L. 92
Liljeros, Fredrik 95, 150
Lindenberg, S. 60
'linear system analysis' 116
Little, D. 24
Llewelly, C. 55
Loewenstein, G. 42
Logic of Collective Action, The (Olson) 152
Lombard, L. B. 14
Luttmer, E. F. P. 123

McAdam, D. 24
Machamer, P. 25
macro-level 29
    outcomes 65
    patterns 88–89, 92
        decision-making and **89**
    phenomena 67
    trends 29
    see also micro–macro
macro-sociological theory of social
        structure 17
Macy, M. W. 36, 76, 111, 149
    agent-based modelling and 117
Mahoney, J. 24
manipulation, consequential 101, 104
Manski, C. F. 47
Mare, R. D. 132
Mark, N. 117
Marsden, P. V. 93

Marshall, Alfred 3
Marx, Karl 69, 81
Matthew effects 99
Mayhew, B. H. 19
Mayntz, R. 24, 30
mechanism
    based approach 107–8, 113, 154
    based explanations 24–30, 30–31
    action-related **59**
    belief-mediated 108
    concatenations of 56–58
    definitions 14, **24**, **25**
    desire-mediated 108
    dissonance-driven desire
        formation 78
    explanations and **14**
    intra-individual 78, 83
    levels 74
        micro- 29, 116
    opportunity-mediated 108
    theoretical 37
    types of 60
    see also social mechanisms and
        explanatory theory
Menzel, H. 8, 89, 92, **99**
    social networks and 149, 150
    social outcomes and 88, 89
Merton, Robert K. 36, 59, **99**, **145**
    analytical tradition and 6, 7, 9
    empirical research and 114, 143
    self-fulfilling prophesy and 48, 65
methodological and ontological distinctions
    70–74
Meyer, M. W. 17
micro level 29
    foundation 90
    mechanisms 29, 116
    process 89, 92, 117
    simulations 117, 119
    theory 65
micro–macro
    graph (Coleman) 115–16, 117
    link 7–8, 131, 145
    relationship 69
Micromotives and Macrobehavior
    (Schelling) 7
Mill, John Stewart 15, 31, 32
Miller, R. W. 27
Mills, C. W. 153
Mills, J. 51
miracle argument 71
models
    actor-based 117–18
    agent-based 87–88, 100, 112, 116,
        117–19, 149
        computational 76

    simulation 78
    unemployment 124–26, 131–36
    building 76
    deductive-nomological 20
    differential equation 89–92, 111
    ECA 100, 114, 116, 117, 131,
        136–43, 153
    generative 110, 111–12, 113
    inductive-probabilistic 20
    regression 102, 106–7, 109–10, **128**, **141**
    simulation 7, 78, 111, 112–13
    'snowball' 92
    statistical 102–3, 112
    stratification **103**
    structural equation 105
    Sugarscape 76
    variable-based 111
Mood, C. 123
Morgan, S. L. 60, 104
morphogenetic approach 70
Mullainathan, S. 123
multi-factoral motivation theories 41
'multivariate structuralists' 106
Myrdal, G. 99

Nagel, E. 16
national level 71
networks 67, 93, 149–50
Newman, M. E. J. 93, 150
Neyman, Jerzy 102, 103
Nisbett, R. E. 43
'non-reductive causal mechanisms' 71
norms, social 67

O'Connor, T. 74
Olson, Mancur 97, 152
ontological and methodological distinctions
    70–74
open/closed systems 77, 118
Opp, K. D. 54
opportunities 38
    based explanation 40
    based interaction 119, 120, 122
    mediated mechanisms 108
    mediated social interaction 54–56
    Chains of Opportunity (White) 55
    see also DBO (desires, beliefs and
        opportunities) theory
organizational differentiation 17–18
organizational structures 32
Oswald, A. J. 121
outcomes *see* social outcomes

Pareto, Vilfredo 3, 57
Parsons, Talcott 108, 145
    analytical tradition and 3, 6

path dependency 99
patterns, distributions and aggregate 67
Pawson, R. 6, 24
Payne, C. 55
Pearce, J. R. 6
Perrone, L. 106
Petersen, R. 97
Pettit, P. 29
'phenomenological laws' 23
Phillips, D. C. 73
Pierson, P. 53
pluralism, theoretical 37
'political opportunity structures' 55
Popper, K. R. 34, 36
precision 3–4, 64–66
predictive accuracy 107–8
predictive tool 37
preferences
    adaptive preferences 40
    counteradaptive preferences 40
'probabilistic law' 17
programme explanation 29–30, **29**
'pure sociology' 18

quantitative analyses 100, 109
quantitative research 8, 112, 113
    and theories of the social 10, 114–44
        agent-based models 117–19, 131–36;
            empirically calibrated (ECA)
            136–43
        social interactions and youth
            unemployment 119–22
        transitions out of unemployment
            123–31; data 123–24,
            neighbourhood variations 124–26,
            social-interaction effects 126–31

Rainwater, L. 54
rational choice theory 60–66, 114
rational imitation 48, **59**
Raub, W. 60
Ravenscroft, I. 41
regression 102, 106–7, 109–10,
    128, 141
research
    empirical 109, 112, 114, 118, 145,
        151–52, 154
    sociological 22
    see also quantitative research
Ritter, M. 12
Ritzer, G. 12, 37, 42
robust dependence 101–3, 104
Rosenbaum, P. R. 103
Ross, L. 43
Rubin, D. B. 102, 103, 104
Rydgren, J. 45

Sacerdote, B. 123
Salmon, W. C. 2, 16, 24
Sandell, R. 97, 123
Sawyer, R. K. 73, 74
Schelling, Thomas 6, 8, 24, 132,
    145, 147
    action, interaction and 45, 50
    micro–macro link and 7, 8
    social interaction, change and 75, 76,
        90, 99
Schweitzer, A. O. 120
Scott, W. R. 17
selection effect 46
self-fulfilling prophesy 48, 59, 65
Sen, A. 12, 62
Shapiro, I. 65
Sheinkman, J. A. 123
Sherif, C. W. 120
Sherif, M. 120
Sica, A. 12
Simmel, Georg 7, 109
simulation **82**
    agent-based 78
    micro- 117, 119
    models 7, 111, 112–13
    see also ECA models
Skocpol, Theda 29, 74
Skog, O. J. 29
Smart, B. 12, 42
Smith, R. E. 120
'snob effects' 46
'snowball model' 92
Sobel, M. E. 104
social interaction
    effects **130**
    of Ego and Alters **80**
    and social change 9–10, 67–100
        individual and the social 70–74; link
            complexity 75–76
        patterns in desires, beliefs and actions
            76–87
        social outcomes and group affiliations
            87–98
    social outcomes and 109–13
    structures **86**
    unemployment and 119–22, 126–31,
        140, 141
    see also action and interaction
social mechanisms and explanatory theory
    9, 11–33
    covering-law explanations 15–20
    differences and similarities 30–32
    mechanism-based explanations 24–30
    sociological theorizing 11–14
    statistical explanations 20–23
social norms 67

social outcomes 75, 92, **96, 109–113,**
    112, 116
  group affiliations and 87–98
  probabilities **98**
social structure theory 17
'social wholes' 87
'sociological dandyism' 64
Sociological Theory 12
Sørensen, A. B. 1, 55, 106, 111
Soule, S. A. 150
sour-grapes syndrome 83, 84, 146
Spilerman, S. 89
Stark, R. 60
'staticism' 105
statistical
  analyses 111, 118
  approaches 104–7, 112–13
  explanations 14, 20–23, 30–31
  models 102–3, 112
Stern, C. 97, 123
Stewman, S. 55
Stich, S. 41
Stinchcombe, A. L. 23, 26, 65
'stopping rules' 27–28
Stouffer, S. A. 58
Strang, D. 150
stratification model **103**
Strogatz, H. 150
strong ties 93
structural
  differentiation 18
  equation models 105
  equivalent blocks 95
  individualism 5
  'multivariate structuralists' 106
Structure of Social Action, The (Parsons) 3
Sugarscape model 76
'supervenience' 73–74
Suppes, Patrick 31
Swedberg, Richard 1, 6, 23, 24, 25

Tarrow, S. 24, 55
taxonomies 13
Taylor, S. E. 43
theories 11–14
  action-based 114–17, 116
  building 34
  causal models and 104–7
  cognitive dissonance 40, 51–52
  descriptively false 66
  micro- 65
  multi-factoral motivation 41
  pluralism 37
  quantitative research 8
  rational choice 60–66, 114

social structure 17
Sociological Theory 12
theoretical mechanism 37
  see also DBO theory; quantitative
    research
Therborn, G. 13
Thomas, D. S. 48
Thomas Theorem 48
Thomas, W. I. 48
threshold effects 99
Tilly, C. 24
tipping points 90, 92–93, 99
Tocqueville, Alexis de 58, 59, 145, 147
  analytical tradition and 6, 7
Tolbert, C. M. 106
topologies of networks 67
torus 80
tradition
  causal modelling **102,** 101–113, 104
  see also analytical tradition
Troitzsch, K. G. 117
Tukey, J. M. 66, 149
Turner, B. S. 12
Turner, J. H. 6, 41
Turner, S. 35
typologies 13

Udehn, L. 5
'understandable action' 153
unemployment 140, **122, 125, 127, 128**
  actual and simulated **138**
  social interactions and 119–122,
    123–131, **140, 141**
uniformity within groups **47**

vacancy chain **59**
validity, external 152
Van den Bulte, C. 92
'variable approach' 23
variable-based models 111
Verba, S. 27
Von Neumann neighbourhood 79, 110
Von Wright, G. H. 17, 19, 36,
    37, 39

Wasserman, S. 93
Watts, D. J. 93, 150
weak ties 93
Weber, Max 109, 145, 153
  action, interaction and 36, 43, 44, 46
  analytical tradition and 3, 6, 7
  mechanism and 34, 35
  social phenomena and 68
Weesie, J. 60
Welch, I. 49

White, Harrison **59**
  catnets and 93, 94, 95
  opportunity and 55
Whitehead, A. N. 14
Willer, R. 36, 76, 111, 117, 149
Williams, B. 43
Wilson, W. J. 120
Winship, C. 104

wishful thinking 40, 59, 83, 146
Wong, H. Y. 74
Wright, E. O. 13, 106
Wrong, D. H. 36

Young, H. P. 50
youth unemployment *see*
  unemployment

Lightning Source UK Ltd.
Milton Keynes UK
UKHW041129291118
333162UK00004B/638/P

9 780521 796675